To Prof. Ray B. Westerfield

with the compliments

and high esteem of

Irving Fisher

Sept., 1942

CONSTRUCTIVE

INCOME

TAXATION

CONSTRUCTIVE INCOME TAXATION

A PROPOSAL FOR REFORM

by

IRVING FISHER, LL.D.
Professor Emeritus of Economics, Yale University

and

HERBERT W. FISHER, LL.B.

HARPER & BROTHERS PUBLISHERS

NEW YORK AND LONDON

1942

To

the memory of

Ogden L. Mills

the first to draw and introduce

a spendings-tax bill

CONTENTS

		PAGE
PREFACE		ix

PART I. PRACTICAL
1. THE PROPOSAL — 3
2. CASH YIELD ACCOUNTING — 18
3. SPENDINGS APPROXIMATE REAL INCOME — 24
4. TAXES ON CORPORATE INCOME — 28
5. ADVANTAGES INDICATED IN PART I — 33

PART II. THEORETICAL
6. YIELD IN GENERAL — 39
7. DISCOUNTING — 46
8. DOUBLE TAXATION — 56
9. DESTRUCTIVENESS OF TAX ON SAVINGS — 61
10. FINANCIAL CONSEQUENCES — 75
11. SOCIAL CONSEQUENCES — 92

PART III. LEGAL
12. "INCOME" ACCORDING TO COMMON USAGE — 109
13. "INCOME" ACCORDING TO LAW — 121
14. STOCK DIVIDENDS — 130
15. THE CAPITAL GAINS TAX — 142
16. WHEN INCOME AND INCOME TAXES FAIL TO SYNCHRONIZE — 153
17. DOUBLE TAXATION AND TAX EVASION — 160
18. COMPLEXITIES — 168
19. LESSONS FROM BRITISH EXPERIENCE — 177
20. CONSTITUTIONALITY — 184
21. CONCLUSIONS — 194

vii

viii   CONTENTS

PAGE

APPENDICES

To Part I: Subsidiary Problems   201
To Chapter 7: The Five Necessary Conditions   210
To Chapter 8: The Duplication Questioned   215
To Chapter 9: A: The Destructiveness Analyzed   220
              B: The Relation of Double Taxa-
                 tion to Destructiveness   222
              C: Some "Realistic" Comments   223
To Chapter 12: "Income" According to Experts   232
To Chapter 20: Miscellaneous Constitutional
               Problems   234

BIBLIOGRAPHY on Double Taxation of Savings
(and closely associated subjects)
    A. Writings of the Author (chronological)   249
    B. Writings of Others (alphabetical)   252

INDEX   261

PREFACE

THIS book was begun in 1938, before World War II had contributed its huge addition to America's tax burden. The book was intended, and still is intended, to present a fundamental solution of the whole income tax problem, and not merely to propose a stop-gap for an emergency.

But the coming of war has intensified the need for the same solution, namely, that we put the income tax on "real" income and take it off of savings; that is, off of the expansion of enterprise which, by becoming war enterprise, has made the need more urgent.

Our present system has functioned largely as a ball-and-chain to hobble business; that is, to retard the growth of the productive equipment of the nation. This has been true since 1913, and especially since 1933, and still more especially since 1940.

Now that income taxes have, of necessity, been raised to unheard-of heights, the evils which come both from the taxation of savings and from the exemption of dissavings have brought about a very critical situation—one threatening the very existence of the American economic system as we have known it.

And a most astonishing fact concerning the present tax laws is the complacency with which their absurdities and injustices are accepted. This complacency is doubtless due, in part, to the lack hitherto of any satisfactory plan for escape. I hope that the escape here offered may appeal to business men as the needed solution and that the recent new taxes, by their very destructiveness and complexity, may soon have the effect of stirring them to action. One of the most intensive students of the problem, Professor Robert H. Montgomery, C.P.A., after

objurgating our present involved system—or lack of system—
said wisely, "there will be no simplification unless business men
get busy."

The root theory of the present book has been in my mind
since 1896. It was then that I made my first attempt to formulate a concept of income. The concept was soon seen to be de-
fective and was amended accordingly the next year.

Since then I have found no reason for further amendments,
as far as fundamental theory is concerned. But how to put the
theory into practice still remained a problem; and only recently did a solution occur to me. Still more recently came the
realization of how destructive is the present system.

Needham has well said that the root of the problem of
income taxation lies in the one question: "What *is* income?"
In this book, several concepts are considered, including the
alleged concept (or concepts) of the so-called "common man";
for our American income tax law avowedly professes to apply
this common man's concept. But there has never been an effort
to question the common man himself prior to the modest effort
which I have made and reported in Chapter 12 of this book.
The fact emerges that we now have to deal with not one but
two versions of the common man's income concept. First there
is what the common man is *presumed* by law to think and,
second, there is what he himself says he thinks, neither of which,
however, is a *workable* concept.

The proposal of this book is simply to make our taxable income approximate our "real income."

This solution received the written approval of Ogden L.
Mills, shortly before he died. Originally I tried to attain a
slightly closer approximation to real income by means of corrections for three small "discrepancies"; but Mills and Sir
Josiah Stamp—(afterward Lord Stamp, who lost his life from
a German bomb)—convinced me that these complicated corrections were not worth making.

By dropping them, the plan becomes, I think, much the
simplest income tax proposal ever made. It would require no

appraisals, and it would levy the tax only where there is the wherewithal to pay it. The central argument is so simple that it is substantially contained in a single paragraph of John Stuart Mill.

One obvious effect of such a tax would be to encourage savings or, rather, to remove the present discouragement of savings. Thus, it is an example of "incentive taxation" as advocated by Mr. C. W. Hazelett.

Nevertheless, the proposal and the arguments for it have been contested by many writers without, it seems to me, adequate study. It is because of these widespread misunderstandings (especially as to the revenue-raising capacity) that so long[1] a book on so simple a plan seems necessary. In fact were it not for existing controversies this book could end with Chapter 1.

Also because of these controversies, the book should be of use to several classes of reader. The cursory reader who starts out with the feeling that he cannot spare the time for all of it is asked to read at least the first and last chapters; though these, if he is endowed with normal curiosity, may lead him to explore at least some other parts. Certain parts, such as Chapters 1, 9, 21 should be of interest to every taxpayer. So far as possible, everything which might seem of special interest only to particular classes of readers has been relegated to Appendices.

The book aims, so far as possible, to avoid repetition of previous writings on the subject. The mathematics of the subject have been excluded; but those who wish to pursue this fascinating aspect may find it in "Income in Theory and Income Taxation in Practice," and "Paradoxes in Income Taxation," published in *Econometrica* in the January 1937 and April 1942 issues respectively.

In Part III the Federal Income Tax is analyzed—chiefly its most typical features which were all present prior to Janu-

[1] Owing chiefly to an effort originally to include complete answers to all possible objections, the manuscript for this book was, at first, more than double the present length and thought unsuitable for a war-time volume. See Appendix to Chapter 8.

ary 1, 1940. The amendments of 1940 and 1941 are largely war measures. Where there is occasion to refer to them, smaller type is used—sometimes with square brackets. No attempt is made to cover statutory law beyond January 1, 1942.

Acknowledgments

Much of the book was included in a course of lectures in the Graduate School of the University of Southern California, in February and March, 1941. Many of the students in that course have contributed valuable suggestions, especially the following:

Andor Beretvas   Walter M. Loder
William Bloodgood   Edmond C. Maroder
George J. Cole   Albert A. Martell, Jr.
Robert J. Dorsey   Proceso Pulido
Asisclo A. Figueroa   Chase Stevens
John E. Firman   Nien-min Sun
Otto F. Fleischer   P. W. Thelander
Luis E. Laso

Some of these are also mentioned in the text or in the appendices, where their special contributions have been utilized.

My economic colleagues have also helped greatly by criticism (sometimes adverse but always helpful) either of parts of the text or of articles on which it has, in part, been based. These colleagues include Professor Fred R. Fairchild of Yale University; Professor E. N. Hong and Professor R. B. Pettengill of the University of Southern California; Professor William W. Hewett of the University of Cincinnati; Professor Harley L. Lutz of Princeton University; Professor Henry C. Simons of the University of Chicago; Professor M. P. Catherwood of Cornell University; Professor Harry G. Brown of the University of Missouri; Professor Willford I. King of New York University; Professor Jacob Marshak of the New School of Social Research; the late Professor E. R. A. Seligman of Columbia University and his associates, Professors Robert M. Haig and Carl Shoup;

Professor Roswell Magill of the Columbia Law School; and Professor Erwin N. Griswold of the Harvard Law School.

Mr. Frits Wynhausen of Los Angeles, a thorough student of law as well as of economics and accounting with special reference to the American income tax, has helped me both by criticism and by translating some of the Dutch literature on the subject. I am also indebted to Mr. Alexander Loverdos, economist of the National Bank of Greece, for helpful suggestions, and to Professor Luigi Einaudi of Turin for data concerning the Italian literature on the subject, including both sides of the chief subject of controversy—the double taxation of savings.

The income accountant who has for years assisted me in filling out my own income tax returns, Mr. W. J. Bissonnette, C.P.A., has offered valuable suggestions; also Professor Frederick W. Woodbridge of the Department of Accountancy of the University of Southern California.

Mr. Hans Cohrssen, formerly my secretary, has helped greatly by way of general criticism of much of the manuscript and also by translating parts of Eduard Pfeiffer's valuable work which he first called to my attention.

Practically the entire manuscript has been subjected to the searching scrutiny of Mr. Irving I. Schachtel, an attorney and author of *Planning for Tax Economy* (with William H. Crow and U. S. Greene)—a book which has had a notable success.

Dr. C. A. LeDeuc, of Los Angeles, a well-known controller and author has read all of the manuscript, and Mr. William Vickrey of Washington, D. C., has read most of it. Both have made important suggestions.

Needless to say these various critics do not necessarily agree with all or any of the views here set forth. For those views I alone am responsible.

The greatest help of all has come from the co-author, my brother, Herbert W. Fisher. After a painstaking study of the American income tax, he wrote most of Part III, specifically the chapter on Constitutionality, its Appendix, and Chapters

13 to 18. Naturally, each of us has made contributions to the work of the other.

I wish to thank *Taxes* for permission to quote from my articles: A Fundamental Reason for Not Taxing Savings, in the issue of January 1941; A Second Reason for Not Taxing Savings, August 1941; Rebuttal to Professor Hewett and Mr. Benjamin, May 1941.

In constructing the bibliography I have received very valuable co-operation from Mr. Donald Patterson of the Library of Congress and from members of his staff, especially Mr. Raymond E. Manning, and also from the staff of the Yale University Library.

IRVING FISHER

Yale University
July 1942

PART I. *PRACTICAL*

CHAPTER 1. THE PROPOSAL

CHAPTER 2. CASH YIELD ACCOUNTING

CHAPTER 3. SPENDINGS APPROXIMATE REAL INCOME

CHAPTER 4. TAXES ON CORPORATE INCOME

CHAPTER 5. ADVANTAGES INDICATED IN PART I

Chapter 1

THE PROPOSAL

ALTHOUGH this book aims primarily to show ways in which income taxation can be improved in wartime—even if only a little—we shall begin by showing what we believe to be the ideal and permanent solution of the whole problem, valid in both peace and war. We fully realize that it is too much to expect such an ideal program to be fully adopted at once. But, by setting the ideal clearly before us as an ultimate goal, we may guide our steps toward it more surely.

An entirely new approach to income tax legislation has long been needed. This is evidenced by the amendments to the laws which have been piling into our statute books, year after year, through a quarter of a century. The volume of them has become stupendous and still grows. Moreover, as this book goes to press, the need of reform has become more urgent than ever, by reason of the new tangles which our Defense and War problems have introduced and the frantic efforts of Congress again to rewrite the tax laws.

In our opinion, the present income taxes are objectionable in many ways. For instance:

(1) They are unfair, both to the taxpayer and to the government, not only because they impose double taxation (by taxing savings and their fruits) and allow double exemption, but also because they thus tax the producers of the nation's wealth more heavily than those who merely spend, especially the "idle rich."

(2) By taxing the increase of capital, they kill the most important geese which lay the most important golden eggs.

3

(3) They are unwise, largely because they actually kill much of the revenue which they should produce.

(4) Their administration is unduly costly and vexatious to the taxpayer; and their uncertainty and complexity require the continuous employment of expensive tax specialists in government, in business, and in private life.

(5) They keep a sword of Damocles hanging over the head of the taxpayer. Several years after his original return has been filed with great care and in good faith, he is still exposed to the chance of receiving from the Treasury a deficiency notice, which it is often difficult and costly to contest.

The remedy, as we see it, is outlined in this chapter. The arguments in favor of this remedy, as well as those alleged against it, will be found in the rest of the book.

The Tax Base

The essential feature of our proposal is that the proposed tax base is *income spent*, that is, income used for consumption purposes, excluding all *income saved*, such as undivided profits and investments, presumably used for productive purposes.

Essentially the same proposal—to tax only so much of the gross income as is spent, not saved—has been praised as "ideal" by John Stuart Mill, Professor Alfred Marshall, Professor Arthur C. Pigou, Professor Luigi Einaudi, and others; but most of these authorities have regarded this ideal as unattainable because (so they thought) "spendings" can be measured only by means of records which might be incomplete and incorrect.

It is strange that those who recognize that "spendings" are the only fair and logical base for taxable income often fail to realize how practical and simple is its application.

How do we figure what we spend in a day? We need only two data:

1. The amount we had to spend; that is, what we had or received during the day.

2. The amount we did not spend; that is, the amount left over as determined by counting at the end of the day.

The application of this simple procedure to the tax problem is the only novelty in the present proposal.

Moreover, the data needed for this calculation are considerably more trustworthy than those used in our present income taxes, which often depend on debatable estimates.

We propose, then, to reckon the taxable spendings, not by adding together the separate items spent for food, clothing, rent, amusements, etc., but by adding together the *gross receipts from all sources* and then deducting all items of outgo *other* than "spendings." The chief deductions under this proposal are: investments, taxes paid during the taxable year, and proper exemptions for the taxpayer and his dependents.

The Tax Would Be a Luxury Tax

It will be seen that our proposed new income tax is not merely a spendings tax; it is practically a *luxury*-spendings tax—"luxury" being defined as any excess above reasonable necessities. These necessities would mostly escape the tax through the "minimum exemptions." Thus, unlike a sales tax, this luxury tax would allow little or no taxing of necessities; and would spare the spendings of the very poor. The middle class and the rich would bear the burden; for, the greater the spendings—which means the more luxurious—the higher the rate.[1]

Such a luxury-spendings tax is more truly a luxury tax than any excise tax on specific luxuries, such as costly automobiles, opera tickets, or Oriental rugs. To define satisfactorily specific objects as "luxuries" is impossible; but to *measure* satisfactorily what constitutes luxurious *spending*, and with definite gradations, is easy.

Would Also Be a Net Cash Yield Tax

To this proposed tax, either of two names may be applied—one, as just indicated, in terms of disbursements and the other in terms of receipts:

[1] For suggested exemptions and progression, see Appendix to Part I.

    (1) it is a tax on spendings;

    (2) it is a tax on what is here called net cash yield.

Net cash yield may be defined as the gross payments received by the taxpayer in the taxable year *from* all income sources, less any payments he may make *into* income sources *during that same year*, and less certain other deductions to be specified by law.

The term "yield tax" merely extends, or generalizes, the idea of yield as commonly applied to shares of stock. For example, a share of stock which "earns" $3 may "yield" only $2, the remaining $1 being reinvested in the business. Even under the present *personal* income tax laws, only the $2 yield is taxed, not the $1 withheld by the company and reinvested. In fact, the courts have ruled (or once ruled) that to tax the $1 to the stockholder would be unconstitutional, since it is not "income" under the Sixteenth Amendment—not income to the stockholder, although it can be taxed as income to the corporation.[2] The present proposal is merely to extend this ruling consistently to *all* cases, always taxing only the *net* yield—never the $1 reinvested even if reinvested without the help of a corporation.

IN TWO PARTS

The total net cash yield received by an individual consists of two parts:

    A. that part which comes from his own *work*—(the *personally* "earned" part)—such as wages, salary, professional fees, business commissions;

    B. and C. that from his property.

Since the first part—that is, net cash yield from work—is practically identical with the personally "earned income" of

---

[2] Eisner v Macomber, 252 U.S. 189 at 218, Mar. 8, 1920. But see Chap. 20 as to recent possible weakening of the Macomber case. In special cases, the penalty may perhaps be put on the stockholder. As to a penal tax on corporate profits, see Helvering v National Grocery, 304 U.S. 282 at 288 (1938); also a note in 133 American Law Reports, Annotated, p. 806.

the present income tax laws, it needs no elaboration here. But the second part—net cash yield from property—is *not* necessarily identical with the "income" from the property, as reckoned under present laws. What the differences are will become clear as we proceed.

SUBDIVISIONS

Meanwhile, we specify the two parts of the net cash yield from property as follows:

B. that from the taxpayer's *"investments, etc."* and

C. that from his *cash balance.*

"Investments" we here define as all the property owned by the taxpayer for the purpose of bringing him cash and not for the purpose of personal use or "consumption." The "etc." is added to insure the inclusion of certain operations closely identified or associated with investments—loan operations, the buying and selling of property, the receipt of windfalls and of money from any sources not explicitly mentioned in the following tax return.

Moreover, to cover the subject fully, we must include, as sources of income and outgo, not only all positive property ("assets") but also all *negative* property ("liabilities").

Thus "investments, etc." includes all sources except the taxpayer himself as a worker for pay, and except his cash balance.

"Cash balance" at any instant comprises the cash on hand in a checking bank account, plus currency in pockets, tills and cash drawers or boxes.

The foregoing basic sources are similar to the basic sources covered by our existing income tax schedules. But there are important differences between the simple "net cash yield" flowing from those sources and what the present law makes of it by many additional bookkeeping adjustments, including "depreciation." All these adjustments are technical complications which are entirely avoided in our proposal.

Following is an outline of what the proposal would include

THE TAX RETURN

To Be Filled Out by Taxpayer For a Given Taxable Year
(Under a Net Cash Yield System)

Reporting all Cash Yields (from: (A) Work; (B) "Investments, Etc.";
and (C) Cash Balance)

A. Work

1. Net cash receipts from Salaries, Wages, Fees, Commissions

B. Investments, etc.

2. Net cash receipts from Private Business, Partnerships, Syndicates, Pools
3. Dividends
4. Rents and Royalties
5. Interest received, less interest paid (the difference may be either plus or minus)
6. (As to principal of loans *to* others) repayments received on such loans less any lendings made in the taxable year (may be plus or minus)
7. (As to principal of loans *from* others) any borrowings less repayments* (either plus or minus)
8. All cash received from sales of investments, less all cash paid out in purchase of investments and less all brokerage and other expenses incidental to said transactions (plus or minus)
9. Cash from windfalls, gifts, bonuses, insurance, bequests, etc.
10. Net cash from any other sources (specify)
11. Total Net Cash Yield from "investments, etc." (sum of lines 2–10)

C. Cash Balance

12. Cash on hand at beginning of year
13. Cash on hand at end of year
14. Net cash yield from Cash Balance (line 12 less line 13) (plus or minus)

SUMMARY

15. (A) From work (line 1 repeated)
16. (B) From "investments, etc." (line 11 repeated)
17. (C) Drawn (net) from cash balance (line 14 repeated)
18. Total Net Cash Yield from all sources (sum of lines 15, 16, 17 but subject to the deductions below)

DEDUCTIONS (OF OUTGO†) TO BE SPECIFICALLY AUTHORIZED BY LAW

19. Payments, made within the taxable year, of *all* taxes
20. Payments of insurance premiums for business purposes and of all life insurance premiums
21. Costs of medical, nursing, surgical, and dental care, subject to specific legal limitations
22. Funeral expenses; birth expenses; both subject to specific legal limitations
23. Fines, forfeitures, penalties, and payments for damages
24. Gifts and contributions made by the taxpayer, subject to specific legal limitations
25. Minimum exemptions of taxpayer and dependents
26. Any other deductions authorized by law
27. Total deductions (sum of lines 19–26)

FINAL RESULT

28. Taxable spendings (line 18 less line 27)

* But when these repayments to others consist of paying off a mortgage *on a dwelling or other consumer good*, the repayment may be treated as spendings. See Appendix to Part I.

† No deductions of income are recommended, such as from tax-exempt securities. For discussion of the deductible items, see Appendix to Part I.

in an individual's tax return in order to arrive at his "net-cash-yield" (or its equal, his "spendings").

The foregoing form of tax return is sufficient for purposes of our exposition. In practice, of course, other details would be supplied, as to the progression brackets, special rates on (or "credits" for) personally "earned income" (line 1), taxes paid at source, allocation of tax between periods and between American and foreign sources, so as to provide for the deduction of foreign taxes, if any, or perhaps the deduction merely of the foreign proportion of an inclusive American tax. We need not discuss these complications here.[3]

Also, of course, the form of return would be accompanied by routine explanations and directions.

SOME COMPARISONS WITH EXISTING FORMS

The very simplest case is that in which only the individual's work yields him income, say $10,000 salary (line 1). In this case, the present proposal does not differ from existing practice nor, apparently, from any other form of personal income tax which has been proposed. We therefore need not pause to illustrate it.

Next in simplicity is the case in which additional cash is received from private business (line 2). In such a case we have:

1. Salary	$10,000
2. Net cash yield from Private Business	5,000
Total net cash yield (subject to legal deductions)	$15,000

In line 2, the present proposal differs radically from most income tax systems now in use and from most systems which have been proposed.

For instance, suppose Smith's private business, besides *yielding* him the $5,000 in net cash, also *earns* $1,000, which is not yielded but is "plowed back." Under existing laws (but not here), this $1,000 is regarded as taxable income like the $5,000 actually taken out of the business. That is, instead of taxing

---

[3] The problem of allocation is discussed in Appendix to Part I.

Smith on only the $5,000 of actual cash *net yield*, as here proposed, existing laws tax him on the whole $6,000 of *earnings*. Serious objections to this practice will be presented in due course.

We next suppose that there is also a yield in the form of dividends (line 3).

1. Salary	$10,000
2. Net Cash Yield from Private Business	5,000
3. Cash Dividends	3,000
Total (subject to legal deductions)	$18,000

Cash dividends from corporations are here treated in exactly the same way as was the cash yield from private business. In both cases only actual cash *yield* is to be taxable—not the taxpayer's interest in undistributed earnings.

But under present laws the two cases—private business and corporate business—are treated inconsistently. If John Smith's business is in corporate form, he will (under his personal income tax) have to pay on the net *cash* yield (dividends) instead of on what the corporation, or his interest in it, earns. This restriction we believe to be correct.

If, however, his business is in a partnership, he will, as in the case of private business, be taxed under the present law, on his part of the earnings even if these are not all in cash. This is, we believe, incorrect.

FURTHER COMPARISONS

Line 4 (rents and royalties) and line 5 (interest) are treated in the present proposal substantially as in all other proposals and practices.

But lines 6, 7, 8, 9 (loans, sales, gifts, etc.) are treated quite differently. No other income tax system includes in the reckoning the *principal* of loans (lines 6 and 7). As to *investment transactions* (line 8) these are, in other income tax systems, partly included and partly excluded.

For instance, the present American law, instead of figuring all

purchases against all sales occurring *in one taxable year*, figures the gain or loss from the sale of any investment item in
the taxable year against the purchase of the same identical investment item even if the purchase occurred in some other
year. This is the famous (or infamous) "capital-gains" tax—a
tax which straddles the years. Only by accident can it correspond with the yield tax, namely, when the purchase and sale
of the same identical item happen to fall within the same taxable year.

Nor does the present law deduct such a purchase or investment *unless* it is followed by a sale, whereas the system here
proposed would deduct *all* investments made in the taxable
year, regardless of what happens before or after.

As to line 9 concerning bequests: It differs from existing systems by including cash bequests; however, any reinvestment of
this cash received is deducted again (line 8). In fact it is deducted even if kept in cash (line 14).

Of course, bequests may—and we believe should—be taxed
under estate and inheritance laws, quite apart from income
taxes.

The foregoing differences, as well as others, between the proposal of this book, on the one hand, and existing income tax
procedures, on the other, are illustrated in the following supposed tax return of "John Smith" for 1941, requisitioning all of
our 28 lines.

INTERPRETATION

We may interpret the figures in this "return" as follows:

John Smith received as cash yield in the taxable year:
$10,000 in salary, $5,000 from private business, $3,000 in divi-
dends, $200 in rents, $300 (net) from interest, $3,500 (net)
from borrowing and lending, $4,000 (net, i.e., $24,000 less
$20,000) from sales and purchases of securities (other than
those from bequest). These make a total, thus far, of $26,000
available for spending purposes. To this he adds $1,000 taken
out of the $100,000 cash bequest, since he reinvested only

$99,000; that is, he does not keep "unimpaired" as capital the whole of the $100,000 received as bequest but decides to use as income (that is, he decides to spend) $1,000 of it.

Cash Yields (*positive and negative*) Received by John Smith in 1941

	Cash	
	Paid in from Income-Sources (A, B, C)	*Paid out to* Income-Sources (A, B, C)
A. WORK		
1. Salary	$10,000	
B. INVESTMENTS, ETC.		
2. Cash from private business	5,000	
3. Dividends	3,000	
4. Rents	200	
5. Interest received by Smith	900	
Interest paid by Smith		600
6. Loans repaid to Smith	8,000	
Lent by Smith		4,000
7. Borrowed by Smith	2,000	
Repaid by Smith		2,500
8. Receipts from *sales* of securities	24,000	
Disbursements for *purchases* of securities		20,000
Paid out for bonds as investment of bequest (see line 9 below)		99,000
9. Cash received from bequest	100,000	
10. Cash from other sources	000	
Total of lines 2–10 first column	143,100	
Total of lines 2–10 last column		126,100
11. Total net of lines 2–10 (from "investments, etc.")	17,000	
C. CASH BALANCE		
12. Cash on hand and in bank at beginning of year $1,001		
13. Cash on hand and in bank at end of year 1,000		
14. Taken out of Cash Balance	$ 1	

	Cash	
	Paid in from Income-Sources (A, B, C)	*Paid out to* Income-Sources (A, B, C)
SUMMARY		
15. A. From work (line 1 repeated)	$10,000	
16. B. From "investments, etc." (line 11 repeated)	17,000	
17. C. Drawn (net) from cash balance (line 14 repeated)	1	
18. Total Net Cash Yield from all sources (sum of lines 15, 16, 17 but subject to the deductions below)	27,001	
DEDUCTIONS (OF OUTGO*) *Authorized by Law*		
19. All taxes† paid in 1941		1,800
20. Business and life insurance premiums		1,000
21. Costs of medical, nursing, surgical and dental care		500
22. Funeral expenses; birth expenses		100
23. Fines, forfeitures, penalties, and payments for damages		0
24. Deductible gifts and contributions		700
25. Minimum exemptions		1,000
26. Other deductions authorized by law		100
27. Total deductions (sum of lines 19–26)		5,200
FINAL RESULT		
28. Taxable spendings (line 18 less line 27)	$21,801	

* If any deductions of income are also authorized, the calculations would be modified accordingly. In that case, line 28 would be subject to said further deductions.

† Subject to allocations in some cases (see Appendix to Part I).

Thus far, the total net available for spending is $27,000.

Finally, Smith took $1 by drawing down his cash balance during the year by that amount. Thus, his total net cash income yielded from work, investments, bequest and all other sources, including the $1 net withdrawal from cash balance, was $27,001.

Deducting the tax-free outgo of $5,200 listed in lines 19-26, he has, as his taxable income for 1941—that is, he has spent—$21,801, the tax on which is to be paid in 1942.

If, to illustrate most simply, we suppose (for simplicity though quite contrary to our recommendations) that his tax is a flat 10 per cent, he will (in 1942) pay $2,180.10 on the 1941 net cash yield of $21,801.

CHECKING YIELD WITH SPENDINGS

In this tax return are entered all of John Smith's cash receipts and disbursements in 1941, except his spendings as a consumer. It follows, therefore, that his taxable income as here defined—his total net cash yield in 1941—must exactly equal those spendings.

Therefore the taxpayer might be asked by the Internal Revenue inspector to declare that, to the best of his knowledge and belief, the final figure, line 28, agrees with his spendings, during the year 1941 for "consumption"—that is, for personal uses and personal-use goods; and that, if challenged, he is prepared to prove such consistency, at least approximately.

We may suppose that such a checkup is made from John Smith's books, as follows:

Spent in 1941 for food	$ 4,000
for clothing	2,000
for rent	2,000
for house operation	2,000
for amusements	2,000
for automobiles (and their care; and all personal transportation paid for and not used for business)	2,000
for education and church	2,000
for miscellaneous (including net actual payments made in financing the purchase of durable consumer goods)	6,801
Total spendings in 1941	$22,801
Less minimum exemptions	1,000
Net total taxable spending	$21,801

The balance of accounts, then, is expressible as follows:

Taxable spendings	$21,801
Nontaxable spendings (line 25)	1,000
Other nontaxable disbursements	4,200
(lines 19–24 and lines 26–27)	
Total Net Cash Yield (line 18)	$27,001

Thus, the tax of $2,180.10 to be paid in 1942 may be said to be either 10 per cent on his taxable *income* (net cash yield) of 1941, or 10 per cent on his taxable *spendings* of 1941. The $21,801 of spendings is a *negative* quantity, that is, an outgo, but necessarily equal to the *positive* $21,801—the income, or net cash yield.

From this relationship between the positive "net cash yield" and the negative "spendings" it follows, not only that every dollar added to a man's net cash yield adds a dollar to his taxable total, but also that every dollar added to his spendings adds a dollar to his taxable total.

Yet spendings and yield play somewhat different rôles. "Spendings" is the more revealing as to the basic philosophy of the tax, because of its closer relationship to real income and to luxury. But "yield" is the more readily calculated and is therefore preferable for entry in the tax return.

Moreover, to employ the concept "yield" instead of "spendings" in the tax return makes it possible to discriminate between the taxable income which arises from work and the taxable income which flows from property, thus enabling us to tax these two at different rates, if we choose. If the spendings figures alone were used, this segregation would be impossible.

But, whether the proposed tax is called an income tax or a spendings tax, it is the positive yield and not the negative spendings on which chief reliance must be placed in computing the tax base.

WHEREWITHAL FOR TAXES ALWAYS AVAILABLE

One merit of the proposed system is that it imposes a tax where and when there is cash out of which to pay the tax. That is, if we go back to the gross receipts before any disbursements are taken out (whether for reinvestments, for spendings, or for any other purpose), there is always *wherewithal* for paying the tax. The attribute of "wherewithal" in taxable income is a desideratum recognized (or once recognized) by the Supreme Court.[4]

This is not always true of other taxes. A tax on property may be imposed when the property yields no cash. In such a case the tax has to be financed from some other source than the property itself. A tax on cash yield need never be financed unless the wherewithal is recklessly dissipated.

Wherewithal Could Be Reserved for Taxes

It should, however, be remembered that, although the yield of 1941 provides the wherewithal for paying the 1941 tax, actual payment will not be made until 1942; so that the best way of providing the money for that payment would be to set it aside in advance out of the 1941 yield as a separate fund "reserved for taxes." This procedure is not explicitly provided for in the above figures, although John Smith in 1941 may have earmarked some of his cash balance or some of his invested funds to be so used in 1942. Or he may "trust to luck" that the tax money required will easily be available out of the early yield of 1942.

If John Smith does wish to set aside in 1941 a special fund for the taxes payable in 1942, he may easily do so, in part or in full, approximately or even exactly, as he may prefer.

Could Be Adopted Gradually

The ultimate objective of this proposal for Income Tax Reform is to substitute the net cash yield tax (or luxury-spendings tax) for all existing income taxes, but this substitution could, if desired, be approached by successive stages, especially if the

---

[4] "Wherewithal" is stressed in Eisner v Macomber, 252 U.S. 189 (1920). Capacity to pay is stressed as an *ideal* in Union Refrigerator Co. v Kentucky, 199 U.S. 194 at 203 (1905) (citing Adam Smith); and in Hawkins v Comm. 6 Board of Tax Appeals 1023 (1927).

start were made in wartime. Without necessarily repealing or even altering the existing income taxes of either individuals or corporations, we could *add* to existing taxes the Luxury-Spendings Tax here proposed, and call it a new war tax. If this recommendation were adopted, it would be easy after the war to continue the new tax while repealing the pre-existing income taxes or gradually reducing them until only the new spendings tax remained.

Another approach would be to transform gradually our existing personal income tax into a net cash yield tax. For instance, we could begin by abolishing the troublesome capital gains tax (see Chapter 15) and substituting the English system (see Chapter 19) or, still better, the tax indicated by line 8 of the above tax return. Next, we could introduce the analogous taxes (plus or minus) indicated by lines 6 and 7, which are seldom important.

These simple changes would accomplish 99 per cent of the desired transformation! For the rest of our tax return is substantially identical with existing laws. All that would be needed to complete the transformation would be the adoption of lines 9 and 10 (rarely applicable) and 14 (of infinitesimal importance).

The above changes refer to personal income taxes. As to corporation income taxes, the important step, if their abolition must also be gradual, would be to reduce and then abolish all taxes on corporate profits, especially profits not distributed as dividends.

We make these suggestions for a gradual transition simply because new ideas must usually win their way slowly. We would greatly prefer to have the plan adopted immediately and in full. If this were done, we believe (for reasons which will appear in due course) that immediate benefits would result, and that these benefits would, as argued in Chapters 9 and 10, speedily grow to colossal proportions, far beyond what, at first blush, would seem possible.

CHAPTER 2

CASH YIELD ACCOUNTING

ONE of the chief merits of the tax return here proposed is that it derives from, and squares perfectly with, double-entry accounting.

This chapter will summarize a year's income entries as they would appear in a double-entry account book. The entries represent payments, in or out. Every receipt of cash is an item of gross yield. It may be said to come out of some source (including man himself as a worker) and every opposite item—disbursement or expenditure—may be said to go into some source. The former may be called the *positive* yield from the source; the latter, its *negative* yield.

Moreover—excepting only the final consumption spendings—every payment out of one source is also a payment into another. The producing source may be said to be *credited* with the item and the receiving source *debited* with it.

In the following examples, we classify the sources of income payments under the headings "I" and "II." "I" includes the initial sources, that is, the worker and his property. "II" is the "cash account" or "cash balance." This usually consists of a demand deposit in a bank. The items opposite "II," therefore, represent merely the payments into and out of the cash balance during the year. (The *size* of the cash balance itself is not indicated by these entries.)

Thus, a man's net cash yield-income is simply the algebraic sum of all the payments, relative to all the sources, the credits being *plus* and the debits *minus*.

The following table summarizes the accounting for a taxable year in a very simple case. Each figure covers many individual

18

transactions during the year. An arrow is used to show the
direction in which the money moved (each item instantaneously)
from the source credited to the source debited.

Example 1. Simplest Case

Source of Yield	Positive Yield from the Source Specified	Negative Yield	Net Yield in the Year
I Work	$10,000	000	$10,000
II Cash Account	(Spent) 10,000	10,000	000

Total Net Cash Yield	$10,000

This first example shows that, during the taxable year, John
Smith's source "I," that is, himself (by his "work"), yielded
him $10,000 and cost him nothing. Therefore, that source is
credited with $10,000 and debited nothing; so the net yield, for
that year from that source, is also $10,000, as shown in the last
column.

The example also shows that the said $10,000 went into source
"II," that is, "cash account" (middle column). Also a total of
$10,000 during that same year came out of that cash account
(first column). This $10,000 *out* is "spendings" for the year.
The net yield from source "II" is therefore zero (last column).

In other words, the asset called "cash," "cash account," "cash
balance," or "cash box" yields nothing net, because what comes
out of it is wholly offset by what goes into it.

Those unfamiliar with such accounting will be most helped
by regarding the "cash box" as a gold mine to be credited with
whatever money comes out of it and debited with whatever
money goes into it.

In this over-simplified example we find five equal entries of
$10,000 each, but all with distinctive meanings: (1) yield from
"work" ("I" in first column); (2) *net* yield from "work" ("I"
in last column); (3) positive yield from "cash" (II, first

column); (4) negative yield from "cash" (II, middle column); and (5) total net cash yield from both sources (bottom of last column).

The first and fourth of these entries (connected by the arrow) are one and the same payment, recorded as *plus yield* from the individual himself who has performed the work and as *minus yield* from the "cash balance" into which this $10,000 was paid. That is, this one transaction is double-entried.

The third $10,000, that is, the cash paid out of the cash balance (first column, II) is evidently the "spendings."

In less simple cases, these five entries may not all be equal. But one of the equalities never fails, namely, the equality between the spendings figure (first column, II) and the total net cash yield (last column, bottom). These two are *necessarily* equal. Their equality will survive any bookkeeping complications, even though these might upset all the other equalities. For both represent the same algebraic sum of all the pluses or credits and all the minuses or debits, but reached by two different methods. The "spendings" figure is arrived at by the "method of couples," that is, by canceling out the equal and opposite entries coupled by double entry (per oblique arrow); whereas, the "total net cash yield" figure is arrived at by the "method of balances," that is, by adding up the net balances in the last column, each arrived at horizontally, so to speak.

This equality between spendings and yield is shown by bold-face type.

Our next example shows what happens to the accounts when more cash is drawn out than paid in.

Example 2. Cash Balance Drawn Down

Source of Yield	Plus Yield from Source Specified	Minus Yield	Net Yield in the Year
I Work	10,000	000	10,000
II Cash Account	(Spent) 11,000	10,000	1,000
Total Net Cash Yield			**11,000**

The total net cash yield is now $11,000 instead of $10,000 because $1,000 more was paid out of "cash" than was paid into it during the year.

The third example is the reverse of the second; that is, it is a case of cash not drawn down but accumulated.

Example 3.   Cash Accumulated

Source of Yield	Plus Yield	Minus Yield	Net Yield in the Year
I Work II Cash Account	10,000 (Spent) 8,000	000 10,000	10,000 −2,000 (Saved)
Total Net Cash Yield			8,000

Here the net cash yield from the cash balance is a minus quantity; for only $8,000 was paid out of the cash balance whereas $10,000 was paid in. The difference, $2,000, was accumulated or *"saved"* as cash. This item of savings (included in the cash-balance debit) automatically reduces by $2,000 both the total net cash yield (last column bottom) and the spendings (line II, first column).

Example 4 shows what happens to the account when the $2,000 of savings is invested, or "plowed back," within the year (per upturned arrow, ending on the "investments" line).

Example 4. The Accumulated Cash Invested

Source of Yield	Plus	Minus	Net
I { Work { Investments	10,000 000	000 2,000	10,000 −2,000
II Cash Account	{ (invested) 2,000 } { (spent) 8,000 }	10,000	000
Total Net Cash Yield			8,000

In this example, we split the first source (line I) into two lines—"work" and "investments." Also we split line II—disbursements from the Cash Account—into "invested" and "spent."

In the figure for what is *spent* (and its equal, total *net cash yield*) no change has been made from Example 3 nor in the figure for savings. Merely the *form* of the savings has been changed—from cash saved to investments.

The fifth example involves a new source—a cash bequest of $100,000 received by John Smith and recorded on a new line.

Example 5. Bequest in Cash

Source of Yield		Plus	Minus	Net
I	Work	10,000	000	10,000
	Investments	000	2,000	-2,000
	Bequest	100,000	000	100,000
II	Cash Account	{ (invested) 2,000	10,000 }	
		{ (spent) 8,000	100,000 }	-100,000
Total Net Cash Yield				8,000

Although John Smith got $100,000 yielded from one source

Example 6. The Bequest Invested and Spent

Source of Yield		Plus	Minus	Net
I	Work	10,000	000	10,000
	Investments	000	{ 2,000	-93,000
			91,000 }	
	Bequest	100,000	000	100,000
II	Cash Account	{ (invested) 2,000		
		{ (invested) 91,000	10,000 }	000
		{ (spent) 17,000	100,000 }	
Total Net Cash Yield				17,000

(bequest), all of it was absorbed by another source (cash balance), so that the taxable income remains unchanged, $8,000.

But let us now suppose, in Example 6 that, out of the $100,000 cash received from the bequest, $91,000 is *invested* and $9,000 is added to the spendings.

Thus the total net cash yield is $17,000—being the $8,000 of the last example plus the $9,000 received from the bequest but *not* reinvested.

CHIEF CONCLUSIONS

The main points are two:

1. The total net cash yield is what we get by simply entering the plus and minus yields relative to the several sources specified.

2. No savings ever appear in said total net cash yield—which is the *final taxable result.*

Chapter 3

SPENDINGS APPROXIMATE REAL INCOME

ANOTHER merit of the tax base here proposed is its simplicity. And this simplicity derives partly from the fact that only cash items are entered.

Nevertheless, money income is, or should be, merely a representative of real income. It is this real income which should be the ultimate objective of income-taxation.

And such it is under our proposed spendings or net cash yield tax. For John Smith's books really accomplish an appraisal of his real income. They show his spendings for real income, or "consumption."

"Consumption," an Inept Term

It is regrettable that the terms "consumption" and "consumer" have come to be used as identifiers of real income. Literally and etymologically "consumption" should mean destroying goods by use—using them up, wearing them out. But, in this literal sense, consumption happens to some articles which do not yield real income, such as coal, wool, cotton and other raw materials, whereas it does *not* happen to some articles which *do* yield real income—such as automobiles, dwellings, paintings and other durable consumer goods.

Yet one economist gravely explained that gazing at a beautiful painting is "consuming" it; and usage insists unflinchingly that the owners of car and picture are the "ultimate consumers" of car and picture.

Better terms than "consumer" and "consumption" would be

"user" and "personal use." Cars, dwelling houses, diamonds and clocks may be used for years without being used up.

It is, therefore, interesting to observe that, as applied to automobiles and other durable goods intended for personal use, the term "use" is gradually displacing "consumption." Dealers offer "used" cars for sale and even "used" rugs. This growing custom, if it becomes prevalent, will be an improvement.

"Personal Uses" Better

We may, therefore, best define real income or so-called consumption (since we cannot altogether shake off the term) as consisting of those particular uses or services which give direct satisfactions to the user, that is, satisfactions without the intervention of further productive processes or of money payments.

Some of the chief of such personal uses are: the use of food; the use of clothes; the use of jewels and other personal adornments; of house furnishings and utensils; of the domestics who manage these; of the dwelling house itself, or of a hotel room; of teachers and trainers; of a seat or a box at the opera; of a pleasure car, a pleasure boat or a pleasure plane; of pianos, radios, art collections, and of all other pleasure-giving objects and persons.

A person's assortment of personal uses constituting his real income is also called his "standard of living." The amount of money he spends for them is called his "cost of living." This amount necessarily varies with the standard of living; and consequently a tax on spendings is a tax that varies with the standard of living.

Real Income

In strict economic theory, as considered in Part II, real income consists of uses pure and simple; but, in order to adhere strictly to a money economy, we wish to avoid appraisals; that is, we wish to tax only net cash yield, which means *spendings*, which means real income as approximately *measured* by spendings.

In some cases, the spending is for a specified use or service. Thus, rent is for the use (shelter) of a house; and the price of a theater ticket is for the services (acting or singing) of certain persons.

On the other hand, there are cases such as food, as to which spendings cannot, for practical purposes, be specifically assigned to the *uses* of an article but only to the article used. This is because the use of the article has no market separate from the article itself.

In some cases, such as a dwelling house, both the article and the use or rental of it have well established markets. In cases of rent paid, our plan, by taxing the spendings for shelter, closely approximates taxing the shelter itself—real income. In case of a house bought outright and then occupied by the buyer, our plan in order to avoid appraisal (and also to escape a constitutional difficulty discussed later) would in effect pre-tax the *future shelter* by taxing the *present price* of the house itself. Fortunately, this price is usually paid in installments, thus more or less approximating rental payments. And the same applies to the cost of building a new house to be occupied by the person paying for it.

Having now introduced real income, let us go back to John Smith's bookkeeping. Hitherto in our examples we got as far as the spendings for real income but not to the real income itself. So here we add a new *Source* (line III) for the consumer goods into which the spendings go and from which the uses, real income, are derived.

In the following example, No. 7, we include this new category of "consumer goods" such as dwelling houses, furniture, wardrobes, larders, and all the other stocks of consumer goods. Their positive yield is their uses; their negative yield is their cost of operation, repairs, and replacements. We enter all these in the new line III.

The $10,000 in the new line III, middle column, includes all the *costs* of such personal uses—i.e., John Smith's cost of living. The $10,000 in line III, first column, is the value of all the *uses*

Example 7. Real Income

Source of Yield	Plus	Minus	Net
I Work	10,000	000	10,000
II Cash Account	(Spent) 10,000	10,000	000
III Consumer Goods	(Real Income) (10,000)	10,000	000

Total Net Cash Yield			**10,000**

or real income from consumer goods enjoyed during the taxable year. This includes the year's uses of larder and wardrobe, of the dwelling, and of all other articles or persons (or rights in articles or persons) which afford uses personally to John Smith.

The real-income figure is placed in parenthesis to segregate it as a *noncash* item. It is equal to the net cash yield (bottom of last column). Both are put in boldface type.

Thus, for all practical purposes, the proposed tax base amounts to *real income*. In no other income tax is this definitely and consistently true.

CHAPTER 4

TAXES ON CORPORATE INCOME

THE tax return in Chapter 1 makes no provision for corporations; and the omission is intentional. Corporations are associations of real people, and should not, in their corporate capacity, be subject to income taxation.

Here again we are admittedly setting up an ideal and not expecting the present heavy taxes on corporations to be suddenly dropped and replaced by a corresponding increase in the taxes on individuals.

Yet it should be more clearly and more generally understood that a corporation is not an independent source of taxes but merely a conduit through which the real taxpayers—the stockholders—pay the so-called corporation taxes.

ONLY REAL PERSONS HAVE REAL INCOME

A corporation, being an "artificial person" conceived as separate and apart from its stockholders and other real persons, can of itself have no capital and no income. These facts find their perfect expression in the corporation's two chief accounts, capital and income, both of which come to zero, because (as to capital account) everything the corporation owns it also owes—if not to its creditors, then to its stockholders; and because (as to income account also) every operation is both positive and negative—double-entried like the items paired by the oblique arrows in Chapter 2.

The old saying that "a corporation has no soul" expresses a genuine economic truth. No "real" income can appear in the corporation's accounts; for a corporation cannot, as such, enjoy

28

food, clothes, or amusements, although its dividends, after being spent, can bring all these to its stockholders.

DOUBLE TAXATION

But when a corporation is considered not as a separate legal person but as a group of real persons (namely, stockholders) its yield-income is, of course, the yield to the stockholders (namely, dividends).

Therefore, to tax the corporation on the profits which it distributes and, at the same time, to tax the stockholders personally on their dividends is to tax the same thing twice—it is double taxation.

Partnerships are treated differently and more logically. All income of a partnership is imputed and taxed to the individual partners.[1]

The corporation has always been considered by economists and accountants as a better form of association than the partnership, except for enterprises requiring only small amounts of capital. But because of this double taxation many corporations are now being dissolved and reorganized as limited partnerships. Aside from the advantage of avoiding double taxation, a change of this sort is, in most cases, not desirable, because under the partnership form it is impossible to obtain the responsible directorship employed by a corporation.

Moreover, such a change of organization is possible only in states having statutes authorizing limited partnerships. Also, only close corporations, with a few large stockholders, can effectuate such a change; and legal talent must make sure that the articles of partnership do not create a situation which the Bureau of Internal Revenue could construe as having the essential attributes of a corporation.

A system is clearly unsound which makes a man's income tax depend essentially not on his income but on the technical form in which the sources of his income are held.

Dr. C. A. Le Deuc shows how two large stockholders holding

[1] Code Sec. 181.

together 85 per cent of the total stock of a corporation with a corporate income of $360,000 could save themselves jointly about $50,000 of income tax by dissolving the corporation and reorganizing it as a limited partnership.

REMEDY

Of course, if the tax on corporations is merely removed, the government will at first lose some revenue; but the loss can be made up by raising the tax rates all along the individual taxpayer line instead of putting these *extra lumps* here and there where the taxpayers happen also to be stockholders. The net effect of both changes—(1) abolishing the extra lumps and (2) raising the other rates—would not be to increase the present burden but to redistribute it and more equitably.

STOPPAGE AT THE SOURCE

However, it would be possible to use the corporation to some extent, as a collection agency for the government, thereby employing the device of "stoppage at the source."[2]

HIGH CORPORATE TAXES AND POOR VS. RICH

A corporate income tax plays havoc with the personal income tax. A poor man who owns dividend-paying stock now has to forfeit some 24 to 70 per cent of his dividends, or rather of what his dividends might be without the corporate tax. In some cases his tax would be zero if figured as a personal tax.

This injustice is widespread. Thus the figures of the United States Steel Corporation show that, out of the 164,000 common stockholders, 60,000 own less than 10 shares each and 115,000

[2] It should be noted, however, that American experience with the "stoppage at the source" principle, has not been favorable. It was thought to complicate rather than simplify collection. But it is the long standing British practice to collect the normal tax (present rate 50 per cent) directly from the corporation at the time the income is earned on an accrual basis; when the individual figures his own income, he includes this tax in his income for surtax purposes; if he is not subject to tax at the full normal rate he may claim a refund.

own less than 25 shares each. Presumably most of these small stockholders have small incomes, yet have to pay high taxes.

Today the common stockholders in the United States who are so "poor" as not to have been subject to personal income tax but who, as common stockholders, are indirectly paying taxes on their incomes—and at high rates—must number many millions.[3]

Nor can this injustice be avoided by any system of progression applied to corporations. For no such progression in a corporate income tax can be made to harmonize with the progression in the personal income taxes of the various stockholders, some poor, some rich. To reconcile the two sorts, it would be necessary for the corporation to *refund* to various stockholders different percentages of the taxes paid by it on their behalf, and then to obtain the same miscellaneous refunds from the government—after due checkups on the books of all three: government, corporation, and stockholders.

Of course, if we were to abolish the progressive principle itself, and substitute the idea of a simple flat tax, the problem would be greatly simplified throughout; and taxes on corporations could be well utilized, under the principle of stoppage at the source, without greatly upsetting, as they do now, the distribution, or incidence, of the income tax.

And when income taxes are levied (as under the present law) not only on yield but also on savings, including corporate savings, there are still other problems of disharmony between the corporate and the private systems of taxation, since corporate savings are included in the taxable income of the corporation but not in the taxable income of its stockholders.

The abolition of all taxes on corporate income would not only rid us of the sort of double taxation described above (relating to the distributed profits) but would largely rid us of another sort of double taxation to be described in Chapter 8, relating to

[3] The February 1942 Bulletin of the New York Stock Exchange states that in 1941 there were 3,700,000 stockholders in the United States and that this is 79 per cent more than in 1929.

the *un*distributed profits. In fact, so destructive is a tax on the undistributed profits (really a tax on business expansion, as shown in Chapter 9) that, if we had our choice between abolishing all taxes on distributed profits alone or abolishing all taxes on undistributed profits alone, we would choose the latter. Such a reform would be a halfway step toward the ideal income taxation described in Chapter 1.

PLUCKING THE GOOSE

One specious argument for heavy taxes on corporations is the old aphorism of a French finance minister, that "The art of taxation is to pluck the most feathers with the least squawking by the goose." But under a sound and fair tax system, the taxpayer should at least be allowed to know what he pays.

CONCLUSION

In our opinion, therefore, corporate income taxes, if employed at all, should be nominal, should be levied solely on dividends, and should be deductible by the stockholders; while any loss of revenue occasioned by such a reform should be made up according to capacity by *all* individuals whose incomes are up to the taxable level.

If any further taxes on corporations can be justified, these should not be in the nature of income taxes but of entirely other sorts, such as franchise taxes or taxes avowedly to check undesirable magnitude or monopoly, or for other nonrevenue purposes, none of which greatly concern us in this book.

CHAPTER 5

ADVANTAGES INDICATED IN PART I

THE TAX WOULD BE ON REAL INCOME

THE most fundamental merit of the proposed "yield" or "spendings" tax is that it would be, in effect, a tax on real income, real income being the most fundamental of economic magnitudes.

No other income tax so closely approximates a tax on real income, chiefly because all others contain a capital ingredient, but also partly because they are so vaguely defined. This vagueness is unavoidable in a system which affords no means of penetrating beneath the money veneer; for money is a veneer common to *all* economic magnitudes, and it gives no sign to distinguish just when it is veneering real income.

On the other hand, to make a tax on real income workable, we must have recourse to some sort of a money measure. "Spendings" serves this purpose.

PRECISION

Precision is another and most vital merit of our proposal. For the determination of yield-income does not require, as does the taxable income under the present system, any appraisal or valuation of assets. It is entirely free from such troublesome questions as what markdowns are to be taken on merchandise, how much shall be written off for bad debts, what is legitimate depreciation and depletion—questions which are uncertain, debatable, and often costly to decide.

AVOIDS CONTROVERSY AND LITIGATION

The proposal reduces to a minimum the possibility not only of errors in the computation of the tax, but also of disagreement between the taxpayer and the tax collector. An honest taxpayer, after once computing the tax, will be able to sleep in peace, free from the nightmare of deficiency notices falling on his head years after the original return was handed in.

WHEREWITHAL ALWAYS AVAILABLE

Another merit is that the proposed tax would be levied only when and where there is wherewithal available for paying the tax.

SIMPLICITY

No other income tax can approach the yield tax in simplicity either as to concept or as to administration. Ogden L. Mills, than whom there could be no better judge, six weeks before he died, wrote to the author approving the spendings tax essentially as here proposed, and commended it especially for its simplicity.

WOULD RID US OF THE DOUBLE TAX ON CORPORATE PROFITS

The proposed tax would put an end to that form of double taxation occasioned by the present taxation of corporate profits, and would stop the inconsistency between taxing corporations and taxing partnerships.

TAX-EXEMPT SECURITIES

As an explicit spendings tax, it would automatically avoid the exemption of tax-exempt securities. Ogden L. Mills, in an article on his proposed spendings tax, mentioned this as a merit. Such an escape, however, would be unfair as applied to existing exemptions granted under guarantee. But one policy of a spendings-tax as of a yield tax would certainly be at least to *discontinue* granting tax exemption on new government securities.

Would Rid Us of Certain Hardships

Also the proposed system would provide for the deduction of certain hardship items which are ignored by the present law, such as medical expenses and even, within limits, the legal expenses of preparing tax returns.

Would Tax Only Luxury

As a luxury tax, it would be fairer than a sales tax or than any other luxury tax system, because it would define luxury by the amount spent and not by the nature of the things purchased.

Would Accord with Accounting Principles

This has been shown in Chapters 2 and 3 as regards currently crediting and debiting all payments. As regards capitalization, this harmony with accounting principles will be further shown in Part II.

Other Advantages

The foregoing advantages will become clearer as we proceed.

And others will make their appearance; such as: less tax evasion; more eventual revenue; escape from the injustices and vexations of the capital gains tax without loss of revenue; escape from the double taxation of savings, and, by the same token, escape from the actual destruction of future enterprise now going on invisibly like compound interest in reverse.

Finally, the proposed tax reform, in conjunction with death duties, would, so we earnestly believe, go far toward rescuing our democracy from the evils of a threatened plutocracy, while retaining and increasing the benefits from an efficient capitalism.

The proposed system would not, of course, be entirely free of difficulties. But, so far as we can discover, it would have only such difficulties as our existing system possesses—and fewer of them. Some of those which would survive will be mentioned later.

And it may even be that experience would disclose difficulties peculiar to the Yield system. But, unless and until any such are pointed out, we are justified in holding the opinion that, with all its advantages, the Yield system has no substantial disadvantage—except newness.

PART II. *THEORETICAL*

CHAPTER 6. YIELD IN GENERAL

CHAPTER 7. DISCOUNTING

CHAPTER 8. DOUBLE TAXATION

CHAPTER 9. DESTRUCTIVENESS OF TAX ON SAVINGS

CHAPTER 10. FINANCIAL CONSEQUENCES

CHAPTER 11. SOCIAL CONSEQUENCES

CHAPTER 6

YIELD IN GENERAL

IN 1906, in *The Nature of Capital and Income*, the present writer set out to analyze the income concept. At that time there was no federal income tax[1] and little thought was given in that book to the practical problem of devising such a tax.

An unfortunate result of this omission was that when, seven years later, America adopted the Sixteenth Amendment, some of those who then proceeded to consult *The Nature of Capital and Income* gained the impression that its theory of income could not be practically applied. Nor did the author himself then realize how easily a near approximation to real income could be made effective in practice. Professor Seligman was substantially correct when he said: "Professor Irving Fisher . . . attempts to give a precise analysis of income, but he concedes that, for purposes of taxation, his scheme, while ideal in theory, would be difficult to carry out in practice."

John Stuart Mill, Professor Alfred Marshall, and Professor Arthur C. Pigou have held that a pure income tax which should leave savings untouched was impracticable, though theoretically ideal.

These writers did not discuss what difficulties they thought stood in the way of adopting spendings, or real income, as the tax base. But apparently the only essential difficulty was that of obtaining an accurate money measure of spendings.

In Part I it has been shown that spendings can be measured

[1] Former income taxation had been pronounced unconstitutional by the Supreme Court in 1895. Pollock v Farmers Loan and Trust, 158 U.S. 601, May 20, 1895.

accurately from any ordinary records including receipts and re-investments—these two being the most accurate and easiest items to verify.

In Part II the purpose is to show how spendings and real income are related to the general theory of income in its two legitimate senses (yield-income and accretion-income) and also to show why one of these two sorts of income and not the other should be the tax base.

First, we consider yield-income.

SERVICES AND THEIR SOURCES

Income, in its fundamental sense of *yield*, is: services rendered by property or persons. A service is the occurrence of a desirable event or the prevention of an undesirable event. Services, when performed by objective capital as distinguished from persons, are often called "uses."

The value of the services or uses flowing from any specified source during a certain period of time is the yield-income obtained during that period from that source.

Capital is wealth owned by human beings at an instant of time. It is owned *solely for the sake of some kind of service or services*, which it is expected to yield.

The capital of society as a whole is all its tangible capital-wealth including lands, railways, factories, dwellings; but, since the ownership of many of these is subdivided, the capital of an individual can often be expressed only in terms of his property rights, such as stocks, bonds, mortgages, and equities in mortgaged property. This capital-*property*, of course, is not in addition to the concrete capital-*wealth*, but is merely a share in the ownership of that wealth.

Wealth and property are coextensive.

For convenience, human beings, so far as their economic function is concerned, may be included in capital or wealth, in the very widest sense of these terms.

The essential relation of capital to *yield*-income is the relation of a service-rendering instrument to the services rendered by it; for instance, between a shovel and its shoveling, a plow and its plowing, a reaper and its reaping, a pump and its pumping, a farmer and his farming, a singer and his singing, a share of stock and its bringing in of dividends.

DURABILITY OF SOURCE NOT ESSENTIAL

An item of capital may be durable like a factory or a dwelling; or it may be perishable like a quart of milk or a cake of ice. Any "good" existing at an instant of time, whether it be concrete wealth or abstract property right, is capital. An instantaneous economic photograph would reveal capital and nothing else. It would show trainloads of meat, eggs and milk in transit, as well as the contents of private storerooms and refrigerators. Even the food on the table or on the fork of a man bolting his dinner would find a place in the snapshot.

NEGATIVE SERVICES AND INTERACTIONS

Capital-wealth falls into two main and usually distinguishable classes: "producers'" capital and "consumers'" capital. The services rendered by consumers' capital—by houses, the land surrounding them, house furnishings, automobiles, clothing, food, and other personal belongings—constitute "real" income—they consist of personal uses; whereas the services rendered by producers' capital—farms, mines, factories, railways, ships, coal or other raw materials, merchandise—are merely *preliminary and preparatory* to such final services or real income.

The essential difference between these two sorts of services—preparatory and final—is that a preparatory service is double-faced, looking backward as well as forward. It is an intermediate link in the chain, whereas a final service is the end link. That is, a preparatory service is not only a service relative to the asset or person which renders it but also a *disservice* relative to some other asset or person which intervenes before the final service. Such a double-faced service, or rather such a service-disservice, may be called an *interaction* between the two assets.

The two items are equal, opposite and simultaneous because they represent the selfsame event looked at from opposite sides.

Such service (or rather service-disservice) should be credited to the giving capital and debited to the receiving capital. In other words, each preparatory service or interaction would, theoretically, be subject to what is called double entry or "couple" accounting—if our bookkeeping went the limit, though, in practice, double entry or "couple" accounting is confined to transactions valued in money, as exemplified in Chapter 2.

But let us assume that *every* preliminary service is, as a service, *credited* to the service-rendering asset, and, as a disservice or cost, *debited* to some other asset.

There can never be doubt as to when a service is to be regarded as positive and when negative. Human desire always settles the question. If the owner of a given asset *desires* that it should occasion a given event, then that event, if it occurs, is a positive service rendered by the asset. If he desires that an instrument should *not* occasion a given event, then that event, if it occurs, is a disservice—a negative service—a cost.

Thus, since the houseowner desires that the house should not occasion repairs, these repairs are disservices or costs of the house; and since he desires that the repair tools should produce repairs, these same repairs are services rendered by the tools. The service event called "repairing" is thus an interaction between the tools and the house—a service credited to the tools and, at the same time, a disservice debited to the house.

This double-entry principle of interaction applies also when the service consists in preventing a change instead of producing one. Thus, consider goods in a warehouse, such as cotton. The storage, preventing loss of injury, is a service on the part of the warehouse but, on the part of the stock of cotton, it is a disservice or cost.

Nor is the principle altered when there are, in either or both of the two interacting capitals, more articles than one, as indeed is usually the case. Plowing, or the transformation of land into a furrowed form, is performed by a man, a plow and a tractor.

The plowing is a cost to be debited to the land, and a service to be credited to the *group* of capital consisting of man, plow and tractor.

Nor is the principle altered if one or more of the transforming agents is a raw material and perishes in the transformation while another service-giver comes for the first time into existence. Breadmaking is a transformation debited to the bread and credited to flour, fuel, range, and cook, of which the flour and the fuel are consumed as soon as they have performed their services.

In general, "production" consists of a succession of such stages, and at each stage the essence of the productive process is an interaction. The finished product of one stage may become the raw material for the next, and its passage from the earlier to the later stage is an interaction between the capitals at those two stages. At each stage, the services, performed by the earlier of the two capital items, add value to the other capital item.

Adding Services Together

The accounting which primarily concerns us in this book is income accounting. Interactions constitute the great majority of the elements which enter into this accounting; it, and most of the entries are the mere interactions which cancel out in the total. The only services which survive are those which are not double-faced, namely, the ultimate services of consumption (that is, personal uses) constituting real income.[2]

Though the two equal and opposite aspects of every interaction are bound to cancel out in the end, they need not do so in any subtotal reckoning *before* the end—that is, before the real income. If, for instance, we wish merely to reckon the net yield *from a given asset* acting on a second asset, only one of the two equal and opposite aspects of the interaction will be included in our reckoning.

[2] If we wish to proceed a step further—from real income to psychic income—what has just been called an "ultimate" service ceases to be ultimate. For we have now added a new link to our chain. This is considered in *The Nature of Capital and Income*, Chap. 10.

For instance, the net yield from a loom is the excess of the value of the weaving credited to it, above the various costs debited to it. That is, the net yield of the loom is the value which the loom adds to the product on its way to completion. In the same way, the net yield from a man's wardrobe is the very small excess (if any) of the value of its uses (the "wear" which the owner gets out of it) over its costs; and the net yield of his larder is the excess (if any) of the value of what is "consumed" out of the larder over what is spent on it during the year.

In the case of more than one asset—say, all the assets, positive and negative, of John Smith—we may arrive at their total net yield to him in either of two ways. We may, as in the examples just mentioned, ascertain the net yield from every single category of assets and add all these balances together. This is the "method of balances." Or we may perform much of the summation of the positive and negative services by a short cut connecting *pairs* of capital assets. That is, we may couple the two equal and opposite aspects of each interaction and cancel out each such pair, thus arriving at a number of zeros which add nothing to the final services of his entire capital and labor. This is the "method of couples," indicated by arrows in the examples given in Chapters 2 and 3.

Each of these two methods has its distinctive advantages, as shown in *The Nature of Capital and Income*.

SOCIAL VS. INDIVIDUAL INCOME

Theoretically, there need be no important distinction between the concepts of individual and national income. Both are aggregates of services, or of their values in terms of money. But practically there are certain items which are difficult or impossible to reckon both in the individual category and in the social category. For instance, an individual's use of the streets is a part of his income but one which he does not and cannot reckon in his income tax return. If he is taxed at all on this part of his income, it will not be under the guise of an avowed income tax but as a payment of tolls, or, more indirectly, as a gasoline tax, and also as that part of his general taxes which the state allocates to the upkeep of the street. Similarly, the individual's use of parks, public buildings and other public works, cannot be explicitly included in his individual income statistics. Yet all these can and should be reckoned, in some fashion, in the *nation's* income.

Assuming that such practical difficulties of reckoning are overcome, we may say that National Income is the sum of individual incomes.

ANOTHER CONCEPT

Besides yield there is a second sort of income which has often been suggested as a suitable income tax base. It has been called, by Professor R. M. Haig, "accretion."

But in order to pass from the concept of yield-income to the concept of accretion-income we need, as a steppingstone, the discounting or capitalization of yield-income. This we consider in the next chapter.

CHAPTER 7

DISCOUNTING

UP TO this point the accounting considered has been a *current* accounting of credits and debits; that is, it has consisted of the addition and subtraction of payments and other services and disservices, all occurring within the taxable year.

We now turn to another aspect of accounting—the one which connects what is current with what is future. This connection is expressed by the valuation of capital at the *present*, derived from the *future* services flowing from said capital.

A study of this time-relationship reveals another merit in yield as a tax base, namely, conformity with the capitalization or discounting principle.

DISCOUNTED YIELD IS CAPITAL

Physically, capital produces income; but, in valuation, income produces capital; or, more explicitly, the value of any sort of capital is the present or discounted value of its expected *net yield*. Ideally, this present value is obtained by discounting each expected payment (or other service) back to the present, and then adding the resulting items together.

The value of any property at a particular instant is the net discounted value of all the future services it is expected to yield, whether those services be in kind or in money. To a real estate dealer, the value of a house which he lets for money rent is the discounted value of all the money he expects it to bring in *less* the discounted value of all the expenses he expects it to cost him. To the owner of a home which he himself occupies, its value is the discounted value of all its expected uses—its

46

"shelter"—less the discounted value of all the expenses and trouble it is expected to cost him.

If the property is a "perpetual annuity," so that the income items are all equal, occur at equal intervals, and go on forever, there is a simple discount formula. By this formula we find, for instance, that if the yield is $50 a year and the rate of interest employed in discounting each successive $50 is 5 per cent (or, in technical language, if the "basis" for discounting is 5 per cent), the value of that asset is exactly $1,000. If the basis is 4 per cent, the value becomes $1,250; if the basis is 8 per cent, the value becomes $625.

EFFECT OF A YIELD TAX

A tax of 50 per cent on this yield of $50 per annum would bring the government $25 per annum, or half the yield. Thus, theoretically at least, a taxpayer could "compound" (pay in advance) for this tax by paying the government in advance a lump sum equal to 50 per cent of the capitalized value of the annuity; that is, 50 per cent of $1,000, or 50 per cent of $1,250, or 50 per cent of $625.

This same principle of time-equivalence applies to any other type of investment. For instance, instead of a perpetual annuity, let us take a 5 per cent $1,000 bond with four years to run. Its yield would be $50 in each year, except the fourth and last when the yield would be $1,050. If purchased on a 5 per cent "basis" the bond would sell for $1,000. But if the $1,000, received at maturity, were at once reinvested in another "5 per cent" bond on the same 5 per cent basis, the net yield in the said fourth year would be changed to only $50 (instead of $1,050), so that the $50 a year would be continued. If such reinvestments were repeated forever, at each successive maturity, the bond would become, in effect, a perpetual annuity of $50 a year.

Now suppose there is put into effect a tax of 50 per cent on net cash yield. It would still produce $25 a year; and, on a 5 per cent basis, the tax could fairly be prepaid by a lump sum of $500, just as before.

The Yield system would involve no tax on the successive $1,000 maturities; for, while each $1,000 received would itself be entered in the tax return as a gross cash yield, its reinvestment would be deducted as illustrated (in the tax return, line 6) in Chapter 1. Only if the $1,000 were *not* all reinvested but were spent (or partly spent and partly reinvested) would the tax reach it (or part of it). In that case no further tax would be derived from the spent part because it would not produce any further yields. But it would still be true that, on a 5 per cent basis, the taxes could be "compounded" (paid in advance) for $500, or 50 per cent of the original capital value.

Now suppose this "5 per cent" bond to be bought, not on a 5 per cent but on a 4 per cent basis, and suppose, as before, that it has four years to run. It is still a bearer of $50 a year for four years and $1,000 at the end; but, on this 4 per cent basis, the initial value comes out approximately $1,041 and the discounted tax of 50 per cent comes out $520, or half. And, as before, this would be true whether the investor reinvested his $1,000 or used it up, or reinvested part and used up the rest. In short, *no matter what the yield or the basis, a tax of 50 per cent of the yield will be equivalent to 50 per cent of the initial value*—of the bond or other property.[1]

The same principles of correct discounting apply not only to valuing a single asset but to valuing any group of assets or to all a person's assets and liabilities put together—his "net worth."

The Three Concepts

We now turn from income in the sense of *yield* to income in its only[2] other legitimate sense, *accretion*, the term proposed by

[1] We have assumed throughout that the tax itself does not have the effect of changing the basis for discounting. This assumption is theoretically true under a yield tax. But, even were it untrue, substantially the same conclusions would follow as are here discussed except that the numerical figures would be somewhat different and more complicated.

[2] See Appendix to (this) Chap. 7.

Professor R. M. Haig. Accretion is yield plus capital-increase. In the stock market, accretion is commonly called "earnings."

We have seen that capital is discounted yield. We shall see that it is not discounted accretion and that, for this reason, accretion cannot be a good tax base.

To illustrate the distinction between the two sorts of income we may repeat here the example used in Chapter 1.

The yield of a certain stock may be only $2 a share, while its earnings are $3 a share, the extra $1 being undistributed profits on the books of the corporation. The $3 of "earnings" are called "income" as to the corporation. The stockholder, however, usually thinks only of the $2 of "yield" as his income. Yet the $1 undistributed is "earned" by his stock.

For many years the present writer argued for confining the use of the word "income" to one of these two concepts—what is here called yield. However, experience has apparently proved that, parodoxically, the best way, in this case, to avoid ambiguity is to recognize income in *both* senses, but always to use the term with a modifier such as *yielded* or *earned*.[3]

Accretion thus consists of the two very unlike ingredients— yield and capital-increase. It represents the extent to which a person acquires *any* addition of economic value from a property during a certain year, whether the addition be in the form of yield during that year, or in the form of increased capital value or savings (reflecting the *prospects* of yield in *future* years).

To denote this increase in capital value, we shall use the term "capital-increase" rather than "capital gain," because the term "capital gain" has acquired special connotations in connection with our American income tax law. Under that law, "capital

[3] There remains ambiguity, and a curious one, of recent origin, in the term "earned." For the phrase "earned income" has, in recent years, come to be identified with remuneration for a person's work—his wages, salary, professional fees, commissions. In this book such earnings will be called *personally earned* income as distinguished from *property-earned* income, such as that "earned," for instance, by a share of stock. The prefixes seem necessary to avoid confusion since personally earned income is an example of *yield* and property-earned income, of *accretion*.

gain" always or usually means a capital gain "realized"[4] by
sale or other disposition of property in the taxable year, and is
measured relatively to an original valuation of the property
(usually its purchase price) *even if this original valuation or
purchase price dates back to a previous year*.[5] Evidently this
"realized" capital gain is not always the same as what is here
called capital-increase. For "capital-increase," unlike "capital
gain," may not be "realized" and must not "straddle" years.

We are now equipped with three concepts: (1) *yield*, (2)
capital-increase, and (3) *accretion*, the last being the sum of
the first two—the "algebraic" sum, since "capital-increase" may
be negative, that is, may be capital-decrease.

Sequence of Thought

To tread safely through this region of theory, we should note
carefully the necessary sequence of concepts. These are as follows: (1) the value of the *services* flowing from a given source
during a given period; i.e., the *yield* in dollars from that source
—for instance, from a stock or a bond during any given period;
(2) the *capital value at the beginning* of that period, found by
discounting the value of the future yield; (3) the *capital value
at the end* of said period, found in the same way; (4) the
difference between these two capital values—i.e., the *capital-
increase* accruing within that period; (5) the sum of said yield
and said capital-increase, which is the total accretion from said
source during said period.

It is sometimes supposed that we can reverse this sequence of
thought; but it cannot be done.

Yield and Earnings Contrasted

While yield is the more fundamental concept, accretion is,
for some purposes (other than taxation), the more useful. For
instance, given the accounts of a corporation for a single year,
we naturally strive to extract from these accounts as much of

[4] Code Sec. 111 (a).
[5] See Chap. 15.

the whole picture as can be expressed in a single figure. Merely to know the yield, or dividends, in that year tells us little. The earnings or accretion tell much more; for the earnings include capital-increase; and from capital-increase (in this case, undistributed profits) we can get some idea as to *future* yields.

In summary, the total net yield-income of a person or a nation during a year is equal to "consumption"; while accretion-income is equal to said consumption plus any net value that has been added to capital during that same year.

Discounted Accretion Is Not Capital

It is often loosely stated that the market value of a stock or other property is the capitalized or discounted value of its expected "earnings"—earnings in the sense of accretion. As we shall see, this is, except in special cases, a misstatement. The statement should be "discounted value of its expected *yield*."

Suppose John Smith to be the beneficiary of a $100,000 trust fund *yielding* him 5 per cent, that is, $5,000 a year. If he had no other source of income and did not save any of his annual items of $5,000 but spent them all for personal uses—that is, if he did not "plow back" anything—his income would indubitably be $5,000 in both senses—yield and accretion.

But suppose that John Smith elects to save for a while $1,000 a year, and that he segregates these savings by buying each year, at par, a 5 per cent $1,000 bond, keeping the bond in a special Bond Portfolio.

And suppose he then segregates, in turn, the bond interest payments of $50 a year by depositing them in a savings bank which allows him 5 per cent compound interest.

Smith now has three sources of income: the Trust Fund, the Bond Portfolio, and the Savings Bank Account.

Suppose Smith continues this policy for ten years, and then goes back to his spending policy—spending all his yield, including the yields of the bonds and of the savings account which he acquired during the ten years by *not* spending some of his yield. Also suppose that his inheritors continue the spending policy forever. We already know that the present value of the income (in the sense of yield) forever must be $100,000. Very well; if we discount (always at 5 per cent) all the yield or spendings and none of the savings, we get $100,000; but if we discount also the savings (i.e., bonds and bank account), we get a much higher figure which, as we know, cannot be the true present value.

Yet we *can* get the true $100,000 in spite of including the savings in the discount process, *provided* we *ex*clude the yield of said savings from said discount process. That is, we can include in our discount *either* the new capital *or* its yield but not both—in a word, not accretion.

First Year's Yield-Income*	Positive Yield	Negative Yield	Balance
Received from Trust Fund	$5,000.00		
Paid into Bond Portfolio		$1,000.00	
Net Yield-Income			$4,000.00

* All interest is, for simplicity, reckoned as if paid only once a year—at the year's end.

First Year's Accretion-Income

Yield (as above)	$4,000
Capital-increase (bond)	1,000
Total accretion	$5,000

Second Year's Yield-Income	Positive Yield	Negative Yield	Balance
Received from Trust Fund	$5,000.00		
Paid into Bond Portfolio		$1,000.00	
Interest received from Bond Portfolio	50.00		
Paid into Savings Bank		50.00	
Net Yield-Income			$4,000.00

Second Year's Accretion-Income

Yield (as above)		$4,000
Capital-increases		
Increase in Portfolio (Second Bond)	$1,000	
Increase in Savings Bank Account (accrued but unpaid interest)	50	1,050
Total accretion		$5,050

Third Year's Yield-Income	Positive Yield	Negative Yield	Balance
Received from Trust Fund	$5,000.00		
Paid into Bond Portfolio		$1,000.00	
Interest received from Bond Portfolio	100.00		
Paid into Savings Bank		100.00	
Interest received from Savings Bank	2.50		
Paid into Savings Bank		2.50	
Net Yield-Income			$4,000.00

Third Year's Accretion-Income

Yield (as above)		$4,000
Capital Increases		
Increase in Portfolio (Third Bond)	$1,000	
Deposited in Savings Bank Account (interest on two bonds)	100	
Interest on Savings Bank Account	2.50	1,102.50
Total Accretion		$5,102.50

Suppose that these same procedures continue for ten years. At the end of that time the *Trust Fund* will still be worth exactly $100,000; but the *Bond Portfolio*, consisting by that time of ten bonds, will be worth $10,000 and the *Savings Bank Account* will amount to $2,577.89, so that John Smith will own a total capital value of $100,000 + $10,000 + $2,578, or $112,578. His aggregate savings or capital-increases in the ten years thus come to $12,578.

Smith now quits saving. Therefore his yield-income henceforth will be

From Trust Fund	$5,000	
From Portfolio	500	(Interest on 10 bonds)
From Bank	129	(Interest on bank deposit of $2,578)
Total Net Yield	$5,629	

In the following chart of Smith's financial history, let us see where the discount process gets us—as to yield and as to accretion, every annual item being discounted on a 5 per cent basis.

	Yield (or spendings)	Accretion (or Yield plus Capital-Increase)	Capital-Increase (or savings)	Total Capital-Value (at year end)	Yield Produced by the Capital-Increase
1st year	$4,000	$5,000	$1,000	$101,000	$000
2nd year	4,000	5,050	1,050	102,050	000
3rd year	4,000	5,102	1,102	103,152	000
4th year	4,000	5,158	1,158	104,310	000
5th year	4,000	5,216	1,216	105,526	000
6th year	4,000	5,276	1,276	106,802	000
7th year	4,000	5,340	1,340	108,142	000
8th year	4,000	5,407	1,407	109,549	000
9th year	4,000	5,477	1,477	111,026	000
10th year	4,000	5,552	1,552	112,578	000
11th year	5,629	5,629	0 000	112,578	629
12th year	5,629	5,629	0 000	112,578	629
forever after	5,629	5,629	0 000	112,578	629

DISCOUNTED YIELD VS. DISCOUNTED ACCRETION

If we discount the yield items in the first column, we get the correct $100,000. If we discount the accretion items in the second column, we get an incorrect figure, $109,522. The extra $9,522 is caused by discounting every saved item twice—i.e., first the saving itself and then its fruits. This excess of $9,522 would disappear if either the discount of the savings or the discount of the yield from those savings were left out.

Moreover, the discount of the yield will *always* give 100,000, no matter what saving-spending policy Smith might adopt—even if he were to spend his entire $105,000 at the end of the first year; whereas the 109,522 would not stay put—it would wobble with almost any change in the saving-spending sequence. In a word, the discounted value of accretion is not a consistent figure. It is a figure without any useful significance.

Also, as to the tax:—there will be, of course, a corresponding inconsistency if we discount it.

Suppose we take a 1 per cent tax on yield—1 per cent of every item in the yield column and discount the series; we get $1,000. But if we take a 1 per cent tax on accretion—1 per cent of every item in the accretion column—and discount the series, we get $1,095—subject to wobble, if Smith's saving-spending policy changes.

There are cases, of course, in which the discount of yield and the discount of accretion come out the same; for instance, when the yield and the accretion are the same in amount each year (there being no capital-increase).

We come now to that saying (derived from the stock market) that the present value of a security is its discounted "earnings," meaning accretion.

This statement is true in the simplest case when only the first year's earnings are known and the *fiction* is adopted that thereafter the earnings and the yield will go on forever and stay identical with the first year's earnings.

But in cases where we are supposed to know the whole future —all the future yields and therefore all the future earnings— the market discounts only the yields. It never sanctions such a figure as the $109,522 above nor any discounted earnings conflicting with the discounted yields.

The nearest approach to perfect foreknowledge is the case of a "safe bond." As those who use the ordinary brokers' bond tables know, the value at any time of a bond, for a given "basis" or market rate of interest, is the discounted value at that time of all its future *yields* (interest payments and return of principal). The discounted value of all its future accretions or earnings (which means including each year's capital-increase or decrease) would be as bizarre a figure as the $109,522 above.

Chapter 8

DOUBLE TAXATION

Thus, if the discount of savings is added to the discount of their fruit, essentially the same thing is *discounted* twice.

It follows, as the night the day, that, if a tax on the savings is added to a tax on the fruit of the savings, essentially the same thing is *taxed* twice.

Fruit Tree and Fruit

To take an analogy, if we lay a tax of 1 per cent on an orange grove of 100 trees, we may (theoretically) do it simply by handing over, once for all, one tree to the government. This is equivalent to handing over annually the oranges which one tree bears. But to do both, to hand over one tree at first and then to hand over annually 1 per cent of the oranges borne by the 99 trees remaining, is virtually to hand over two series of oranges and reduce the fruit of the orchard twice; for the only value of an orange tree lies in its yield of oranges. That is, one tree is handed over outright and, in effect, a second tree is set aside, or earmarked for the government, since its fruit or 99 per cent of it, must go to the government.

So also the value of $100 of savings lies in its fruit—its interest. To pay a tax of $1 on $100 and then, in addition, to pay a 1 per cent tax on the fruit of the remaining $99 is virtually to hand over two sets of fruit.

Any tax on savings is merely a pre-tax on their yield. If we are to tax yield *after* it comes, we should not also tax it *before* it comes—unless, of course, we really *want* for some special reason to tax the same thing twice.

THE DUPLICATION OFTEN OVERLOOKED

This fundamental effect (double taxation) wrought by an accretion tax has been the subject of much controversy.[1] Many able writers have tried to defend it or even to deny its existence. Here we are primarily concerned to show that it exists. In Chapters 9 and 10 we show that, in general, it is undesirable.

We cannot escape the existence of this double taxation as some have tried to do, by mere verbal quibbles such as the suggestion that taxing fruit trees and taxing their fruit are not taxing literally the "same thing"; for the fruit bearer merely stands for the fruit—foreshadows and discounts it in value.

It matters little whether the foreshadow and the substance foreshadowed are called the "same thing" or two different things. We may well waive the point. If a poll tax were levied on a man and a totally distinct tax on his shadow, we might, if we wish, say that this is not taxing the "same thing" twice, as long as we are willing to admit that the real man has to bear both taxes.

Probably the great majority of people find it difficult, at first, to detect the double counting and double taxation of savings, or capital-increase. But such duplication will be easy to perceive if we imagine a tax on a large bequest, say a perpetual annuity of $1,000,000 a year, like the old French *rentes*. If interest is 4 per cent, this property is worth $25,000,000. The recipient of a $25,000,000 bequest is really the recipient only of what the bequest yields him, $1,000,000 a year, and not of two separate items—$25,000,000 inherited at the death of the testator and, *in addition* thereto, $1,000,000 in each subsequent year.

If it were desired to tax this bequest 50 per cent and only 50 per cent, the levy could be imposed *either* at the start, by taking $12,500,000, *or* thereafter, by taking $500,000 yearly, but not both ways. A tax of 50 per cent on both the bequest and the fruit of the bequest would take, in all, 75 per cent of the

[1] See Appendix to (this) Chap. 8.

annuity—half at the start and half of the other half by the 50 per cent tax on the annual $500,000.

Exactly the same recognition of double taxation should be accorded when a man saves $25 in one year and from it gets thereafter $1 a year and is taxed on both.

UNCLE SAM AS PARTNER

The advocates of Accretion as a tax base sometimes suggest that we regard Uncle Sam as a "partner" of the taxpayer. Now a true partner does not claim cash for accruals. No private partner would think of such a thing. Suppose John Smith has a brother James, a 50-50 silent partner; and suppose John, for both himself and James, puts $1,000 of the savings of their joint business into a bond. James now has an undivided half-interest in that bond, but no cash. They both wait for cash. And, meanwhile, since John gets no cash, James gets no cash. And when, later, John deposits the $50 interest on that bond in a savings bank, James has an undivided half-interest in that deposit; but since John withdraws no cash, James withdraws no cash. And when, still later, that savings bank account earns $2.50, which accrual is added to the savings account, James has an undivided half-interest in that $2.50 accrual, but he gets no cash, any more than John does. Under these conditions the interests of the two partners would run exactly parallel.

If, now, Uncle Sam be substituted for James and becomes the 50-50 silent partner, he should be content to do as James did: get cash when John gets cash and get an undivided interest in accruals when John gets an undivided interest in accruals. In other words, if John and Uncle Sam are to go share and share alike in every way, there would be a cash tax only when there is a cash income.

THE REVERSE CASE—DOUBLE REDUCTION

Such appeals to common sense seem to be even more convincing when applied in reverse—to dissaving.

Under an accretion tax, when a rich spendthrift spends some

of his capital, the accretion base would give him a double reduction. First, he deducts from his taxable income the reduction in value of his capital and later his annual tax shrinks because his annual yield shrinks. A life annuitant (under a full-fledged accretion tax) would be in the same too-happy situation without being stigmatized as a spendthrift.

Moreover, the discount principle still applies. The discounted value of the spendings *including* the wastings is the true present value, whereas the discounted value of the spendings *less* the waste of capital is too small.

Adhering to the 5 per cent discount basis, let us figure on a million dollars of capital wasted in fifteen years by spending. The present value of a 50 per cent tax, if figured on *all* the spendings, will be half a million; but if figured on accretion—that is, on the spendings *minus the wastings*—it will come out only a quarter million.

Whether the capital-shrinkage is caused by extravagance or by mismanagement or by blameless accident, fire, flood, drought, storm, shipwreck, earthquake, or by studied and wise design, or by any other cause, such loss of capital merely symbolizes a reduction of *future* spendings or yield-income. If John Smith's income in future years will be lessened because his factory burns this year, he will in those future years have correspondingly less taxes to pay. He should not have any less to pay *this* year, if his yield-income is not less this year.

For instance, after the 1936 hurricane there were many capital-decreases. These represented lower future yields from property—from the damaged forests, damaged factories, etc. But the government, instead of suffering merely a reduction of taxes on these *future* yields, which would automatically occur after 1936, allowed a lessening of income taxation for the capital reductions of 1936 itself.

Few examples of a thoroughgoing accretion tax exist. The actual law vacillates between it and a spendings tax. In England, for instance, a *life* annuity is taxed without deductibility for depreciation, whereas a *fixed-term* annuity allows such de-

ductibility which is the same thing as taxing the interest on
the capital value of the annuity.

A paradox of Accretion is that, under it, people can eat and
drink on an income of less than zero. The same is true of our
existing tax system, as was widely advertised in the recent depression by J. P. Morgan's statement that neither he nor his
partners had paid income tax in several years.

CHAPTER 9

DESTRUCTIVENESS OF TAX ON SAVINGS

THERE is a famous saying, based on a decision of Chief Justice Marshall, that: "the power to tax is the power to destroy."[1] But apparently no one has pointed out that this power to destroy is many times greater when savings are taxed than when merely spendings are taxed.

The destructiveness works in two ways: *indirectly*, by discouraging the saver from saving, and *directly*, by taking over in taxes some of the savings which he actually makes.

Let us consider this direct destruction of savings.

And by savings we mean any sort of capital-increase, whether of individuals, partnerships or corporations; and whether in the form of a savings bank account accumulating at 2 per cent compound interest; or in the form of the development (sometimes at 50 per cent per annum compounded) of new inventions, such as railways, automobiles, airplanes, radios, and motion pictures.

In the last chapter, the taxes used as examples were mostly restricted to an uncharacteristic 1 per cent. The destruction wrought by such taxes would be almost negligible. But let us now consider *heavy* taxes on chronic savers.

DESTRUCTIVENESS MAGNIFIED BY REINVESTMENT

The case of a great new invention or even of a great new enterprise based on technological improvements of an old invention is typical of the origin of American capital. To tax the annual growth (which is what savings mean) of such typical

[1] McCulloch v Maryland, 4 Wheat. 316 (1819).

61

enterprises destroys that growth to an amazing degree—like compound interest in reverse. It destroys the growth of our capital equipment, the income and social benefits therefrom, and finally, and by the same token, the tax revenue itself.

A once-for-all tax, at the same rate, on the final total—that is, on the inheritable estate after the accumulator has finished his lifework—would produce far more revenue.

At first sight, the opposite result might be expected. It would seem obvious that a 20 per cent tax on these yearly increments, levied in advance, would yield, at any rate, as much revenue as a 20 per cent tax on the final estate.

But this is not true.

It might seem still more obvious that the most revenue of all could be obtained by taxing *both* the yearly installments *and* the estate at the end of the accumulator's life.

But even this is not true.

It might seem most obvious of all that the higher the tax on accumulations the more the revenue from said accumulations.

But exactly the *opposite* is true—the higher the tax the lower the revenue![2]

Suppose No Tax on Savings

It is said that, in a period of forty years, the fortune of Henry Ford rose from a net worth of $1,000 to a million times $1,000, namely, a billion dollars—a doubling every two years. This would be accomplished by a constant annual rate of increase of 41.42 per cent compounded.

But, for the sake of round figures, let us take an imaginary case—the case of a man named Henry Forward—a blacksmith to start with; and let him live in a land where savings and capital gains of any sort are exempt from income tax. Only spendings are taxed—spendings for real income.

After 1900, namely, on January 1, 1901, young Forward converts his smithy into a shop for making automobiles by a new

[2] For discussion of these paradoxes, see "Paradoxes in Taxing Savings," Econometrica, April, 1942.

method of his own devising. His net worth at this time is $1,000. This proceeds to grow at the rate of 40 per cent per year, so that in 1921 it reaches the $1,000,000 mark and at the end of 1940 comes to $700,500,000. This value is embodied in a huge automobile plant which he has constructed on River Rouge.

In the first year, 1901, the capital-increase was from $1,000 to $1,400—a gain of $400. In 1921 the increase was from $1,000,000 to $1,400,000, a gain of $400,000. This looks as if at the end of 1921 there would be $400,000 which, under a tax on capital-increase, could be taxed.

But not if there had already been such a tax during the previous years. For the 20 annual applications of such a tax prior to 1921 would have prevented most of the $400,000 from coming into existence.

SUPPOSE A 100 PER CENT TAX ON SAVINGS

To show more clearly the effects of such taxation, let us change our assumption. Instead of no savings tax, suppose there was a 100 per cent savings tax from the beginning—that is, a 100 per cent tax on savings alone. This impossible rate is chosen, in our first example, for simplicity of exposition. And in order to exclude the indirect destruction by discouragement, we shall suppose further that even this 100 per cent tax did not deter our Henry Forward. He was fool enough, or saint enough, to keep on each year adding 40 per cent to his net worth, despite the fact that the government forthwith confiscated the entire increase.

In the first year, having faithfully increased his initial $1,000 to $1,400, Forward paid the whole $400 over to the government. This would leave him exactly what he started with, $1,000. He could not enlarge his little shop at all—not out of his own capital. At the end of the next year, the same thing would happen— he would have only $1,000—and the same every succeeding year. Also, the savings which he pays over every year would remain the same. In the twenty-first year, for instance, the savings would be not $400,000, but just the usual $400, and in the fortieth year not $200,100,000 but $400. And, after the forty years were up, he would have not $700,500,000 but only $1,000.

That is, the $700,500,000 fortune embodied in a River Rouge plant (which *would* have come into existence, had there been no tax on savings) has died aborning—died, in fact, forty times in succession.

But did the government gain what the taxpayer lost? No, the taxpayer (and the country) lost $700,499,000 of capital, while the government gained only $16,000; that is, $400 a year through forty years. Thus the government, too, was really a loser, losing, among other things, the chance to tax, after forty years, an estate of $700,500,000 instead of an estate of $1,000. For the sake of that $16,000 collected through forty years, the government deprived itself of untold millions in taxes.

Worst of all, the public was deprived of the benefits of that $700,500,000 capital. It was as if the Ford plant, the General Motors plant, the Chrysler plant, and all other automobile plants had been prevented by the tax from ever coming into existence. Surely, no government could so sorely need $400 a year for forty years that it could not wait forty years for millions!

"Ah, but the expenses of government must be paid every year, not just once every forty years."

This is palpably a weak argument; for the government, more easily than any other person or organization, could finance itself over a forty-year period. If it needed $16,000 during those forty years, it could borrow it at rates so low that, at the end of the forty years, it would owe less than $25,000. Even if it had to pay 5 per cent interest compounded during those forty years, its accumulated debt at the end would be only $48,320. Such a trifle could then be repaid out of the millions obtainable from an inheritance tax on $700,500,000. Even a 1 per cent inheritance tax would bring in over $7,000,000. Clearly the policy of taxing the savings as they accrue is "penny wise and pound foolish"—anyhow, in the case of a 100 per cent tax.

SUPPOSE AN 80 PER CENT TAX ON SAVINGS

"But a 100 per cent tax is inconceivable!"

Very well; try it at 80 per cent—a rate actually approximated today in the higher income brackets, applied, be it observed, to income *saved* quite as ruthlessly as to income spent.

In the first year, the capital-increase is, as in the former example, $400. On this, an 80 per cent tax is $320, leaving only $80 net capital-increase after the tax. That is, though the 80 per cent tax does not, like the 100 per cent tax, *totally* destroy the capital-increase, it sets back the increase enormously.

However, the main point is that the setback is cumulative. The setback in the first year has an after effect in the next year; for the fortune then starts, not at $1,400 but at $1,080, and clearly a 40 per cent increase on $1,080 is less than a 40 per cent increase on $1,400.

The second year's tax again sets back the increase, whereupon *both* setbacks have after effects on the *third* year's capital-increase. And the fourth year will feel the effects of all three previous setbacks, and so on cumulatively. At the end of forty years, forty successive setbacks have had their disastrous effects.

Constituting a sort of compounded setback, the 80 per cent each year knocks off 32 points from the 40 points gained each year, so that the *net* increase is only 8 per cent. The fortune thus grows, not at 40 per cent compounded as it would without the tax, but only at 8 per cent compounded. After forty such annual setbacks, each reducing a 40 per cent increase to an 8 per cent increase, and each setting back all that follow it, the final fortune is not $700,500,000 but $21,700! That is, whereas the 100 per cent tax destroyed exactly 100 per cent of the potential increase, the 80 per cent destroyed *more* than 80 per cent of the potential increase—it destroyed 99.97 per cent of that potential increase. The little $1,000 smithy has, it is true, grown in forty years, but only to a small shop worth $21,700, not to a River Rouge plant worth $700,500,000.

And, "out of" the $700,500,000 that might have been, how much did the government get in taxes? In the first year it collected $320; in the second, $346, and so on up to $6,437 in the fortieth year—the total for the forty years being only $82,600! For the sake of this $82,600 the government destroyed over $700,000,000!

Again we see that the government would have done better to borrow. It would have had to borrow only $320 the first year, $346 the second, and so on up to $6,437 in the fortieth. Even if it had paid on all these loans as high as 5 per cent compound interest, its accumulated debt in forty years would be only $164,500. Evidently it would be good business to go into debt that much in order to have, at Forward's death on December 31, 1940, a taxable estate of $700,500,000 instead of $21,700.

We conclude that, paradoxically, delay in taxing the savings actually increases the revenue, while also helping the saver and the public.

THE 100 PER CENT AND 80 PER CENT COMPARED

If, now, we compare the results of the 100 per cent and the 80 per cent tax (as applied yearly for forty years) and count no inheritance tax, we observe another paradox. The *lower* of the two rates affords the *higher* revenue, that is, the 100 per cent tax yields during the forty years $16,000; the 80 per cent, $82,600.

Also, of course, this lower tax permits the eventual Forward estate to rise from $1,000 (to which it was glued by a 100 per cent tax) to $21,700, with corresponding benefit to the public.

Thus, lowering the tax rate on savings from 100 per cent to 80 per cent is beneficial all around—to the public, to the Henry Forward estate, and to Uncle Sam's revenue, both before Forward's death and after.

As to this last paradox (increasing the revenue by lowering the tax), let us record the revenues year by year at each of the two rates.

Government Revenue from

	100 Per Cent	80 Per Cent
1901	400	320
1902	400	346
1903	400	373
1904	400	403

We see that the 100 per cent savings tax does yield more revenue at first, but in the fourth year the 80 per cent tax passes it, and thereafter has an advantage which increases every year. By the end of 1940, as we have seen, it has brought in a total of $82,600 instead of the $16,000 from the 100 per cent tax.

SUPPOSE A 50 PER CENT TAX ON SAVINGS

Let us now lower our annual savings tax from 80 per cent to 50 per cent. The revenue results compared with those of 80 per cent will be as follows:

Government Revenue from

	80 Per Cent	50 Per Cent
1901	320	200
1902	346	240
1903	373	288
1904	403	346
1905	436	415
1906	470	497

In this case, since the lower tax starts with a bigger immediate handicap, it requires six years instead of four to overtake the higher tax. But at the end of the forty years, its total collections would be $1,500,000 instead of the $82,600 under an 80 per cent tax, and the fortune of Henry Forward would be $1,470,000 instead of $21,700—with corresponding benefits to all concerned.

It would again be good business for the government, instead of collecting this $1,500,000 from savings, to exempt the savings entirely and to borrow the amount elsewhere, even at 5 per cent compound interest. At the end of forty years the government's debt would then be $2,050,000, but the fortune available for death duties, instead of $1,470,000, would be $700,500,000, on which a 50 per cent tax would, if fully collectible, produce over $300,000,000; or, if the government wanted only the $1,500,000, it could get it with a tax of less than ¼ of 1 per cent!

Suppose a 20 Per Cent Tax on Savings

Under a 20 per cent tax we find the same threefold advantage from lowering the tax rate on savings—advantages to public, to Mr. Forward, and to Uncle Sam. It takes longer for the 20 per cent revenue to overtake the 50 per cent revenue—namely, eleven years; but the total tax yielded in forty years would be $16,600,000 as against $1,500,000 from the 50 per cent rate, and the Forward plant would reach $66,500,000 instead of $1,470,000.

And here again it would pay the government many times over to wait, and meanwhile borrow even at 5 per cent compounded if necessary. The debt at the end of the forty years would be only $20,700,000; and to pay it there would be needed only a 3 per cent tax on $700,500,000.

Suppose the Growth Rate 20 Per Cent or Less

In all the foregoing illustrations, a 40 per cent annual growth of capital was assumed. But, even with a 20 per cent growth of capital, there would be corresponding advantages from successively lowering the tax.

At a 20 per cent growth rate, the fortune, if untaxed, would in forty years amount to $1,480,000 and would be cut down by a 100 per cent tax to $1,000; by an 80 per cent tax to $4,800; by a 50 per cent tax, to $45,300; by a 20 per cent tax, to $379,000; and by a 10 per cent tax, to $750,500.

Even in this last case (a 20 per cent growth rate and a 10 per cent tax rate on savings) it would pay the government to wait forty years for an estate of $1,480,000. The annual tax would produce in forty years only $83,200. If this were "passed up" and the same sum borrowed (even at the high rate of 5 per cent compounded), the whole debt in forty years would be only $114,300, which could be easily paid by taxing at the same 10

per cent rate the estate of $1,480,000 which would have existed
if not half destroyed by the annual 10 per cent.

LOWER RATES OF GROWTH

Thus far, we have supposed only the two growth rates—40
per cent and 20 per cent.

Even at low rates of accumulation and taxation, a parallel
destructiveness appears. Thus, suppose $1,000 growing at 5 per
cent for forty years without any annual savings tax. It would
reach $7,040. But a 20 per cent annual tax on savings would cut
it to $4,801, thus destroying 30 per cent of it; and a 50 per cent
tax would cut it down to $2,685, destroying 60 per cent of it.

Most of the nation's capital equipment now existing—railways, ships, factories—must, almost certainly, have grown at
first at much higher rates than 5 per cent; for their chief growth
occurred during their development as new inventions. If this is
accepted as correct, we need not descend to a 5 per cent growth
rate to prove the destructiveness of taxing the growth or expansion of a plant.

RAISING THE TAX RATE DEFEATS ITSELF

This paradox has already been mentioned, but is repeated for
emphasis. It has no exceptions under our hypotheses. As shown
mathematically in the *Econometrica* article, if we take a period
of time long enough, the lower the rate of tax on the capital-
increase, the greater is the total revenue obtained during that
period.

"PERPETUAL" SAVING

Even a 1 per cent annual tax rate on savings would yield
more than a 10 per cent rate, still more than a 20 per cent rate
and still more than 50 per cent, 80 per cent, 100 per cent—provided only we wait long enough and the potential rate of growth
continues.

A skeptical reader may point out that, according to what has
just been stated, an "infinitesimal" rate would eventually pro-

duce the most revenue. But to do this would require an "infinite" time. Here, of course, we find ourselves entering a theoretical realm of mathematics. One objector insists that somebody and his heirs might continue to save perpetually and *never* spend a cent beyond the minimum of necessities supposed to be exempted. In that case he and his heirs would be tax-free indefinitely.

Without taking the time here to discuss the various theoretical implications of such an hypothesis,[3] we may cut the Gordian knot by stipulating that death duties or succession taxes (that is, taxes on estates and inheritances) shall be an integral part of our tax system, complementary to the net yield or spendings tax. There could then certainly be no fear of any *perpetually* untaxed savings unless we assume a perpetual lifetime.

WHEN WOULD IT NOT PAY TO FINANCE THE WAITING?

Suppose we now reduce the growth rate to 10 per cent. With so low a growth rate as 10 per cent we find, for the first time, that it would no longer pay the government during the forty years to skip the 20 per cent annual tax and borrow the equivalent at 5 per cent compound interest. For its debt at the end would be $2,220 and the inheritable estate would be only $7,040, on which 20 per cent would bring only $1,408.

But, in arriving at this checkmate in the case of a low rate of savings, we have not only restricted the period of accumulation to 40 years but we have been much too liberal in our other hypotheses. To be realistic, we ought to assume that the government would borrow at rates far below 5 per cent. At a 3 per cent rate its debt would be only $1,510 and at lower rates the debt would, of course, be much lower, certainly lower than the $1,408 which we supposed could be obtained by a 20 per cent death duty.

We have imagined a fixed rate of tax on all amounts, whereas the present tax is progressive. But while some of our figures are higher than in practice, some are lower; and the

[3] For some of these, see The Nature of Capital and Income, p. 224.

compounding applies in practice on a rising scale. There can be no doubt of a tremendous rising compound destruction under present practice.

The table at the end of this chapter embodies most of the figures which have been discussed, and some others.

MORE REVENUE FROM A "PART" THAN FROM THE "WHOLE"

The tables even indicate that more taxes can be raised by taxing only accumulations at death than by taxing *both* the accumulations at death *and* the annual increments out of which those accumulations were formed.

For instance, in the case of Henry Forward, with a growth rate of 40 per cent per year for forty years, a 20 per cent annual savings tax would bring in $16,600,000 and would cut the estate left from $700,500,000 to $66,500,000. Even this tax of $16,600,000 plus a 100 per cent death duty on the $66,500,000 would aggregate a revenue of only $83,100,000; whereas, if the estate were allowed to reach its potential $700,500,000, a tax of *less* than 20 per cent would produce far more than the $83,100,000, and with ample margin for interest on any interim borrowing by the government.

And to raise the annual tax rate above 20 per cent only makes matters worse, as has been seen.

In a less degree, these same inequalities apply to the case of slower accumulations, as may be seen by examining the table appended to this chapter.[4]

INFLUENCE OF DISCOURAGEMENT

We have not yet taken into account the important factor of discouragement. This leads a saver to quit saving or greatly reduce the rate of it when the government punishes his thrift. A 100 per cent tax would not, in practice, bring in the supposed $16,000. That figure was the result of assuming that

[4] The mathematical formulas by which these tables were constructed appeared in the April, 1942, number of Econometrica. The derivation of these formulas proves the truth of the various paradoxes cited above and gives their limitations.

Henry Forward would pile up 40 per cent each year despite having to turn it all over to the government. What would actually happen would be that he would shut up shop entirely. The government would get nothing nor would anyone else.

So also the 80 per cent tax would not bring in anything like the $82,600 calculated. Nor would 50 per cent bring in $1,470,000; nor 20 per cent, $16,600,000. This discouragement factor would lessen every figure in the tables.[5]

How much the lessening would be there is no way of knowing. Therefore we cannot calculate any figures, though, in our opinion, the discouragement factor is probably even more important than the direct destruction already considered.

We may, then, conclude that, in *all* realistic cases, it would pay the government to borrow until the death of the saver rather than to tax the savings annually as they accrue.

It might not even be necessary to assume that the rate of interest at which the government could borrow must be less than the rate of capital-increase of the business in question. Even if these two rates were the same (without the tax) the discouragement caused by the tax would probably operate destructively enough to make it "pay" and pay well for the government to wait rather than tax the capital-increase currently.

Conclusions

The automobile industry was essentially established before the American income tax began to put high rates on capital-increase of corporations and before there was any personal income tax. It seems certain that such an income tax as is now in force, and the added taxes which are being proposed as this book is written, would never have permitted any such industrial developments as have actually occurred in the past. That is a very disconcerting thought.

On the basis of our cited calculations, we may conclude that, if we were today to repeal all our present taxes on capital-

---

[5] It would also lessen spendings. That is, the tax would drive a wedge between spendings and savings.

increase—or even merely to exempt from taxation that part of the earnings of corporations which is plowed back (the undivided profits)—the result would be, in the end, not a reduction of tax revenue but a tremendous increase, as well as a tremendous boost to our whole economy. There would be more immediate savings, and consequently *more future spendings to tax, plus bigger estates to tax.* Even if the rates for taxing them were unchanged, the tax revenue from large estates would probably be vastly increased. Perhaps they would be multiplied many times.

Even if this plan required the government to borrow substantially, that would, as we have seen, be "the smart thing to do." It would generate more income.

But this borrowing, even temporarily, might not be necessary. For our plan not only takes off taxes on savings but it puts taxes on dissavings. It gains revenue from both these procedures and the gain from putting taxes on dissavings would be immediate.[6]

In other words, our present handling of savings and dissavings is doubly destructive of revenue. It loses immediate revenue by exempting dissavings and it loses ultimate revenue by taxing savings, thereby killing the goose that lays the golden egg.

Nothing else in the field of taxation is quite comparable to the tragic harm[7] done by a tax which thus destroys and discourages saving. Perhaps the nearest parallel is the old French window tax, which discouraged windows so that people preferred to live in the dark, thereby falling prey to tuberculosis. The tax collections were light in terms of money, but in terms of distress and disease the tax burden was, so goes the tradition, enormous.

[6] See Chap. 10.
[7] For factors explaining the destructiveness, see Appendix A to (this) Chap. 9; as to its relation to Double Taxation, see Appendix B; as to whether the illustrative figures in this chapter are sufficiently realistic, see Appendix C.

Table I

The Forward Fortune after Forty Years

(For Specified Rates of Growth and Taxation)

Potential Rate of Growth of Fortune Per Cent	Tax Rate				
	100 Per Cent	80 Per Cent	50 Per Cent	20 Per Cent	No Tax
40	$1,000	$21,700	$1,470,000	$66,500,000	$700,500,000
20	1,000	4,800	45,300	379,000	1,480,000
10	1,000	2,210	7,040	21,700	45,300
5	1,000	1,490	2,685	4,801	7,040

Table II

Tax Collection through Forty Years

(For Specified Rates of Growth and Taxation)

Potential Rate of Growth of Fortune Per Cent	Tax Rate			
	100 Per Cent	80 Per Cent	50 Per Cent	20 Per Cent
40	$16,000	$82,600	$1,470,000	$16,600,000
20	8,000	15,000	44,200	94,400
10	4,000	4,750	5,990	5,160
5	2,000	1,916	1,660	940

Table III

Government's Debt Accumulated in Forty Years

(Including 5% compound interest, from borrowing instead of collecting as per the preceding table)

Potential Rate of Growth of Fortune Per Cent	Tax Rate			
	100 Per Cent	80 Per Cent	50 Per Cent	20 Per Cent
40	$48,320	$164,500	$2,050,000	$20,700,000
20	24,160	37,600	80,300	142,000
10	12,080	13,500	14,080	10,300
5	6,040	5,590	4,355	2,220

CHAPTER 10

FINANCIAL CONSEQUENCES

BUT these destructive effects of a tax on savings are overlooked by those who argue for such a tax, whether under an accretion tax or under the present law.

THE "BROADER BASE" FALLACY

It is commonly supposed that a given rate of tax will draw in more revenue from accretion than from yield. This seems, at first blush, perfectly obvious because accretion, so it is claimed, "provides a broader tax base" than yield; for accretion includes capital increase and yield does not. Professor Simons[1] and Mr. Harold S. Benjamin,[2] C.P.A., have argued that, in order to equal the present revenue through a spendings tax, the rates would have to be increased enormously—in fact, in some cases, impossibly.

Thus, it is claimed that if a man's accretion in a given year is $20,000 and if his spendings included therein are only $10,000, and if the accretion tax at, say, 10 per cent produces $2,000, then a tax on only the spendings would, in order to produce as much revenue, have to be at least 20 per cent.

If the accretion is $100,000 and the spendings included therein are $40,000, and the accretion tax at an average of, say, 50 per cent produces $50,000, a spendings tax, to produce as much, would have to be at least 125 per cent!

If the accretion is $1,000,000 and the spendings included

---

[1] Personal Income Taxation, p. 230. University of Chicago Press, 1938.
[2] Taxes, May, 1941, p. 274.

therein are $75,000 and if the accretion tax at an average of, say, 67.5 per cent, produces $675,000, then a spendings tax, to produce as much, would by the same sort of calculation have to be 900 per cent.

But, obvious as the foregoing may seem, it is fallacious as a generalization and for two reasons.

First, it ignores the *future* broadening of the base from the savings reinvested, as explained in the preceding chapter. The very essence of savings is to provide for the future. To ignore that future and discuss only the year in which the savings are made, is a case of "Hamlet with Hamlet left out."

Second, the claim of narrowed base, even as an immediate and temporary condition, takes no account of capital decrease per spendthrift as a new and immediate source of revenue under a proper spendings tax.

This new tax on the spendthrifts would *immediately* add to the tax revenue.

Le Deuc's Illustrations

The American income tax is not in all ways an accretion tax but, as will be shown in Part III, it allows no deduction for saving and it counts many forms of capital gain and loss; so that it operates largely as an accretion tax.

Dr. C. A. Le Deuc of Los Angeles, a controller, is hopeful as to the speed (in fact, the possible immediacy) of a net gain in revenue from a spendings tax without increasing the rates. He offers the following three cases—typical and based on actual cases in his own experience.

First, a Mr. Neutral who neither saves nor wastes; then a Mr. Spender, and finally a Mr. Saver.

All three derived their incomes from private business. We need not specify the gross receipts; but all three withdrew from their respective coffers exactly $13,500.

Mr. Neutral both received it and spent it, and after deducting "personal exemption and credits" of $3,800 (leaving $9,700) and an earned income credit of $300 (leaving $9,400), he figured his tax as follows: The normal tax of 4 per cent was $376; the surtax of 5 per cent was $180, and at 6 per cent, $102. These three elements made a total tax of $658.

Mr. Spender gave himself $13,500 under the name of salary; but through this burdensome expense plus bad management, his business operations resulted in a "net loss" to his business—a loss of $9,500. Under the law he was entitled to deduct this loss from his personal income of $13,500 so that his net income, according to the tax base, became only $4,000. But even out of this $4,000 there came "deductions, personal exemption, and credits" of $3,800, leaving a "net income" of only $200 against which he was entitled to an "earned income credit" of $300. The final result was that, though he spent $13,500, he paid *no* tax whatever. He was actually rewarded (so far as tax was concerned) for his dissaving.

We now come to Mr. Saver. His business showed a net profit of $13,500, but he plowed back $8,500. That is, he drew and spent on himself only $5,000. Yet under the law he was taxed on the whole net accretion of $13,500. Thus, after "deductions, personal exemption and credit" (of $3,800) and "earned income credit" (of $300), Mr. Saver figured his tax as follows: "Normal tax net income," $9,400 on which the "normal tax" of 4 per cent was $376; surtax at 5 per cent, $180, and at 6 per cent, $102, making a total tax of $658.

Summary:

	Under Accretion Tax	Under Yield Tax
Mr. Neutral's tax	$ 658	$ 658
Mr. Spender's tax	0	658
Mr. Saver's tax	658	36
	$1,316	$1,352

Thus, a switch from the accretion basis to the yield basis would, in these cases, not only not immediately decrease the total revenue but would immediately increase it by $36.

Dr. Le Deuc insists that there are many such dissavers, and he frankly believes that, under a yield-plus-estate tax, there would be an immediate gain in revenue for the country as a whole. At any rate, we believe that gains would not be long in coming without any increase in rates other than those representing the mere transfer of corporation taxes to personal incomes.

MAXIMUM RATES MORE SIGNIFICANT THAN AVERAGE RATES

"But," it is said, "Henry Forward is not typical; his net worth was supposed to grow at the rate of 40 per cent per annum. The 'average' savings would not grow with any such speed."

This is like the statistician who, when consulted as to the proper height for a bridge under which ships were to pass, replied that the height should be so as to permit the masts of average height to pass under it!

Clearly, in some cases, maximums and not averages are what signify. Students of population from Malthus on, and biologists from Darwin on, have observed that the organisms which survive and therefore characterize the future—whether plants, animals, or races of man—are those whose increase in numbers is *not* at the average rate but at the highest rate, however small their numbers may be at the start. That is, in biology as in industry, the really significant effects are those of the most rapid rates of growth, especially when long continued in geometric progression like compound interest. The survival of the fittest is largely a survival of the fastest.

The capital-formation of an industrial country is predominantly the result of new and great inventions, relatively few in number but growing at prodigious rates. This is exemplified by automobile, airplane, radio and "movie." The dramatic growth of these industries is vivid in men's memories today. By the creative force of great, new and useful inventions, a thousand-dollar shop may indeed become a billion-dollar plant in forty years, all from the genius of a few individuals; whereas, to equal *one* such plant by, say, a 5 per cent growth per annum, would require 140,000 shops each starting at $1,000. And when it comes to a *thousand* potential Henry Forwards (and there are probably more than that number in America) they contribute, in forty short years, more to the nation's capital than would be contributed by the other 130,000,000 men, women and children of the nation if each had $1,000 to begin with and if each saved at 5 per cent.

In fact, the term "savings," though we have used it so freely, is somewhat misleading because it suggests mere thrift and not the creation or innovation associated with the most important examples of capital-increase.

It is strange how little attention economists have given to *invention* as the great economic creator. The literature in this field is remarkably meager, consisting chiefly of the writings of Rae,[3] myself,[4] Taussig,[5] Snyder,[6] and Schumpeter.[7]

We Don't Appreciate

It is tragic how little the 130,000,000 of us appreciate the benefits we get from a few thousand inventors and their associated enterprisers. In fact, too often these pioneers are regarded as people to be pilloried for having gained "at the expense of" the rest of us.

On the contrary, when we wear clothes we should thank Hargreaves, Arkwright, Eli Whitney, and Elias Howe.

When we travel we should thank Watts and Fulton (if it be by steamship) and Watts and Stevenson (if it be by train).

When we telephone, we should thank Alexander Graham Bell. When we turn on an electric light, we should thank Thomas Edison. When we enjoy the radio, we should thank Marconi

[3] John Rae, New Principles of Political Economy (1834), now available as The Sociological Theory of Capital. New York, Macmillan, 1905. 485 pp.

[4] The Rate of Interest (1907), rewritten as The Theory of Interest (1930). New York, Macmillan Co. 566 pp.

[5] Frank W. Taussig, Inventors and Money-makers. New York, Macmillan, 1915. 138 pp.

[6] Carl Snyder, Capitalism the Creator. New York, Macmillan, 1940. 473 pp.

[7] Joseph Schumpeter, Business Cycles. New York, McGraw-Hill, 1939. 2 vols. 1095 pp.

and DeForest. When we buy our bread so cheaply today, we should thank McCormick.

And, in each case, besides the inventor, some business enterpriser is involved. In a word, the creative work of both inventors and developers is one important key—in our opinion *the* important key—to the continual improvement of the standard of living in America.[8]

LIMIT TO 6 PER CENT?

Among the many misconceptions in this field is the idea that these high rates of profit, and so of growth, could and should be forced down to an ordinary rate of interest. Even some persons of high standing have suggested such a policy. If their idea be to limit *dividends* to 6 per cent, it is in line with the proposal of this book which would tax spendings and spare savings. But such is not the proposal of most advocates of "soak-the-rich." They say in effect: "Why allow anyone to 'make' more than 6 per cent on his capital?" Apparently these critics think of high earnings as money and as taken *out* of the business by the investor and spent by him; whereas, in fact, these earnings, when undistributed, go back *into* the business and spell expansion in brick and mortar.

And *during* expansion the chief beneficiaries are the public. Only *after* expansion, if at all, come the excessive dividends, the private spending, the extravagant consumption on the part of the rich inheritors. But precisely then, under our proposed system, would come also the taxes.

RISK

During the expansion period one answer to the question, "Why let men 'make' more than 6 per cent?" is that the men who set out to "make" extra high profits have to take extra high risks. The mortality of business enterprises is very high. For example, the life expectancy of a retail business is about seven years.

---

[8] For further discussion of rapid growth as "realistic" see Appendix C to Chapter 9.

"Each year about one out of seven retail stores passes out of existence."[9] When a man is engaged in an undertaking which involves a new invention or a new principle or a new method, the risk of failure increases tremendously. Of the few who can take such risks, only a very few will do so unless the risks are counterbalanced by a chance of big profits. It is hardly fair to limit severely the gains of such men unless their losses are also limited. And it is most certainly unwise. For the prospective victim will simply refuse to play the game of "heads you win, tails I lose."

In fact, even after success, the risks are not over, since another new invention may supplant the once successful enterprise and destroy the old fortune. Thus, the coming of the automobile involved the going of the horse and buggy. As far as private fortunes are concerned, the *average* gain from technological progress is not so great as it appears. What *is* great is the gain to the consuming public, owing to the superior minority of enterprisers who notably succeed.

Do Low Profits on New Inventions Help the Consumer?

"Would it not be better for the masses, that the rate of profit on all capital owned be restricted to 6 per cent instead of the sky as the limit? Would not prices then be lower and so the consumers more numerous?"

Here we meet the same misconception in another form. And the answer is: On the contrary, as anyone can calculate, if the profit is only 6 per cent, and if it is reinvested and so compounded, a capital of $1,000 could, in forty years, reach only $7,000! Such capital, embodied in a tiny shop, could hardly supply the world with as many automobiles as a plant worth nearly a billion! A business, to grow great, requires rapid rates of growth, which means high profits—not per car, but on the invested capital.

The Ford Company, in its whole history through 1940, is reported to have turned out over 29,000,000 machines of all

[9] Eaton Van Wert Read (in Retail Executive, Jan. 3, 1940).

types. Even if all the Ford profits—(*mostly undistributed, and constituting not "money" but the plants now owned by the Company*)—have aggregated a billion dollars, yet the average profit per machine must then have been (on the average) less than $35. A mere $35 net per machine (if correct) must have brought about the 40 per cent compound rate of growth (if correct). Suppose this 40 per cent were reduced to 6 per cent! The growth would be negligible and so would the number of automobiles in existence. And the prices per car would probably be higher, lacking mass production.

High *undistributed* profits represent the most creative influence in our economic life. To shut them off by some such limitation as 6 per cent on the capital invested would be to shut off the main chance for economic development. Relatively backward countries, like Mexico, are backward largely because, in those countries, such inventions have not been developed. On the other hand, countries which were formerly backward and which in the last century have leaped forward—such countries as Japan and Russia—have accomplished this change largely by transplanting American inventions and methods.

Any country that would limit profits on new inventions to 6 per cent would so retard its own industrial development as to become literally a backward country.

And in wartime to limit the profits saved and reinvested in expansion is worse than to limit them in peacetime. For wartime is a time of destruction, and is therefore the time when every creative effort is especially needed to counteract that destruction.

Growth Through Outside Capital

One critic, seeking to escape this conclusion, asks why Henry Ford's business could not have grown by means of outside capital contributed in exchange for stocks or bonds instead of capital earned in the business itself and plowed back.

It is quite true that outside capital might enable a net worth of a thousand dollars to grow to a net worth of a billion in the supposed forty years. But such business borrowing, or other forms of outside financing, would mean to increase, not decrease, the rate of growth and the rate of profit—a result which is, of course, the opposite of what the profit limiters are aiming at. They want the inventor, the developer, all the stockholders and the bondholders to be content with 6 per cent as a maximum, including profits plowed back.

If, as the objector may have had in mind, the introduction of outside capital were supposed to admit of a rapid expansion of plant in spite of a low rate of profit, we may point out that the rate of profit (undistributed) is identical with the rate of expansion (of net worth).

It is quite true that, if the outside capital were put in as loans, not stock, the plant expansion and the expansion of net worth would be different. But to suppose that the plant will expand to $700,500,000 (40 per cent per annum), while the net worth expanded only to $7,040 (5 per cent per annum) is to suppose the impossible; it would mean a company worth $7,040 while saddled with a debt of $700,492,960! If we are to be "realistic" the loan part of the financing must be small and the expansion of net worth nearly as rapid as the expansion of plant.

In short, high "profits" (plowed back) are absolutely necessary for rapid plant expansion.

Moreover, when a great revolutionary invention is in its earliest stages, if it starts with a poor and unknown inventor, as has usually been the case, it has small chance of getting private capital outside the original group. Practically its only hope lies in reinvesting its own profits. If these are limited to 6 per cent it simply cannot grow.

Under such a limitation, "venture capital" simply will not be furnished, unless to a small extent by the government itself under special circumstances, such as a depression or for war.

But for the government deliberately to tax enterprises almost out of existence and then to resuscitate them by the artificial oxygen pumping of government loans is to stultify itself. If, as in wartime, the government wants an airplane factory to expand, it should at the outset take off, not put on, any tax on that expansion. A tax on the plant's income should be on that part of it which is distributed and spent, not on the part used for the expansion desired.

This does not mean that a selfish enterpriser should, especially in wartime, be given *carte blanche* to take advantage of the government as its only or chief customer. Unreasonable *prices* need a curb. But to tax expansion is certainly not the right curb, if, indeed, it is a curb on prices at all.

Undue selfishness finds its expression in *distributed* profits and spendings, not in undistributed profits and expansion.

At present we do not discriminate. War profiteers, who already have adequate plant facilities, are now free to declare huge dividends. Even this would not be so bad if they reinvested these dividends in some useful way. Our tax plan would work in that direction—discourage waste. The present corporation taxes work in the opposite direction—they discourage saving. We cannot make a selfish man unselfish by law. But we can harness up his selfishness and make him pull our load.

Philanthropic Financing and Co-operatives

Occasionally a philanthropist will offer the public the benefit of a new invention, without profit. But the few cases of this sort known to the author, including one in which he himself was involved; failed by far to accomplish as much good as would have been accomplished by ordinary self-interested exploitation.

Such a case was that of an invalid chair invented by Herbert Spencer. He decided "to give it to the world." Result: only one chair ever made! Spencer moralized on his folly in not getting his invention commercialized. Other cases have been similar. One was that of a tent for the treatment of tuberculosis. This was awarded a prize by the *New York Medical Journal* as the best tent for this purpose; and it might have earned a small fortune. In fact, however, only a few dozen have ever been constructed.

Co-operatives have often succeeded on a basis of restricted

profits, but only when the industries had become routinized; that is, long after the pioneering period. During that earlier period, ordinary commercial exploitation had prevailed. Pioneering, so essential for progress, seems to be almost exclusively a job requiring the lure of high profits, not only to attract capital but also to permit rapid growth.

Our proposal to exempt savings would be an inducement to enterprising men to promote the use of new inventions—the same sort of inducement for which the patent laws were made.

Static vs. Dynamic Profits

Another mistake constantly made by the enemies of high profits is their failure to distinguish between the category of static business and the category of dynamic new enterprise. It is true that in a grocery business or a department store high profits can serve no useful purpose to the public. Such lines are too old, too well established and too stable to need much expansion-capital. They are good subjects for consumer co-operatives. And, as a matter of fact, such establishments usually make low profits and so are nongrowing or slow growing. Competition compels this. Almost all the profits, little being needed for expansion, can be spent. And, if spent, the yield (or spendings) tax would "get" them.

We must, of course, distinguish between 6 per cent net profit on sales, and 6 per cent per annum net return on the proprietor's capital.

It is, generally speaking, in the public interest that profits *per sale* should be kept as low as possible.

But the general consuming public would probably be very much surprised to know that the chief department stores of America, for the period 1935-1940, averaged a yearly profit of only 1.67 per cent on sales, even without deducting interest on their borrowings; and a meat-packing company, selling in 1941 a billion dollars' worth, made a profit of only 2 cents per dollar of sales.

New Enterprises

But, as we have seen, new pioneering dynamic types are quite different. It is in the public interest that they grow fast, and, to enable them to grow fast, high profits per dollar invested are indispensable; and to provide high profits per dollar invested it may be necessary, at first, to have high profits per dollar of sales.

The most rapid rate of growth occurs when a potentially great enterprise is young and small. Thus, the proposal which this book offers is really a "friend of small business"—that is, small dynamic businesses.

It is true that high profits on capital often come out of low profits on sales, even sometimes in a new business.

At first great inventions were sporadic, the products chiefly of a few poor men's lonely thinking, or by-products of the scientific work of laboratories in the universities. Such men were Eli Whitney and many other great inventors. James Watt, inventor of the steam engine, was not a professional inventor. He was a maker of mathematical instruments. Richard Arkwright, who invented the spinning jenny, was a barber. Edmund Cartwright, who invented the power loom, was a clergyman. Robert Fulton, who invented the steamboat, was a portrait painter.

Making invention a business began with Edison. He pointed the way toward rapid progress. Today the industries have added gigantic research laboratories to their equipment. In the laboratory of the American Telephone and Telegraph Company there have been over 4,000 scientific men. These commercial research laboratories have called men away from universities. The result of this deliberate commercial subsidizing of inventions has been a tremendous spurt in technological improvements.

In the report for 1928-1929 of Commissioner of Patents Thomas E. Robertson, we find:

It is a noteworthy fact that more patents have been granted during the last ten years than during the 100 years from President Washington's inauguration in 1789 until President Harrison's inauguration in 1889.

But our heavy income taxes on "rich" corporations are now crowding out research, and industrial laboratories are being reduced. Of all the indictments against our present system of income taxation, this is one of the worst. For the tendency of such high taxes, on companies formerly supporting laboratories, must be to reduce the rapidity of developing new inventions.

WOULD A SPENDINGS TAX DECREASE SPENDINGS AND ESTATES?

Opponents may argue that the spendings tax would itself so decrease *spendings* as to decrease the *revenue* therefrom. To this, the perfect answer is: By the same token, *savings* would *grow*, which would mean bigger estates, therefore added revenue both from the estates and from the increased future spendings.

"But," the objectors come back, "if we increase the taxes on great estates and inheritances, there will be little incentive to create such estates. People accumulate in order to leave wealth to their children."

There is a grain of truth in this, but only a small one.

And there are four answers:

(1) No increase in tax rates on estates and inheritances is needed for our purpose. For the revenue would increase *without* any increase in rates, simply because the estates that bear the rates would increase. That is precisely what the yield system would accomplish—by sparing the savings beforehand.

(2) True, in the case of a *small* estate—(or of a big estate *before* it becomes big)—the accumulator *is* of course much concerned for his children. Therefore, *small* estates should not be heavily taxed. But this does not apply to the very big estates. Certainly Ford never accumulated a billion for his son; and even if he should object to a 90 per cent inheritance tax, it would not be on behalf of Edsel,

who, in that case (poor fellow), would get only some $100,000,000!

(3) What, then, is the motive for building big estates? We recently talked with a budding multimillionaire who is developing a useful invention. His comment was that the real fun of making a fortune is not the having of it nor the spending of it nor the bequeathing of it for others to spend, but the thrill of achievement and of service for mankind.

Charles M. Schwab said: "I am not working for money. I have made more money than I'll ever spend. I am working for the sake of my work. Not long ago I had a fabulous offer for my business. I refused it. What would I do without my work?"

(4) Another motive for big savings is philanthropy, especially if philanthropic bequests are exempt. Many rich men build useful charities and are more interested in them than in adding to their own or their family's spendings. As this is being written, the will of a multimillionaire is published showing that four-fifths of his estate is left to charity. Clearly he did not accumulate that four-fifths for his children. Whether or not he definitely had the good of mankind as his original purpose, certainly mankind should not, in advance, destroy that good by premature taxation.

Shortly before this example of philanthropy, the newspapers reported that the well-named town of Mount Joy, Pennsylvania, had become "the amazed inheritor of a thriving million dollar oil company, the gift of the owner, Clarence Schock, who believes that 'a man's estate should go to the general welfare.' "

The author knows personally of cases in which fortunes have been deliberately sought and won expressly in order to finance great philanthropic projects.

Often there may be no such deliberate purpose in seeking the fortune. But it is not uncommon after a big fortune has been won, from whatever motive, for the winner to turn philanthropist. Carnegie was a good example and wrote enthusiastically of such a disposition of surplus wealth, even starting the aphorism "it is a disgrace to die rich." Our present tax laws encourage philanthropic giving. A spendings tax would encourage it further.

We assume, of course, that only a small fraction of accumulated capital is used for *anti*social purposes. When it is so used, as in the case of narcotic drugs, special and exceptional measures should be taken to frustrate the evil.

The Three Chief Uses for Big Incomes and Fortunes

The incomes from great fortunes may be disbursed in three ways (not counting taxes):

    (1) in luxurious spendings for the owner and his family;
    (2) in philanthropy; and
    (3) in capital-increase.

According to the author's views, only the first of these three should be taxed. Public opinion has already sanctioned some exemption of the second. The task remains to obtain exemption for the third.

This third use of large incomes may, in its practical effects, be quite as socially useful as the second. It means, of course, the building of equipment from which future income will flow and become available for the same three purposes.

"Government Can Invest Better"

Another alleged argument for the accretion tax, with its government appropriation of private savings, is that the government can invest the savings thus appropriated better than the private saver could.

In some exceptional cases, this is true. We may cite at least the Post Office and the Panama Canal—the Canal, because of its size and military importance; the Post Office, because private enterprise could not be relied on to make such a service universal, and universality is necessary.

There is, in fact, a great field for public investment where private enterprise would not repay the private investor; for instance, in the elimination of the smoke nuisance, in sanitation, public health work generally, the drainage of swamps, the extermination of mosquitoes and our other insect enemies. Many other sources of disease such as the hookworm could be enormously reduced by known measures of public health if sufficient funds were invested in such work.

But in few, if any, cases is the government enterprise "better" because of better management or more skillful investment in the ordinary sense.

In general, as Professor Warren Persons and others have shown, government management of business in the United States is distinctly inferior. A recent striking example is described in *Reader's Digest*:[10]

While the government is losing millions in farm resettlement projects, this business development of run down farms is already bringing the Metropolitan and its tenants $12,000,000 a year. [From farms on which mortgages were foreclosed.]

The superiority of business management over government management is especially marked in the pioneering of new inventions, though government bureaus often excel in *promoting the scientific studies* which lead to such inventions.

The inventor in many cases, as shown by Professor Taussig in his book on the subject, usually cares little about making money and sometimes functions better on a small fixed salary than when risking any capital.

Private enterprise and government enterprise have naturally distinct and separate spheres for their activities. There is a "twilight zone" between, but we can never expect government, as we now know it, to supersede successfully all private enterprise.

But (and this seems conclusive), even if the government as

[10] Ralph Wallace, in October, 1938, issue. (Condensed from Country Home Magazine.)

an investor were superior in general, that fact would not justify a savings tax, so long as we allow private enterprise at all. For by waiting till the death of the private accumulator, the government would as shown in Chapter 9 get far *larger* revenues on which to practice its superior skills.

Chapter 11

SOCIAL CONSEQUENCES

DOUBLE taxation and double exemption, punishing the thrifty and rewarding the spendthrift, are presumably unjust.

Compound destructiveness, punishing invention and the pioneering of inventions, is presumably unjust.

But justice is a difficult concept. And before struggling with it in the abstract, let us strengthen our presumption of injustice by observing that an annual accretion tax carries a threat to democracy.

DEMOCRACY

Recently we talked with an American "self-made" man.[1] A few years ago he had been a wage-earner—a foreign-born toolmaker. His American employer set him a puzzling problem in airplane safety. By a simple but almost epoch-making invention he solved it. Today he is himself an employer and seems destined to become one of the country's richest men, though he will never be a big spender. He said that in "the old country" he would not have been "allowed" to rise; but here the thing could happen and did. The result is that he loves America as a land of opportunity, individual initiative and self-expression.

And yet, under present tendencies, it is said that most of our manual workers have already given up the idea of ever rising out of their economic class. This may largely explain the recent growth of class consciousness in America. Naturally enough, those who are down impeach the institutions which seem to keep them down.

[1] The man quoted in Chap. 10 on the fun of building a business.

Social Mobility

A democratic state should be socially fluid. Just as the chance to become president is valued by every small boy and may serve as a strong incentive to be useful, so his chance to become a Henry Ford is valued and may be an incentive to usefulness. Some studies like those of Colin Clark would indicate that, although the inequalities in the distribution of income and of wealth seem to remain almost fixed in degree, the economic status of the individual grows more mobile with time. This, if true, is a good omen.

But there are factors which work precisely the other way; for any tax which includes savings must tend to keep the poor from ascending the economic ladder and the rich from descending it. And this indictment applies to existing income taxes in so far as they tax savings and exempt dissavings.

Primogeniture

As to death duties, reform is needed in order to discourage large bequests to individuals. There has been in America a tendency toward an hereditary plutocracy and even toward primogeniture, as in England.

This is due, not to great factories, which can survive a change of hands and can even survive a split-up of ownership, but to large luxurious landed estates, which cannot survive such a split-up, but in order to stay whole have to be passed on to one special heir.

In England, the eldest son is usually chosen as such heir. If we in America are to escape such undemocratic institutions as primogeniture, the escape, we venture to say, can probably be effected only through the adoption of the tax policy here advocated.

Discouraged by Tax Policy

By this means, the formation of luxurious landed estates would be penalized in life and thereby discouraged; and at death, the inheritor of such an estate would find its expensiveness magnified—in fact, magnified twice. The bigger the mansion the higher the tax on the inheritor to start with. Later, like his father before him, the inheritor would be penalized by the progressive spendings tax.

Such a tax policy would discourage mansions and encourage factories.

When rich men are an offense in the eyes of the relatively poor, it is because of their big domestic establishments and their big spendings, not because of their big savings and big industrial plants. Snobbery goes with the idle and extravagant way of living—with diamonds and retinues of servants; but snobbery is seldom seen in a big factory where the owner himself works. In fact, few workers in democratic America object to the rich man who lives and works like a poor man—who puts his gains into instruments of production, not into instruments of consumption.

Graduated spendings and death duties would show the way back from our threat of hereditary plutocracy toward simonpure democracy.

Too Much Capital?

In this connection we may cite an alleged objection to our emphasis on a "continual" accumulation of the national capital: "If the present generation is to subsist on a modest standard of living in order that generations yet unborn may have great luxury, I cannot subscribe to any such goal, nor, I think will most of your readers."

But a graduated spendings tax would not tend toward such a goal. On the contrary, it would curb the luxury of the rich while raising, generation by generation, the standard of living of the poor—"leveling up," not down, with more cheap cars, radios, refrigerators. There is so much room for improvement in this direction that we need not yet worry about universal luxury. If and when such a result ever confronts us we need only to raise the luxury rates still further.

It is quite true that our plan would result in bigger estates (though in factories not palaces); but any danger from such added "bigness" would be curbed by death duties.

JUSTICE IN WHAT YOU GET

Like democracy, justice is rooted in some idea of equality.

"All men are created free and equal," says the Declaration of Independence. But here at once the proposition has to be edited. It really means: "the man who is born is entitled, not necessarily to equal success, but to as nearly as possible an equal chance of success, and the equal protection of the law while he's trying. Of course, he must earn what he gets."

But here again, in the words "equal chance" and in the word "earn," common sense accepts the need of compromise. Chance is chance. It *cannot* be really equal.

THE SUBNORMAL ECONOMIC CONDITION

One object of both science and organization is to minimize chance. Also, that is the great idea of insurance. And the insurance idea grows ever broader. It has grown so broad as to provide, through the RFC, in the beginning of this War, for insurance *with no premium at all*, to every property owner in the United States against damage from Axis bombs. The damage, if it came, would fall principally on coast cities, but the expense would affect also the taxpayers in the interior. Yet, if any among these taxpayers were to protest against such unequal treatment, common sense would simply laugh him to scorn.

We are all "in the same boat," so that those among us who are unfortunate and even those who are down-and-out must be rescued. Of course, the factor of "deserving" may enter and distinguish between the "deserving poor" and the undeserving. Just the same, both must be rescued. The phrasemakers may explain this as "not justice, but justice tempered with mercy"; but common sense will come back: "two words, if you prefer, but fundamentally one thing;—anyhow, one *scheme* of things."

For the original purpose of society was and is mutual protection. Call it mercy sometimes and sometimes justice, but always it is the duty of somebody—and of society if there is nobody else—to throw a protecting arm around the unfortunate.

Is this justice?

Today we think so. We call it "social justice." But the author's first and most revered teacher in economics, William Graham Sumner, though himself full of human sympathy and having even started his career as a clergyman, had no such theory of justice. His able and sprightly book, *"What Social Classes Owe Each Other,"* answered that question by an almost unqualified "nothing."

Common sense rebelled. Beatrice Webb said, "that book made me a Socialist." At any rate, the invincible swimmer who allows a poor swimmer to drown, even if the law does not punish him, is just as obnoxious to common opinion as is the man who cheats.

When "workmen's compensation" was introduced under Theodore Roosevelt, many trained technicians said, "It's unjust. If a workman is injured without the fault of his employer, and with his own contributory negligence, surely it's unjust to make the employer pay." The Chief Justice of Connecticut took this view and brought forth such vituperation from Theodore Roosevelt—the most powerful advocate of workman's compensation—that a libel suit against the then ex-President was narrowly averted.

But the final answer was on the ex-President's side: "The workman," said the voters, "works not only for his employer but for society. *Both* of them work for society. Society must save the workman. Under 'workmen's compensation,' society simply chooses the employer as its agent for that purpose—and gives him the aid of an insurance company." Perhaps the same protection could be accomplished in a better way, but this way, under human imperfections, is good enough for today's practice. It "works" better for all concerned than the old theory that made the "neglectful" workman wholly responsible.

"Justice" is as good a name for this protection as "mercy" or "charity," and the same applies to the so-called Legal Aid Societies which furnish poor people with legal service, either free of charge or in proportion to their ability to pay. Otherwise, "equal protection of the law" is impossible.

And again, such organizations as the Mayo Clinic sometimes charge sheer nothing for the most difficult operations.

Doctors and lawyers, as a matter of course, regulate their charges in proportion to ability to pay. They are, in a sense, society's agents for saving life. True, the agency thus far is inchoate; but the lawyers and the doctors do not boast, and their clients are not ashamed.

JUSTICE IN WHAT YOU PAY

So much for what you get.

But now, as a step toward taxation, let us take the converse case in which the salary earner goes out into the market to buy at market prices. Here, instead of receiving money in proportion to the service he gives, he gives money in proportion to the service he gets; and if he is poor and pays only in proportion to his ability, he buys poorer grades of service or of goods.

Or if he does insist on bread as fine as the rich consume, he gets in proportion as he pays—that is, he pays *out* of proportion to his ability or he buys less.

But when it comes to paying for *government* services—paying in the form of taxes—the government first *compels* him to receive the service and then dictates the price.

Here justice would seem to require the government to be at least as generous as the surgeon and the lawyer and to figure its charge in proportion to the citizen's ability to pay.

And this is the prevailing method.

Yet in some departments of public service, the citizen pays in proportion to what he gets and not in proportion to his ability—for instance, for postage stamps; for bridge tolls; for local improvements, which he pays for per front footage of his real estate and not per ability. And though he is free to refuse to buy a stamp or cross a bridge, he is not free to refuse the local improvement.

But when it comes to such public services as sanitation and police protection and the general cost of government, the individual pays—or is supposed to pay—in proportion to his ability. He may even pay sheer nothing and yet get as much of the service in question as Rockefeller.

Here are the two chief principles: (1) the benefit principle—be taxed in proportion to what you get (usually for an occasional service); (2) the ability principle—be taxed in proportion to your ability—usually for a permanent day-and-night condition—the general maintenance of the state. This is like a family burden. All chip in.

Two principles for two different conditions: (1) Pay in proportion to the service to your individual self. (2) Chip in, in proportion to your ability.

We Use Discordant Principles

Who can prove that either of these principles is universally right? Life is a jumble. It cannot altogether escape rule of thumb. It must cut many Gordian knots. And we are quite willing to accept *both* methods of taxation as reasonably tending, under their respective circumstances, to produce "the greatest good for the greatest number."

Our own tentative formulation would be: "Let's have equality of chance to acquire the strength to bear the country's burdens; but, when it comes to bearing those burdens, let the weight rest on us in proportion to our strength."

We have shown the practical advantages to the country of a yield or spendings tax as compared with a yield-plus-capital-increase tax which we found to be definitely a double tax. But, query: Might not this double tax, after all, be more in proportion to the taxpayer's ability to pay? Would not a simple spendings tax let the saver off too easy?

OPPONENTS OF YIELD

This is where the opposition takes up the case of A and B, regardless of the country as a whole and of the future.

They say that, even though the savings of rich Mr. B do not stand for immediate real income in the sense of bread and butter, they do stand for some sort of immediate "psychic income," in the sense of joy and security. Did not Schwab and others boast that they worked largely for the "fun" of the thing? In a word, the rich man who chooses to live outwardly like a poor man does not really live like a poor man; for, in place of diamonds, he has the safety and the thrill. He should be taxed on these overtones. He has the pleasure of hope and anticipation; he has the satisfactions of accomplishment in accumulating wealth; and all these gratify him regardless of what, if anything, is ever done with the money (or wealth) which he accumulates. This present pleasure of anticipation and imagination should be taxed—so the argument runs—taxed *in addition to* any future *realizations* of the present dreams.

This idea is a persistent one. It appears in the writings of Guillebaud and of others cited in Appendix to Chapter 8.

It is burlesqued in the story of a Jew who, while cooking one of his savory meals, observed a Scotch neighbor poking his nose through the fence to enjoy the smell. The Jew demanded that the Scotchman pay for the privilege of sniffing. The Scotchman retreated but came back the next day, clinking some coins in his pocket; and he said, "I'll give you the sound of my money for the smell of your dinner!"

Undoubtedly, in the mysterious working of our psychic machinery, the image of a future wished-for pleasure may be itself pleasurable (and tantalizing!). But the image can scarcely, if ever, equal the reality. In the markets, the price of sniffing never equals the price of a square meal, nor can the value of clinking equal that of real cash. No matter how much a man may protest that he enjoys making money more than using it later, such joys do not seem greatly to affect the stock market.

The rule that market value is future *realization* discounted still holds true.

The same rule applies to gifts. A man may enjoy giving a Christmas present to his wife or bequeathing a fortune to his son. But the market value of the gift or fortune is the discounted value of the future uses made of the gift by the wife, and of the fortune by the son. In fact, if it should be arranged that there shall be no such future uses, the anticipatory pleasure of the giving would immediately collapse. Mere anticipation without realization amounts to nothing, though the realization be experienced by one person and the anticipation by another.

Those who would put psychic overtones on a level with realized experiences are mixing dreams with waking realities.

Here, as in so many other cases, we doubtless have a case of rationalization. That is, the idea that we ought to tax these alleged psychic incomes is an attempt to justify an unjustifiable levy.

Moreover, the accumulator does not always feel the pleasurable overtones of safety and thrill of anticipations. Sometimes he is paralyzed by fears for his future. Sometimes he is even driven to suicide. Should we, then, *un*tax him?

Psychic income is of fundamental importance in economic theory but has, as yet, no clear and definite place in common-sense practical taxation. We can't measure all psychic income in dollars and cents, and, if we could and applied the measure to taxation, many a happy poor man would be taxed heavily and many an unhappy rich man would get off scot free.

Shall we say that Eli Whitney whose cotton gin has enriched the world by billions of dollars was justly treated? He made no money out of it because his invention was stolen and utilized before he could get patent protection; yet he had the delectable experience of doing the inventing and serving his country. Common sense says he was unjustly treated. Common sense believes in patent protection. Even if we could prove that patent protection is unjust, common sense would accept it as good policy. At any rate, common sense would not tax Whitney on the joy

of achievement not followed by material advantage. We can far
better justify giving the successful man a negative tax, that is
a bounty for his services to mankind when he creates an
industry.

Or, again, if a man likes to make money irrespective of any
use he or his family or others may have for it, the sensible
thing for the state to do is to subsidize him rather than tax him.

ABILITY TO PAY

It is said that the rich man who, in order to save, chooses to
live like a poor man, can *afford* to pay more than the really
poor man.

John Stuart Mill answered this with characteristic incisive-
ness. He said:

It has been further objected that, since the rich have the greatest
means of saving, any privilege given to savings is an advantage bestowed on the rich at the expense of the poor. I answer that it is
bestowed on them only in proportion as they divert their income from
the supply of their own wants to a productive investment, through
which, instead of being consumed by themselves, it is distributed in
wages among the poor. If this be favoring the rich, I should like to
have it pointed out what mode of assessing taxation can deserve the
name of favoring the poor.

PROGRESSIVENESS

But, once we choose our tax basis—our income *available* for
taxation—we are confronted with the question of rates. Certainly the sacrifice of one dollar out of an available income of
$1,000 "hurts" more than the sacrifice of one dollar out of an
income of $10,000—other things equal (as we must assume).

And here it is our belief that both theory and practice must
take into account the marginal utility of income—or "marginal
desirability," as Marshall proposed to call it; or "ophelimity"
(to use Pareto's term); or the "want for one more dollar," as
the present writer once proposed to call it.

Steps Toward Measurement

The present writer once attempted to block out a method of statistically *measuring* the marginal factor—a method which could be applied when sufficient statistics sufficiently reliable should have been made available.[2] Later, Professor Ragnar Frisch, combining our method with one which he had previously suggested, made a first attempt to obtain actual statistical results.[3] These were, however, startlingly different from what many people would have expected. According to his results (very tentative, of course), if a man's income is halved, his marginal want for one more dollar is not *more* than doubled, as commonly supposed—not even *doubled*—but *less* than doubled.

Or, conversely, if his income is doubled his desire for one more dollar, though reduced, is reduced by less than half.

Frisch's Tentative Conclusion

Let us, for argument (as we are inclined to do in practice), accept Edgeworth's rule that equal marginal sacrifice must be the criterion. If the top bracket of a person's income of $10,000 (say the portion of his income between $9,000 and $10,000) were taxed 20 per cent (or $200), then the uppermost bracket of a person's income of $20,000 (the bracket between $18,000 and $20,000) should, if the Frisch calculation is correct, be taxed *less* than 20 per cent (or less than $400; say $300). That is, we would have, in the successive higher brackets, not progressive, but *re*gressive rates.

This result may well be correct as to *accretion*-income, and presumably the income statistics employed by Frisch were nearer to accretion-income than to yield-income, as probably all income statistics are.

---

[2] The study referred to was "A Statistical Method for Measuring 'Marginal Utility' and Testing the Justice of a Progressive Income Tax." (*In* Economic Essays Contributed in Honor of John Bates Clark. Macmillan, 1927).

[3] New Methods of Measuring Marginal Utility. Verlag von J. C. B. Mohr (Paul Siebeck). Tübingen, 1932, 142 pp.

But, as to *yield*-income, it could still be true—and probably is true—that if the yield (i.e., spendings) is doubled, the desire for one more dollar will be reduced not only to half but to far below half, so that, if the spendings are doubled, the tax should be more than doubled. In fact, Dr. Hans Staehle of Harvard has obtained such results (as yet unpublished) based on spendings and worked out by the present writer's method.

And perhaps those who take for granted that the dollar sinks in our estimation faster than our income rises are unconsciously thinking of income as spent.

Marginal Wants and the Spendings Tax

If we are to consider marginal desirability of money as a "function" of *one* variable only, that variable should, we believe, be consumption—that is, spendings. That is, the marginal want for bread depends much on the amount of bread consumed and little, if at all, on the amount the consumer *could* buy. The same is true of his marginal desire for clothing, shelter, music. A rich man who lives like a poor man will hunger almost equally with the poor man. Because of his "abstinence" through saving he will not be much more nearly sated than the poor man. Certainly his desires for these things will be nearer the poor man's than will the desires of his equally rich, but more self-indulgent and less saving brother.

If this is correct, it is reasonable to think that a saver's "want for one more dollar" should be reckoned in relation to the dollars he spends rather than to the dollars he spends plus the dollars he saves.

Many Variables Involved

Apparently the most comprehensive and intensive study of theories of progression and their merits was made by Professor Elmer B. Fagan[4] of Stanford University.

[4] Recent and Contemporary Theories of Progressive Taxation. (*In* Journal of Political Economy, August, 1938 pp. 457-98).

Among his conclusions is this:

According to my version of the socio-political theory, the question of progressive versus proportional or regressive taxation is one which must be decided by ethical judgment rather than by psychological measurement.

We agree that "ethical" rather than "psychological" considerations are paramount. While Fagan does not clearly define the concept, we assume that the essential point is this: in taxing a person, it is not his personal interest but the public interest which should prevail.

Such a distinction covers what we have so much emphasized in this book, namely, the effect of a tax on the nation's capital equipment. While we are gravely theorizing about the unsolved—perhaps unsolvable—problem of how to equalize some sort of psychical magnitude among taxpayers, we must not forget the practical effects on the nation's capital and income as a whole. If we attain some ideal equalization only by making almost everybody poorer, we are making a mockery of justice. It is better to improve the lot of all, even if this involves great inequalities, than to injure all by the equalization. Sumner's aphorism is roughly apt: "We should level up not level down."

CONCLUSIONS

That we are a long way from agreement or certainty in this field is evidenced by the change in views now going on. Professor Lutz[5] of Princeton represents a movement toward a flat tax rate, relinquishing altogether the usual idea of progression.

At the other extreme is a movement represented by an Ohio reformer who is proposing that an acre of real estate should be taxed not in proportion to its value but in proportion to the total wealth of its owner.

In comparing rival tax systems on the score of justice, we

[5] See Harley L. Lutz, Some Errors and Fallacies of Taxation as Exemplified by the Federal Income Tax. (*In* Proceedings of the National Tax Association. 34th Annual Conference, 1941. Washington, D. C. National Tax Association pp. 354-350).

cannot take for granted, as so many do, that the tax systems compared are equal in other respects than justice and that, in particular, there are no great differences between them as to their practical effects on the general level of incomes. We have seen that this assumption is not true when we compare a tax on spendings plus savings with a tax on spendings plus successions.

Thus again we point out that the transcendent consideration must be the *general effects* of the tax system on the *general welfare*.

So we come back, as always, to the most practical consideration of all: that it is good policy to harness up the saver as we would harness up a willing race horse and let him have his head, rewarding him with a little sugar instead of whipping him (which only makes him sulk)—all this on the theory that his race is our race and it is to our interest to promote his saving but restrict his spending.

PART III. *LEGAL*

CHAPTER 12. "INCOME" ACCORDING TO COMMON USAGE

CHAPTER 13. "INCOME" ACCORDING TO LAW

CHAPTER 14. STOCK DIVIDENDS

CHAPTER 15. THE CAPITAL GAINS TAX

CHAPTER 16. WHEN INCOME AND INCOME TAXES FAIL TO SYN-
CHRONIZE

CHAPTER 17. DOUBLE TAXATION AND TAX EVASION

CHAPTER 18. COMPLEXITIES

CHAPTER 19. LESSONS FROM BRITISH EXPERIENCE

CHAPTER 20. CONSTITUTIONALITY

CHAPTER 21. CONCLUSIONS

"INCOME" ACCORDING TO COMMON USAGE[1]

UP TO this point we have argued the merits of Yield vs. Accretion.

In Part III we shall show how the actual American law is a mixture of both concepts, affected by the worst faults of accretion.

The fundamental principle of the law is that it aims to conform with common usage.

First of all, then, what is common usage—or is there such a thing?

Second, does the law succeed in conforming with it?

The most authoritative of all dictionaries, *Murray's English Dictionary on Historical Principles,* concludes (after many citations): "Income, in its usual acceptation, is a loose and vague term." The correctness of this characterization cannot be doubted by anyone who has made any careful study of the subject.

If economics is to be a genuine science, comparable in definiteness and usefulness with other sciences, it ought to be possible to frame such concepts as will serve the needs of scientific analysis, even if those concepts only approximately fit the "loose and vague" usage of the "man in the street." He will gladly accept such a concept if it "works."

In physics, scientists have framed exact definitions for many terms used less exactly by laymen—such terms as speed, acceleration, force, momentum, work, energy, heat, density; and we find that laymen, without hesitation or objection, accept

---

[1] For "Income" according to experts see Appendix to (this) Chap. 12.

these technical definitions and recognize them as more precise formulations of what they themselves had been groping for in daily usage. Nor is the layman at all troubled when he finds that common usage and technical science do not and cannot wholly coincide. When informed that there is some "heat" in ice, he is surprised and amused, but accepts the fact. He knows that the technical concept of heat *"works"* better than the corresponding "loose and vague" popular notion. In the same way he would, we believe, be just as acquiescent as to "income," if economists were to furnish him with scientific concepts which "work" better than his own "loose and vague" ones.

QUESTIONING THE COMMON MAN

It is certainly strange that, so far as we know, no economist, statistician, legislator, or court, however much they all may profess to reverence the notions of the common man, has ever yet taken the trouble to ask this common man himself—though his name is legion—what his idea of income is.

Two of the author's students, Mr. John E. Firman of Buffalo, N. Y., and Edmond C. Maroder of Pasadena, Calif., have, under the author's supervision, made such an inquiry. They put twelve typical questions to one hundred typical laymen. Each of these questions was so framed as to admit of two answers, one covering what we have called yield-income, excluding capital-increase, and the other what we have called accretion-income, including capital-increase.

Of course, those who were questioned were not given any information concerning these concepts, nor were they asked leading questions. They were simply asked to state which of two figures, in a given case, seemed to them properly to be called the true income.

Economists were, of course, excluded from the canvass as being too sophisticated on the subject to serve as specimens of the unsuspecting, unbiased common man.

In the following report, for convenience of reference, the answers conforming with yield are labeled "Y" and the answers conforming with accretion are labeled "A," though these letters were not, of course, used on the questionnaire.

The first question was:

1. Suppose a certain stock "earns" $3 a share during a certain year, but "yields" in dividends $2 per share, the other $1 being undivided profits on the books of the company.

You own 1,000 shares, so that you receive in that year $2,000 in dividends. What would you ordinarily consider your income from that stock?

    Y. $2,000 (81 so thought)
    A. $3,000 (17 so thought)
    U. Undecided (2 were undecided)

The second question:

2. Suppose your income from all sources (before savings) to be $4,000, and, out of this, you save and reinvest $1,000 (by depositing it in a savings bank, buying a bond, putting it into your business, or otherwise). Would you think of your total income as

    Y. $3,000 (14 so thought)
    A. $4,000 (84 so thought)
    U. (2 undecided)?

In this case, the preference was almost exactly reversed. Evidently the common man is not consistent with himself nor even always sure of himself.

But, if we wish to give him the benefit of every doubt, we may say, as to the second question, that in answering A, perhaps he did not really have the accretion point of view but was thinking of that $4,000 as "gross" yield. For, in this case, *unlike* the preceding one, the larger sum was actually received in cash. It could be argued, therefore, that 84 thought of the income in the second question as gross yield and 14 thought of it as net yield but that both thought in terms of yield.

The third question:

3. Suppose you have stock worth $100,000 on the market January 1, 1940. On December 31, 1940 (12 months later), this stock has increased in value to $107,000. No dividends are paid by the company

for that year, and you neither buy nor sell any of the stock during 1940. Do you regard this $7,000 increase in paper profits as income?

    Y. No (84)
    A. Yes (13)
    U. Undecided (3)

These answers are nearly consistent with the answers to Question 1.

The next question:

4. Suppose you have $100 in a savings bank. The bank allows 5% interest on this and so increases your account by $5 during a period of one year, but does not pay it to you. Would you consider this $5 as part of your income?

    Y. No (24)
    A. Yes (75)
    U. Undecided (1)

Here is a definite preponderance in favor of accretion income.

But, though technically the $5 credit in the savings bank is not paid to and received by the owner of the account, most laymen think of a savings bank deposit as cash, just as truly as a checking deposit. If this is true, we may still maintain that the preponderant vote, thus far, is in favor of *some* sort of yield concept.

5. You have in a savings bank $150. The bank allows you 5% interest and so increases your account by $7.50 during a period of one year. On December 31 you withdraw $6 of this accrued interest. What would be your income from this savings account?

    Y. $6.00 (14)
    A. $7.50 (82)
    U. (4)

6. On January 1, 1940, you have a savings account of $50. The bank paid 5% interest. On December 31, 1940, twelve months later, your accrued interest amounted to $2.50, and you withdrew it. Later, during the same day, you changed your mind and deposited the same $2.50 in the same account. What was your income from that account for that year?

Y. $0.00 (11)
A. $2.50 (85)
U. (4)

7. For many years your income has been $5,000 a year. Last year in your spare time you diligently worked a small mining claim, which suddenly brought you $500,000. You spent $50,000 and invested $450,000 in bonds. What was your income for that year?

Y. $55,000 (9)
A. $505,000 (81)
U. (10)

Here the number favoring net cash yield is smaller than for any other question among the twelve; and the number of those perplexed is greater than for any other question but No. 9.

Nevertheless, in this seventh question, as in No. 2, we may regard A as gross yield.

8. Suppose your investments were worth $100,000. Last year you received $5,000 from those investments. This year you also received $5,000, but your investments shrank in value to $99,000. Which of the following items would be your "income" for this year?

Y. $5,000 (69)
A. $4,000 (28)
U. (3)

The majority are for yield; but a large minority are for accretion.

9. You have purchased from an insurance company a $6,000 a year life annuity, and on the basis of your age it costs you $50,000. The same policy, if taken out one year later, would have cost you only $49,000. During the year you spent the whole $6,000. Your annuity meanwhile decreased in value (as was stated) by $1,000. What do you consider as your income for that year?

Y. $6,000 (64)
A. $5,000 (25)
U. (11)

10. Several years ago you purchased an orange grove. The trees were very young and had not yet reached their period of peak pro-

duction; lack of sufficient water had also prevented the trees from attaining their best growth and productivity. But during the twelve month period of time, January 1, 1940 to December 31, 1940, there was more than sufficient rainfall, and your trees reached a high level of productivity. Real estate experts informed you that your orange grove had increased in value during this twelve month period, and that, whereas it had been worth only $30,000 on January 1, 1940, it was now worth $40,000 on December 31, 1940. This represented an increase of $10,000. During this period of twelve months your income from other sources was $5,000. Which of the following figures do you regard as your income for the specified twelve-month period?

    Y. $5,000 (92)

    A. $15,000 (7)

    U. (1)

11. You own a vacant lot which is tax free. On January 1, 1940, the lot was evaluated by a real estate expert at $2,000. On December 31, 1940, twelve months later, the same real estate expert informed you that your lot was now worth $3,000. He also stated that the reason for the $1,000 increase in value was due to the fact that a big corporation was going to build a large factory in the vicinity. During this twelve-month period your income from all other sources amounted to $8,000. Which of the following figures represented your income for the twelve-month period?

    Y. $8,000 (85)

    A. $9,000 (12)

    U. (3)

12. You own a large factory worth $800,000. From January 1, 1940 to December 31, 1940, this factory paid you $40,000. During this period of twelve months the factory was damaged by fire to the extent of $200,000. Which of the following figures represents your income for that period of time?

    Y. $40,000 (68)

    A. $—160,000 (27)

    U. (5)

REVIEWING THE ANSWERS

On the face of the returns, we find that the two concepts are about equally popular. The Y's are 51 per cent, the A's 45 per cent, and the U's 4 per cent.

And, as usually happens when people cannot give convincing reasons for their opinions, they often defended them all the more fanatically. The questionnaires became in some cases the subject of debate in corner drugstores in Los Angeles, with the debaters in some instances nearly coming to blows.

And not only is there a wide diversity of opinion, but there is some confessed uncertainty, especially in the case of Question 9 (presumably because of unfamiliarity with annuity problems) and Question 7 (presumably because income is expected to be more regular).

But the common man has some method in his madness. If we rank the twelve questions in the order of the number of "A" answers we find that they fall into three well defined groups, as follows:

Ques. 6. Savings bank interest withdrawn but immediately redeposited   A = 85

" 2. Savings made out of income and reinvested   A = 84

" 5. Part of savings bank interest withdrawn   A = 82

" 7. Large and sudden mining profit partly spent, partly reinvested   A = 81

" 4. Savings bank interest accrued but not paid out   A = 75

Ques. 8. Depreciation of investments   A = 28

" 12. Factory damaged and reduced in value by fire   A = 27

" 9. Depreciation in value of a life annuity, with age   A = 25

Ques. 1. Whether the yield or the earnings of stock should be called income   A = 17

" 3. Appreciation of investments   A = 13

" 11. Appreciation of vacant lot   A = 12

" 10. Appreciation of orange grove   A = 7

The first group, in which a large majority (from 75 to 85 per cent) of the votes are "A" votes, consists of the savings bank cases and the mining profit case in all of which the capital-increase was realized in cash or so considered. They are all, therefore, cases in which the accretion-income is, at the same time, gross yield income.

In the other two groups, where the A votes are in a small minority, the capital-increase (or capital-decrease) is merely an appraised figure, not realized in cash.

It appears, therefore, that the common man usually thinks of income as yield though not always as *net* yield.

But the most interesting contrast is that between the second and third groups. Fundamentally these two groups are the same except that one is in terms of capital-increase, and the other, in terms of capital-decrease. Yet the contrast is great. Only 13 voted that appreciation of investments is to be regarded as (positive) income while 28 voted that depreciation is (negative) income!

This seems to mean that modern corporation accounting (which is accretion accounting) has accustomed the common man to expect depreciation to be written off and so has caused him to deviate a little from his natural Yield instincts; while, as such accounting seldom sanctions writing *up*, the common man's idea contains, in this case, a smaller admixture of Accretion.

The Commonest Concept-Mixture

It would seem, therefore, that the typical common man has a fairly definite concept of "income," muddled as it is. The typical, that is the commonest, common man thinks of his "income" as cash yield—a net cash yield if the capital-increase is only appraised but gross cash yield if the capital-increase is realized in cash.

He seldom deducts depreciation; and still more seldom does he add appreciation. His "income" is simply his cash receipts.

It therefore includes (generally) private savings and partnership savings but not (generally) corporation savings.

Following is the vote for this illogical concept mixing gross and net Yield and so mixing Yield and Accretion:

	For the Cash Concept	Against the Cash Concept	Undecided
Question 1	81 (Y)	17 (A)	2 (U)
Question 2	84 (A)	14 (Y)	2 (U)
Question 3	84 (Y)	13 (A)	3 (U)
Question 4	75 (A)	24 (Y)	1 (U)
Question 5	82 (A)	14 (Y)	4 (U)
Question 6	85 (A)	11 (Y)	4 (U)
Question 7	81 (A)	9 (Y)	10 (U)
Question 8	69 (Y)	28 (A)	3 (U)
Question 9	64 (Y)	25 (A)	11 (U)
Question 10	92 (Y)	7 (A)	1 (U)
Question 11	85 (Y)	12 (A)	3 (U)
Question 12	68 (Y)	27 (A)	5 (U)
	950	201	49

A "fair average" of these votes is indicated by the totals. These show 950 votes conforming to the more typical common man's set of answers, with 201 votes against and 49 undecided.

We may analyze the results one step further. Of the 100 individuals, the number that answered with complete consistency (according to the three types of answers) was very small—as follows:

The common man's cash norm   26
Net cash yield   1
Accretion   1

Also there was one individual who answered "undecided" for all twelve questions!

But, many were *nearly* consistent, as follows:

Voters who had not more than 3 inconsistencies:

72 for the illogical cash norm
4 for net cash yield
3 for accretion

That is, 79 were nearly self-consistent.

Conclusions

We conclude that the majority of "common" men and women are roughly self-consistent according to the common man's norm above set up—cash received or credited as if received.

This "income" of the common man usually includes whatever is saved by him after it is received and so put at his disposal, but usually excludes whatever was saved *for* him as corporate profits or in trust.

But what is accumulated in a savings bank is usually included, this being almost as easily disposable as demand deposits or pocket cash. The common man's concept is, as we have seen, clearly a mixture of gross and net yield and probably also of yield and accretion—certainly in a minority of the 100 answers.

Yet, illogical as is such a mixture, it serves the chief practical purpose of "income" in the mind of the ordinary man having a small and simple income, namely, the purpose of disposing of what is disposable by him. For this simple purpose he does not need to take into account the undistributed profits on any stock he owns but he does need to take into account whatever he saves himself.

This characterization seems to be the best answer we can extract from the replies to the questionnaire.

It is true that 100 is a small number from which to generalize; but the number is sufficient to create a strong presumption. Moreover, all the six classes included in the 100 cases—clerks, sales and managerial, professional, skilled labor, manual labor, domestic and personal service, college students—arrived at similar results except as to one[2] of the twelve questions.

Besides the above 100 questionnaires studied intensively by the two students, there were 44 other cases reported by other students. Their replies were of much the same pattern. Of these

[2] To that one (No. 8) 5 of the skilled labor group voted Y, 6 voted A, and 1 voted U, whereas in each of the other five groups the majority voted Y.

44, there were 23 who voted the straight ticket, that of the typical common man. The other 21 were scattered. None was always A.

It will be seen that, at best, *the common man's concept of income is not thoroughly self-consistent.* Moreover, *his typical self-consistent norm as expressed by a majority vote is an illogical mixture* of gross yield and net yield; and a still more illogical mixture of yield and accretion. Even our 100 cases are sufficient to establish these two conclusions which we put in italics; and it is unlikely that a thousand or a million cases would change them.

To found our whole system of income taxation, as legislated and as judicially interpreted, on the common man's notions, so hybrid, self-inconsistent, confused, uncertain, and vague is preposterous—just as preposterous as for physicists to found their theory of thermodynamics on what the common man thinks is "heat."

It is hardly just, even for the Supreme Court, to "decide" what is income in cases involving countless millions of dollars by guessing what the common man guesses is income.

PHRASES OF USAGE

Let us now see what our "man in the street" says spontaneously in many popular phrases.

When he talks of living "inside" his income (if we have correctly interpreted him in the questionnaire), he is thinking of that income as gross yield and of regulating his spendings with reference to that gross yield. It does not occur to him—it does not seem to him worth while—to subtract a small margin of savings in order to construct a separate concept of *net* yield.

When he speaks of *"spending* $1,000 *as income* instead of *investing it as capital,"* he is clearly thinking of income as something to be spent, not something to be invested.

Again, and more fundamentally, when he talks of his "real income" or "real wages" he most definitely means something coextensive with yield income—namely, what he gets from spending. It is significant that savings are never, apparently, included in the idea of "real" income.

OUR FOUR INCOME CONCEPTS

As we saw in Part II, there are two and only two legitimate concepts of income, one including and the other excluding savings. We have now seen that the common man sometimes includes savings and sometimes excludes them—illogically but usually consistently.

But none of these three concepts is as yet embodied in law although the common man's is presumed to be.

Thus, in all, we have to consider in this book four concepts of taxable income:

1. Net cash yield-income as set forth in Part I—equal to spendings and approximately equivalent to real income.

2. Accretion income (or enrichment or earnings) as set forth in Part II—suitable for business accounting for the important reason that it includes capital-increase as representnig future yield, but, for that same important reason, unsuitable as a tax base, since it pre-taxes said future yield and later, when it occurs, taxes it again.

3. The common man's "income" set forth in this chapter—a mixture of gross and net yield, being cash receipts including savings made from those receipts but not including savings withheld, unsuitable either for a tax base or for business accounting.

4. Legal "income," to be set forth in the following chapters, faintly resembling the common man's concept in that it includes private savings and excludes corporate savings, but resembling also accretion income and coinciding with it when applied to the taxation of corporate income.

Chapter 13

"INCOME" ACCORDING TO LAW

Magill

THE most exhaustive treatise on the American income tax law and its gropings for a concept is *Taxable Income* by Roswell Magill,[1] member of the New York bar, professor of law in Columbia University, and once Undersecretary of the Treasury.

The introduction is written by Professor Robert Murray Haig.

And from these two, who rank among the highest authorities on the subject, we gather that the original income tax law of 1913 was so "incredibly naïve" as to leave "numerous difficult problems" to be solved "by the off-hand conceptions of those to whom it was addressed"; that, as a consequence of this confused thinking, a new revenue act has had to follow almost annually; that Magill's big book became necessary to interpret the judicial interpretations; that he found "conflicts and internal inconsistencies"; that the judges had made various "assumptions" of which they had "often been unconscious"; so that Justice Holmes saw "nothing to be gained by the discussion of judicial definitions"; that this thrust was "perhaps" aimed at the most important attempt at such a definition, which was so unsatisfactory as to be called "cryptic" by Magill; that Magill after "four hundred pages" could triumphantly report that "one can trace with some accuracy the *outlines* of a concept of income through the decisions of the past twenty-three years"; and that even these outlines are in some particulars "rather vague."

---

[1] New York, Ronald Press, 1936.

Professor Magill entitles his closing chapter (italics ours) *"Toward* a Concept of Income," and sums up the approximation as follows:

The taxable income of an individual consists of (1) his total gross receipts during the period (other than gifts, bequests and devises), after subtracting its cost from the proceeds of any sale or other disposition of stock-in-trade or an investment, plus (2) any increase in his economic worth resulting from the discharge of his obligations.

1. Income so determined is considered to belong to the person who earned it, or who owned or controlled the investment which produced it.

2. The gross receipts of an individual include: (1) any item of money; and (2) any interests in property, having a money value, and differing in kind or in extent from those previously held by the recipient, which he has actually received, which he may obtain upon demand, or which have accrued during the period according to a recognized method of accounting employed in keeping his books.

3. Obligations for this purpose include not only one's debts, but recognized obligations to support and maintain one's family.

GRISWOLD

At our request, other income tax experts have kindly constructed outlines "toward" a concept of income as roughly traceable in our American law (since these statements were written, the law has been changed in some details of computation).

The first authority is Professor Erwin N. Griswold of the Harvard Law School. He says:

There are at least three elements in taxable income, which must be carefully considered, and often distinguished. These may be indicated by the words: (1) *what* is income? (2) *whose* income is it? and (3) *when* is it income? To a considerable extent these elements merge and blend, but they are, I believe, essential parts of any concept of taxable income.

It seems to me quite accurate to say today that taxable income includes any item of receipt or increment or benefit that Congress chooses to make taxable, except that probably that part of the receipts

from the sale of property equivalent to the cost of the property sold
may not be taxed as income. And Congress has in fact said, and the
Court has held, that virtually all of such receipts, increments, and
benefits are taxable, except (1) gifts and inheritances, (2) use income,
and (3) unrealized capital gains. It seems to me not impossible that
these three present exceptions may be put to some extent in the taxable class before present developments are over.

Le Deuc

Another outline toward a concept is kindly provided for us
by the controller, Dr. C. A. Le Deuc of Los Angeles. He says:
"The law was not built upon any scientific and logical concept
of income, but grew out of the necessity of raising revenue for
immediate needs, with very little concern about its long-range
effects upon the economic life of the nation. With this reserva-
tion, we may then venture the following definition":

Taxable income is the money value (so far as it is realized) of the
net increase in proprietorship during the taxable year from all
causes other than gifts and inheritance. It is the result of three elements: gross income, deductions, and credits.

Gross income, according to the revenue law, includes: all compensa-
tions for personal services, business profits, interest and dividends, and
all capital gains.

Deductions from gross income are such costs of getting the gross
income as are not already included in the figures stated as gross income. Moreover, contributions to philanthropic and scientific organizations are deductible up to 15% of the taxpayer's net income for
the year as computed without the benefit of this deduction.

Net income is the difference between gross income and authorized
deductions.

Moreover, from net income certain credits are deducted in order to
establish the base for the computation of the tax. Those credits are
of two kinds and deducted in two successive steps:

1. Personal exemption and credit for dependents are deducted. The
balance is the surtax net income, which is the base for a progressive
surtax percentage rate.

2. Then interest on Government obligations and earned income

credits are deducted from the surtax net income. The balance is the normal net income, which is the base for a constant percentage rate.

To determine gross income, deductions from gross income, and the resulting balance of net income, the Treasury has laid down the principle that "net income shall be reported on the basis of sound accounting practice." . . . If those rules had consistently been applied by the Treasury, the concept of taxable income would have been kept in harmony with that of business income, as the latter is understood by accountants.

In actual practice, however, the two concepts of income have drawn farther apart every year, because there exists a radical difference between the accountant's purpose and that of the Treasury in measuring the income of a year of business operations.

The accountant measures the income of a business enterprise solely for the purpose of getting an index of operating accomplishments during an accounting year. He is conscious that a balance of net profit is not to be considered as an indisputable fact, but merely as an approximation and an estimate. Knowing how uncertain his ground is, he is deeply concerned in excluding from his summation all income not fully realized, and in including every item of expense he may discover.

On the other hand, the Treasury looks at income as a well from which to draw revenue. Therefore, in its measurement of income, its understanding of what is, and what is not "sound accounting practice" is affected more by the desire of serving the immediate needs of the government by raising large amounts than by any care for keeping unharmed the productive agencies of the nation.

Dr. Le Deuc continues:

The federal taxing powers have made matters worse: they have revised the accounting procedure from the standpoint of tax collecting, and produced a bulky, intricate, and obscure system of taxation, which is a goldmine for tax counsellors and the despair of taxpayers.

Would not the economic concept of income, which is simple and scientific, be a better basis for taxation than the accounting concept of income which is technical and complex?

Dr. Le Deuc approves of our Yield system.

MONTGOMERY

Another authority, Robert H. Montgomery, says:[2]

I cannot refrain from reiterating my conviction that the Commissioner of Internal Revenue and the lawmakers have been continuously flagrant in their disregard of good accounting methods in the determination of taxable net income. . . . Thousands of disputes have arisen and hundreds of Court and Board cases have been decided on narrow technical grounds which completely disregard sound accounting practices.

It isn't the taxpayers' books and records and returns which are so complicated; it isn't the revenue agents and their superior officers in the Bureau of Internal Revenue; it isn't the lawyers in the Department of Justice; it isn't the Tax Board Members nor the Judges in our Court. It's the infernal law. No one pretends to understand what it says or means.

HOPE FOR PROGRESS

We now make our own examination of the law.

We do not propose to deny that the law is in a deplorable state. No one does. Even some of the lawmakers have called their own handiwork a "mess" and a "monstrosity."[3]

But these and other criticisms including our own must not be misunderstood. They are by no means a denial that much labor and great ability have gone into the making of the law. Especially admirable has been the skill and the beaglelike vigilance with which the Commissioner and his staff have kept up with the law—both statutory and judicial—and translated it into rules and especially into "forms" for tax returns.

The dire results are due to the lack of a simple concept at the start. And no such concept was ever submitted to the authorities, legislative or judicial. The economists themselves,

[2] Federal Tax Handbook, 1940-41. Volume I. Preface pages v and vi by Robert H. Montgomery, C.P.A. and Counsellor-at-Law, of Lybrand, Ross Bros., and Montgomery.

[3] See the Oct. 12, 1940 report of Tax Research Institute referring to Second Revenue Act of 1940 (Research Institute of America, New York City).

though diligent in the pursuit of theory, were not too much interested in the practical job of taxation. At any rate, the job got off to a false start; the false start has led to trouble; trouble has led to correction; and, in the absence of an absolutely fresh start, each correction has grown more tangled than the one corrected; each builder of a new and better extension has been handicapped instead of helped, by the very ability of his predecessors, until, by 1940, in spite of Professor Magill's hopeful expression "*toward* a concept," the aggregate structure, instead of being simplified, grows more and more like a labyrinth. And, in spite of all the simplification achieved by the Commissioner, we have heard the suggestion that the taxpayer should have a deduction for the legal expense of preparing his return.

Nevertheless, where there is good intention plus brains, an eventual solution ought to be sure. In fact, let us hope that the hard work already done will prove to be but a long process of crystallizing which will suddenly bear the predestined crystal.

How Did It Start?[4]

The Sixteenth Amendment under which the law has developed was made necessary by one of those 5-to-4 votes of the Supreme Court.

The Constitution had already given Congress full powers of taxation[5]—enough to cover income taxes; but, whereas so-called *indirect* taxes could be in proportion to the values of the items taxed,[6] so-called *direct* taxes had to be distributed among the states in proportion to their respective populations.[7]

[4] In the following pages "sec." refers to the Code as first adopted in 1939. "Sec." accompanied by a year numeral, etc., refers to the various amending acts including that of 1939. Discussions of the various acts of '40 and '41 are in smaller type, and references to them are in square brackets. "19." is prefixed to the references to sections of Treasury Regulations 103. "Stats." refers to U.S. "Statutes at Large."

[5] Article I, Section 8, Clause 1, with Section 2, Clause 3; Section 9, Cl. 4.

[6] Article I, Section 8, Clause 1 as interpreted by Knowlton v Moore, 178 U.S. 41, May 14, 1900. The exact requirement is "uniformity," interpreted in Chap. 20.

[7] Article I, Section 2, Clause 3.

In 1895, five members of the Court held that taxes on incomes *from property*, whether real or personal, were direct taxes and that, if the law contained such direct taxes without apportionment according to state populations, the entire law was unconstitutional though not all of its items were thus direct.[8]

Not many years earlier the Court had held that income taxes were not direct taxes, and even intimated that the *only* direct taxes were capitation taxes and taxes on real estate,[9] but it now excused itself for that oversight on the ground that its attention had not been called to the features of the act of 1864 involving income from property—real and personal.

But four of its members still insisted with great vigor, in four separate dissenting opinions, that taxes on income from property are not direct taxes on the property. Some of the arguments were: that really direct taxes could be apportioned per population without substantial unfairness, whereas an *income* tax thus apportioned would be so cruelly out of proportion to individual incomes that the Constitutional Convention could not have intended any such injustice; that the majority opinion was contrary to all American precedents for one hundred years; and that the Court should not invalidate an act of Congress, anyhow, if there was a reasonable doubt of its guilt.

But these views were defeated by one vote; so that, to relieve income taxes of this unjust apportionment rule, the Sixteenth Amendment had to be adopted in 1913.[10]

This was the first explicit appearance in the Constitution of the word "income," and though it added no new taxable items[11] (merely changing the apportionment rule), the Court decided that "income" must be defined, so as to determine how far an

[8] Pollock v Farmers Loan & Trust (as re-argued), 158 U.S. 601, May 20, 1895 (first argued in 157 U.S. 429, Apr. 8, 1895). (Partial unconstitutionality does not always result thus in total loss).

[9] Springer v U.S., 102 U.S. 586, Jan. 24, 1881.

[10] February 25, 1913. The first Income Tax Law thereafter became effective March 1, 1913. U.S. Statutes at Large, Vol. 38, p. 166 at 168, Chap. 16, Sec. II (D).

[11] Eisner v Macomber, 252 U.S. 189 at 206 (Mar. 8, 1920).

"income tax" might go without exceeding the power conferred by the Sixteenth Amendment.

EFFORTS TO DEFINE INCOME

Before the Sixteenth Amendment there was a corporate tax which successfully professed to be an excise tax and was therefore held to be constitutional. However, the excise was *measured* by income, so that, when disputes arose, the Supreme Court had to define "income"—as used by Congress in a statute. The question was what Congress meant.[12]

And after the Sixteenth Amendment, naturally, the Court had to define "income" as used in the Constitution, the question being what the Constitution meant.

And there turned out to be no difference.[13]

What was the definition?

Let us look at the cornerstone case of *Eisner* vs. *Macomber*[14] (after the Sixteenth Amendment).

First, the Court looked at the dictionaries and at books on economics, and from the latter cited a few figures of speech, such as: "The fundamental relation of 'capital' to 'income' has been much discussed by economists, the former being likened to the tree or the land, the latter to the fruit or the crop; the former depicted as a reservoir supplied from springs, the latter as the outlet stream, to be measured by its flow during a period of time";[15] but, on the theory that "the people" wrote the Constitution,[16] the Court concluded that income is whatever it means in "common speech,"[17] and that in common speech it

[12] Corporation Law of 1909. Flint v Stone Tracy Co., 220 U.S. 107 (Mar. 13, 1911); McCoach v Minehill, 228 U.S. 295 (Apr. 7, 1913); U.S. v Whiteridge, 231 U.S. 144 (Nov. 10, 1913); Stratton's Independence, Ltd. v Howbert, 231 U.S. 399, Dec. 1, 1913.

[13] Stratton's Independence v Howbert, 231 U.S. 399, Dec. 1, 1913.

[14] 252 U.S. 189, Mar. 8, 1920.

[15] From Macomber case. See Fisher, The Nature of Capital and Income, Chap. VII.

[16] I.e. "adopted." Merchants Loan & Trust v Smietanka, 255 U.S. 509 at 519, Mar. 28, 1921.

[17] Eisner v Macomber, 252 U.S. 189 at 206-207, Mar. 8, 1920.

means "gain derived from capital, from labor, or from both combined."

This is Magill's "cryptic" definition. It fits yield; it fits accretion; it fits almost any concept of income. It is not a definition. It tells the *sources* of income but not its *nature*. It does not even discuss the nature of the sources, such as capital. It merely substitutes the word "gain" for the word "income," without any real gain in understanding.

And then the trouble started.

In the following chapters we propose to show that the Court began with certain statements of principle which had an apparent leaning toward the Yield concept; that since then the law has swerved more and more toward the Accretion concept; that it has taken over the vices of Accretion but not its virtues; that despite the apparent liberality of the initial definition, the Court has so applied it as perhaps to render unconstitutional a full adoption of *either* concept—either Yield or Accretion.

The resulting law has a number of defects but the chief of them is the taxation of capital in a number of forms, including some stock dividends but emphatically not others.

Results:

1. Double Taxation.
2. Needless provocations for tax evasion and needless openings for it.
3. Prolix complexity.

Let us begin with the problem of stock dividends.

CHAPTER 14

STOCK DIVIDENDS

I. *Common on Common*

In the *Macomber* case,[1] a tax had been levied on a stock dividend; and it was in arguing against the constitutionality of such a tax that the Court defined income and used arguments which seemed to lean in the direction of the Yield concept, though without definitely reaching it.

The dividend was Common on Common, and represented profits plowed back.

No member of the Court quarreled with the definition— "gain from capital or labor or both." Nor with the citation of "common speech"—in other words, the man in the street—as the proper guide. Nevertheless, four members quarreled with the way in which the other five applied the alleged common man's definition.

The four, including Holmes and Brandeis, held that the dividend was income and therefore taxable to the stockholder. The five held it to be capital and therefore not taxable to the stockholder. Yet one of the four laid particular stress on the popular usage adopted by all nine as the ultimate test.

The majority, by the pen of Justice Pitney, argued that "nothing is distributed except paper certificates that evidence an antecedent increase"; that the distribution does "not alter the pre-existing proportionate interest of any stockholder"; that it takes nothing from the corporation and gives nothing *new* to the stockholder.

[1] Eisner v Macomber, 252 U.S. 189, Mar. 8, 1920.

And to the argument that the stock measured an "enrich-ment" of the stockholders, Pitney replied, "first, it would depend upon how long the stockholder had held the stock . . . Sec-ondly, enrichment through increase in value of capital invest-ment is not income."

Finally, the Court pointed out that a stock dividend does not, of itself, furnish the "wherewithal" to pay a tax upon it. "Noth-ing," said Justice Pitney, "could more clearly show that to tax a stock dividend is to tax a capital-increase, and not income, than this demonstration that it requires conversion of capital in order to pay the tax."[2]

Thus the Court seemed to lean rather clearly toward yield income and against enrichment income, or "accretion," which, on the other hand, was almost as clearly the objective of counsel for the government.

The Court also insisted that income must be "realized" and "severed" (from the capital).

ABOUT-FACE

But both "realized" and "severed" are figures of speech. They could easily be applied to any stock dividend. And, as a matter of fact, the ink of the *Macomber* case was scarcely dry before the Court began seizing almost any departure from the *Ma-comber form* as a reason for departing from the *Macomber substance*.

The first departures occurred in four reorganization cases: the *Phellis* case; the *Rockefeller* case; the *Cullinan* case; the *Marr* case.[3]

In all these, the general purpose was to revamp the stock issues of an existing business so as to make the new stock rep-resent in some way the accumulated, undistributed earnings which had been, in effect, added to the capital of the business

[2] Ibid., p. 213.

[3] U.S. v Phellis, 257 U.S. 156, Nov. 21, 1921; Rockefeller v U.S., 257 U.S. 176, Nov. 21, 1921; Cullinan v Walker, 262 U.S. 134, Apr. 30, 1923; Marr v U.S. 268 U.S. 536, June 1, 1925.

before reorganization. Before and after reorganization there was a substantial continuity of the business, without change of the physical assets or of personnel.

In the first two cases (*Phellis* and *Rockefeller*), the initial company continued to exist.

In the other two (*Cullinan* and *Marr*), the initial company was dissolved.

In all four, the instant before reorganization, the capital increases were, according to the Court, not taxable, but the instant after reorganization, these increases (so far as embodied in nominally new securities) became taxable.

In the two nondissolution cases, the new securities, being added to the old, were called a stock dividend and were taxed under that name.[4]

In the two dissolution cases, the new securities entirely replaced the old, and the increase in value, *which they took over from the old,* was taxed under the name of "gain."

There would seem to be one more difference—a difference in the degree of antecedence exposed to the tax by the reorganization. A stock dividend of the sort we have been considering may embody all the growth in capital value since incorporation,[5] and that entire growth is then exposed to the tax, so that, even if the stockholder purchased his stock shortly before the stock dividend, he is held tax accountable for the entire gain in value including any that may have preceded his purchase. This was definitely asserted in the *Phellis* case.

But in the "gain," or dissolution, cases, only the gain since the purchase by the individual and up to the dissolution is taxable; that is, the difference between the purchase price to the individual and the value of what he receives from the new company.

Nevertheless, these "gain" cases cited the "dividend" cases as authority.

[4] Phellis, 257 U.S. at 175, 170; Rockefeller, 257 U.S. at 183 "in effect."
[5] Or, of course, since the last stock dividend.

WHAT NEW FEATURE

What was the new feature of these four cases—both the dividend cases and the gain, or quasi-dividend, cases—which led the Court to differentiate them from the *Macomber* case, so as to transform antecedent untaxable gain into taxable gain?

The new feature was expressed in a variety of ways, but it all boiled down to a change in *legal complexion* of the new certificates; that is, *a qualitative and not a quantitative change*. And such a change might come about in either of two ways. It might be due to a change in the legal class of the certificate (as when a bond replaces a share of stock) or it might be due to a change in the identity of the corporation issuing the security.

HAIRSPLITTING

Even when the new stock in a reorganization was of the same class as the old, if it was *postponed* differently (because the preferred was different), it thereby became not only different but "essentially" different.[6]

On the other hand, if it is a change of corporate identity that changes the legal complexion of the stock, it must be a change of just the right degree. Before the *Marr* reorganization there occurred the *Weiss* reorganization,[7] which was held insufficient to make any of the new stock taxable, because the new stock was of the same kind as the old; the new company was incorporated in the same state as the old; its powers were "similar to those of the old."

And the conclusion was that the stockholder emerged without any "thing really different from what he theretofore had."

CONSISTENCY?

On three points, as it seems to us, the *Macomber* and *Phellis* decisions are fundamentally inconsistent, though both were from the same pen—that of Justice Pitney.

[6] Marr case, supra at 541.
[7] Weiss v Stern, 265 U.S. 242, May 26, 1924.

1. What became of his "wherewithal" argument, than which he said "nothing could more clearly show . . ."?

2. What became of his attack against "enrichment" as income—an argument which he said was "insuperable"?

3. What became of his objection (which also he called insuperable) that a man who buys the stock just before the issue of the stock dividend cannot fairly be taxed on a gain antecedent to his purchase? This last objection, when raised in the *Phellis* case, he answered by calling it simply a harder-than-usual case of buying stock, "dividend on."

"A layman or an economist," says Professor Magill, "would have extreme difficulty in seeing distinctions of substance" between the *Macomber* and *Phellis* cases, while the taxpayer in the *Marr* case, "privately, no doubt . . . called the law an ass."[8]

Nor were any of the cases unanimous, including the following two.

II. *Common on Preferred and Preferred on Common*

After a while the Court was confronted by two cases in which the problem was a straight stock dividend of an unchanged corporation. In this respect these new cases resembled the *Macomber* case, but in each there were two classes of stockholders; and in one—the *Koshland* case—the dividend was common on preferred; and in the other—the *Gowran* case—it was preferred on common.[9] And apparently these stock dividends did not represent a long capital growth but were regular current dividends in the form of stock instead of cash.[10]

Both the *Koshland* and *Gowran* cases seem to rely explicitly

[8] Taxable Income, pp. 66 and 123.

[9] Koshland v Helvering, 298 U.S. 441, May 18, 1936; Helvering v Gowran 302 U.S. 238, Dec. 6, 1937. The statute at the time of these cases did not actually tax stock dividends, but the Court held the dividends to be constitutionally taxable income. It was a premise for deciding another issue.

[10] In the Koshland case, the articles of incorporation provided for either $7 cash or a share of common as dividend; and in the Gowran case, though the articles of incorporation were not mentioned, the dividend was only $14 worth of stock on a par of $100.

on change of legal complexion. The *Koshland* case says: "an interest different from that which his former stock represented." The *Gowran* case says: an "interest . . . essentially different," and certainly accepts the Koshland case as its authority.

CHANGE OF PROPORTIONATE INTEREST?

But the *Marr* case has a summarizing phrase which might be interpreted as embodying a second reason for the tax, namely, change of proportionate interest, evidently meaning a change of any stockholder's interest in proportion to the total. The summarizing phrase is: "The case at bar is not one in which . . . the stockholders have the same proportional interest of the same kind in essentially the same corporation."

We are not sure that mathematics could not work out changes of proportion among the *kinds* of security—both in the *Marr* case and in the *Cullinan* case; but so far as the security *holders* were concerned, the distribution among them was undoubtedly pro rata, and the tax was levied on the pre-existing gain taken over by the new securities as a whole—not merely by one disproportionate class of security. Moreover, in another passage, the Court admitted that "the business enterprise . . . remained exactly the same," but answered that it was not a case (italics ours) of "*merely* the same proportional interest" in the enterprise. And the Court cited the *Phellis* case,[11] which pointed out explicitly the absence of any change of proportional interest, but taxed the stock dividend just the same—for change of legal character—as did the *Marr* case.

We think, therefore, that, both in the *Marr* and in the *Phellis* case, expressions like "the same proportional interest" were merely somewhat more meticulous synonyms for "his share"— the conclusion being that such a "*mere*" or *taken-for-granted* sameness of share in the same enterprise is *not enough* to deliver it from the tax on pre-existing gain when that gain gets a new legal character.

And would not sameness of proportion be naturally taken for

[11] It was the government's citation, but the Court obviously approved.

granted, since the only change in proportion which could justify a tax would be an *increase* in proportion; and would not an *increase* in proportion be illegal as robbing one set of stockholders for the enrichment of another set?

Nevertheless, in the *Koshland* case (common on preferred), we again run into a summarizing sentence which might or might not be interpreted to imply that a change of "proportional interest" was involved. The sentence merely cites *Phellis, Rockefeller, Cullinan,* and *Marr* as holding stock dividends taxable "where there had either been changes of corporate identity or a change in the nature of the shares whereby the proportional interest of the stockholder after the distribution was essentially different from his former interest."[12]

This phrase might mean either

(A) an essentially different proportion, or

(B) the *same* proportion made essentially different in *character*, either by a change in the corporation underlying the interest or by a change in the terms of the certificate representing the interest.

Both A and B fit the syntax, but only B fits the logic, because only B fits the cases cited—*Phellis, Rockefeller, Cullinan, Marr.* No other case was cited. No independent argument was added. The sentence professed to say only what these cases said.

Also, while there can be such a thing as an *"essentially"* different quality, there can*not* be such a thing as an *"essentially"* different proportion—only a *different* proportion—unless "essential" in this case means "big"—but certainly the Court did not mean that a big increase is taxable and a small increase is not taxable!

Nevertheless, in the *Koshland* and also in the *Gowran* case (common on preferred and preferred on common), there was in a sense a change of proportion. Moreover, it was an *increase* of proportion. Moreover, it was not accomplished by taking anything away from one person or class and handing it over to another person or class. What happened as between common

[12] Koshland case, supra, p. 445.

and preferred was that one class of capital was made to take its antecedent gain in the form of stock.

THREE CIRCUIT COURTS OF APPEALS[13]

Before the *Koshland* and *Gowran* cases, the *Tillotson* case had occurred in a Circuit Court of Appeals. Its facts were similar to those of the *Koshland-Gowran* cases, and the Court reached a similar conclusion—taxing the stock dividend—but, this time, distinctly on the ground of changed proportionate interest. The *Macomber* case, when *refusing* to tax common on common had pointed out that the proportionate interest was unchanged; and the *Tillotson* case treated this as a separate premise, and argued the converse: if not taxable in the absence of change in proportionate interest, then taxable in the presence of such change.

The *Tillotson* case played a part in causing the appeals in the *Koshland* and *Gowran* cases, as recited in those cases, but the Supreme Court's reasoning ignored the *Tillotson* case and rested, we think, on change of legal quality alone.

But after the *Koshland* and *Gowran* cases, two other Circuit Courts of Appeals were drawn into the debate at a slightly different angle. It was still two kinds of stock in one company, but the stock dividends were more impartial—clearly no stockholder's proportionate interest was increased.

Held (in the Second Circuit—the *Strassberger* case): the dividend was taxable just the same, because of the change in the "legal quality" of the stock.

But the Ninth Circuit (in the *Sprouse* case) refused the tax because there was no change of proportionate interest.

In this ruling the Court (page 977, by implication) appar-

[13] Comm. v Tillotson Mfg. 76 F 2nd 189, CCA 6th, Mar. 14, 1935. Strassberger v Comm., 124 F 2nd 315, Dec. 22, 1941, CCA 2nd (only one stockholder); Sprouse v Comm., 122 F 2nd 973, Oct. 22, 1941, CCA 9th. Also Dreyfuss v Manning, 44 F.S. 383, Dist. Ct., Dist. of N. J., Mar. 24, 1942. Certiorari denied in Sprouse case, but later granted in both Sprouse and Strassberger cases: May 11, 1942 62 S. Ct. 1266, 1267.

ently meant to escape conflict with the *Phellis*, *Rockefeller*, *Cullinan* and *Marr* precedents, on the ground that, in those cases, *besides* the change of quality there had been a change in corporate identity—a hair-splitting distinction because those earlier cases were interested in change of corporate identity only because this entailed a change in the legal quality of the stock. The *Phellis* case labored to prove that such a change of quality actually resulted, and on the other hand, the *Weiss* case, in which no change of quality could be traced, was not further interested in corporate identity.

Both the *Strassberger* and the *Sprouse* cases are now pending before the Supreme Court, though at first the Court (with three dissents) refused certiorari in the *Sprouse* case.

For the present, therefore, neither the taxpayers nor the judges have more than a gambler's chance of guessing what will happen; and, after it happens, the next case will doubtless bring in a new gamble.

But thus it must be, so long as there is no income concept.

Congress

Congress probably stands nearer to the man in the street than does the Supreme Court. Accordingly, in 1921, Congress followed the dissenting views of Justices McReynolds and Van Devanter in the *Phellis* case, who accused the majority of putting "an embargo upon legitimate reorganizations"; that is, since Congress need *not* tax all the Court says it can tax,[14] it decided in 1921 *not* to tax certain gains registered in reorganizations, though later this step was partly canceled.[15]

But, though Congress need not tax all that the Court says is constitutionally income, it cannot tax what the Court says is *not* constitutionally income. And since the judges, in almost every new case of stock dividends and quasi dividends, have split on the meaning of the last preceding case, Congress has

[14] Brushaber v Union Pacific, 240 U.S. 1, Jan. 24, 1916.
[15] The Definition of Income, by Professor William Wallace Hewett, Philadelphia, Westbrook Publishing Co., 1925, p. 74; Magill, p. 146.

sometimes been misled and found itself seesawing with the Court. After the *Macomber* decision, Congress exempted *all* stock dividends.[16] But eventually, in view of the judicial departures from the *Macomber* case, Congress tried to make itself safe by providing that "a distribution . . . in stock or in rights to acquire stock shall not be treated as a dividend to the extent that it does not constitute income within the meaning of the Sixteenth Amendment."[17]

DEPARTURES FROM YIELD

Thus, after the *Macomber* case, American law has definitely diverged from the Yield concept by taxing capital as income.

The Yield system would, of course, enter a *cash* dividend in the gross income. A stock dividend it would ignore. But if the stock dividend, or, for that matter, the original stock, were sold for cash—in fact, if *any* form of capital were sold for cash —the net cash Yield system would enter the resulting intake in the gross.

But thereafter, in conformity with logical and complete "double entry," the Yield system would deduct from said gross all reinvestments in capital, thus leaving uncanceled and therefore taxable only the final spendings, equal to "real income."

Nevertheless, taxing stock dividends does not square with the Accretion concept either, since Accretion would tax the gain annually without waiting for it to be declared.

However, the law seems to be getting further away from Yield and closer to Accretion. Let us examine some judicial approaches toward accretion.

REALIZATION

The *Macomber* case denies the status of income to any gain that is not "realized," and so long as a gain in capital value must be realized before taxed, the Accretion method is barred.

[16] Sec. 201 (d) of the 1921 Act as cited in the Koshland case at p. 444 footnote.
[17] Code Sec. 115 (f) (1).

But whatever realization is, it has eased up since the *Macomber* case. The *Macomber* case used the word "sever" as a synonym for "realize"; but in 1940, the Court repudiated "sever" without quite repudiating "realize."

This, however, was not in a stock dividend case. The case dealt with real estate.

It is common law that anything "permanently" attached to real estate becomes the same real estate; so that, if a tenant builds an improvement on rented premises, the improvement at once and automatically becomes the property of the landlord, unless they have agreed to the contrary.

The improvement is certainly capital and, in the *Macomber* sense, not "realized."

But in 1940 occurred the *Bruun* case in which the Supreme Court says that land improvements are income if "realized" and that they *are* realized at the expiration of the lease when the landlord takes over.[18]

In this case, the improvements were not rent. There was already explicit rent. The tenant simply had *permission* under the lease to tear down old buildings and erect new ones; and this, of course, was consideration *to*, not *from*, the tenant. But the landlord, at the termination of the lease, was taxed on the increase in value caused by the tenant's improvements.

The landlord protested the tax, both on the ground that the improvements were capital and on the ground that they were not realized since they did not come within the *Macomber* expressions, "severed from," "proceeding from," "something of exchangeable value," something for the "separate use, benefit and disposal" of the recipient.

But the Court answered that the *Macomber* case had dealt only with dividends; that, therefore, these expressions were in-

---

[18] During the lease, it is not realized unless, perhaps, the parties, when making the lease, agree to regard the improvements as rent; and perhaps if the monthly increments of improvement can be appraised. Blatt v U. S., 305 U.S. 267, Dec. 5, 1938 (held not realized); Helvering v Bruun, 309 U.S. 461, Mar. 25, 1940 (held realized). In this Bruun case, the landlord took over through forfeiture.

applicable to improvements on real estate; and that if severance "were necessary, no income could arise from an exchange of property, whereas," said the Court, "such gain has always been recognized as realized taxable gain."

"Sever" is, of course, a figure of speech. But so is "realize" a figure of speech. Should not the Court, in 1940, have traced its conclusion back to the *Macomber definition*? That definition might well be held to include *"an exchange of property,"* as the Court in 1940 said it did; but to make it include a *lessee's improvements on property* would seem to require further reasoning or figures of speech so as to connect the improvements with the definition as limited by the word "realize."

It would seem that the Court is still engaged in stretching "realization" and thus getting nearer and nearer to the Accretion concept. Yet the simon-pure Accretion concept which would tax a *silent* accretion—an accretion not realized even by figure of speech—is still not attained. Under the *Macomber* decision, it would seem to be unconstitutional to tax an unrealized capital gain. In 1936, Professor Magill inferred this with "little doubt";[19] and even this 1940 decision still maintains that "economic gain is not always taxable." Nevertheless, the decisions *continue* to approach Accretion, like the mouse approaching the wall but never quite reaching it, because he stops halfway and then halfway again.

However, after the *Bruun* case, the *Horst* case arose in which, by dictum, the Court has perhaps abolished the requirement of realization altogether.[20]

But we postpone the discussion of this till the chapter on constitutional requirements.

[19] Taxable Income, p. 103.
[20] Helvering v Horst, 311 U.S. 112, Nov. 25, 1940.

CHAPTER 15

THE CAPITAL GAINS TAX

To ITS general definition of income, the *Macomber* case added these words: "provided it be understood to include profit gained through a sale or conversion of capital assets."

This means that, if you buy assets in 1930 for $10,000 and sell them in 1960 for $50,000, your 1960 tax will be based on a "gain" of $40,000—*not* allocated among the years 1930-1960, but levied at one swoop on 1960 alone.

The Yield system, of course, would deal separately with 1930 and 1960, each on its own merits. Thus, in 1930, Yield would reckon an *out* of $10,000 against any *ins* occurring in 1930; and, in 1960, Yield would reckon an *in* of $50,000 against any *outs* occurring in 1960.

Of course, the present law's *ins* and *outs* correspond only in part with the *ins* and *outs* of Yield. But the present law does, in general, profess to compute its tax only on the *ins* and *outs* of each separate year.[1] Nevertheless, Congress is free to reckon the *ins* and *outs* not per year but per transaction, even if the transaction straddles more than a year. And the chief example of taxing the whole straddle at its front end is the capital gains tax. (And, of course, the statute figures capital losses in the same way.)[2]

[1] Secs. 11, 13 (b) ('39, Sec. 201) ['41, Sec. 103 (a)], Sec. 23 [2nd 1940, Sec. 301; '41, Sec. 202 (a)]; Secs. 41-48 ['41, Secs. 114, 115 (a)]. Burnet v Sanford & Brooks, 282 U.S. 359, Jan. 5, 1931.

[2] Secs. 111-118 ('39 Secs. 212-215, 223) [2nd 1940, Sec. 501; 1941, Sec. 115 (b)] all in connection with Secs. 22 & 23 ('39, Secs. 215, 219) [1941, Sec. 202 (a)]. See also the inventory overlap in next chapter and: Bowers v Kerbaugh-Empire Co., 271 U.S. 170 (1926); U.S. v Kirby

MAJOR PREMISE

What was the origin of this capital gain concept—gain per transaction instead of a gain per year? The *Macomber* case inherited the concept chiefly from a case on a law preceding the Sixteenth Amendment—the case of *Doyle* vs. *Mitchell*.[3] Its major premise was that compensation for capital must be treated as capital—or, let us say, constructively as capital—or, at all events, not as income, *except* so far as it exceeds the original value of the capital, thus producing the "gain" considered indispensable to a definition of income. The Court even treated this "gain," not as *net* income but as *gross* income.

CONSEQUENCES—THE DEALER

A professional dealer in capital items—for instance, a dealer in stock market securities—will not necessarily be greatly troubled by the capital gains tax with its straddle of the years. If his business is fairly regular, the total gains which fall within a given year may well approximate what the Yield figure would be.[4]

In fact, under the present law, the securities or other capital goods of the professional dealer are treated as stock-in-trade and several forms of inventory are customarily used,[5] one of which brings the income pretty close to accretion.

CONSEQUENCES—THE NONPROFESSIONAL

Thus the chief hardship of a straddle tax falls on the isolated transactions of nonprofessionals. One taxpayer tried to convince the Court that the straddle tax was for professionals alone. But he did not succeed.[6] And the results are often cruel.

Lumber Co., 284 U.S. 1 (1931), and Burnet v Sanford (1931) in preceding footnote. The provisions seem to cover "property" in general, but the Commissioner does not recognize loss when dwellings or household goods are sold: Regs. 19.23 (e)—1, par. 5.

[3] 247 U.S. 179, May 20, 1918.

[4] See Chap. 19 concerning British practice.

[5] Sec. 117 (a) ['41, Sec. 115 (b)] Sec. 22 (c) and Regs. 19.22 (c)-5.

[6] Merchants Loan & Trust v Smietanka, 255 U.S. 509, Mar. 28, 1921.

EXAMPLES

Nearly any taxpayer can cite examples. We had a neighbor who, in 1929, held most of his fortune in stock of Allied Chemical and Dye. Since the time of his investment, the stock had appreciated from $35 to over $300 per share. He wanted to sell in order to diversify, but felt obliged to refrain, clinging to his lopsided condition in order to escape the practical confiscation which would have overtaken him had he sold.

Another neighbor was a widow, with only moderate means. A few years ago, under the publicity provisions of a law now repealed, her name appeared in the newspapers, among those of the very rich. Her income was listed as $331,000. What this impossible figure really meant was that, because of financial misfortunes, she had been forced to resort to distress selling; that is, she sold family property which had been acquired many years before at low prices, and the "capital gain" resulting from the sale amounted to several hundred thousand dollars which she needed to pay insistent creditors. The absurd conclusion that her income was therefore suddenly swollen to $331,000 made the man in the street laugh, while doubtless it made her cry.

MITIGATIONS

Of course, *after* the straddle of the years, it is too late to allocate the burden *among* the years. Accordingly, the remedy proposed by the advocates of accretion, including Professor Haig and the National Tax Association,[7] is the use of annual market value inventories by ordinary taxpayers as well as by dealers, thus taxing only one year's capital-increase at a time, whether "realized" by a sale or not. This plan, in addition to the objections discussed in Chapters 8 and 9, would, of course, entail the practical and administrative troubles involved in appraisals and in the checking and correcting of them.

[7] "Proceedings" of said association, 1915, p. 303. See Magill, Taxable Income, p. 102 with footnote.

The lawmakers themselves have sought ways to soften this hardship, but without giving up the straddle. At present their chief mitigating expedient does not mitigate the rates, but applies the regular rates to only a fraction of the capital gain: half of it, if it straddles more than 24 months; two-thirds, if it straddles anything from 18 to 24 months. If the straddle is only 18 months or less, the entire gain bears the tax.

The statutory rules are complicated and not quite the same for corporations as for individuals.[8]

CAPITAL CONTINUITY AND DISCONTINUITY

This expression is not known to the present law, but it aptly expresses some of the tangled consequences of the present law.

Under the Yield concept, if what you get in return for capital is itself capital (either at once or by investment after a split second), there would be capital continuity, gain or no gain, loss or no loss. Even during the split second—in fact, for any length of time—the cash itself would, under the Yield system, rank as capital waiting to perform its services.

Under the present law, capital continuity is, in effect, recognized if there is no taxable gain or loss, *even if the proceeds of a capital sale are spent at once for food or fun.* But such capital continuity is purely make-believe. This is inconsistent with any concept of income!

And this is not the only inconsistency, for the law is inconsistent with itself; it recognizes capital continuity in *some* cases of capital gain or loss.

For instance:

PROPERTY FOR PROPERTY

Under the present law, payment in kind, like payments in money, may result in taxable gain or loss. But if both properties are for productive use and are not only in kind but of the

[8] Sec. 117 ('39, Secs. 212, 214) ['41 Sec. 115 (b)]. There is a complicated carry-over of short-term losses. Sec. 117 (d) (e) ('39 Sec. 212 (a) (b)). One hundred per cent of a gain in property subject to depreciation allowance can be taxed (Form 1040, schedule G).

same kind, there is capital continuity, gain or no gain, loss or no loss.[9] Thus, if a plow plant is exchanged for an electric shaver plant, any gain or loss is counted; but if a plow plant is exchanged for another plow plant, no gain or loss is recognized.

SECURITIES—CAPITAL—CONTINUITY

When you dip into your purse for a dollar bill, you are not interested in the particular numeral it happens to bear. This ought to be true of different stock certificates of the same stock. But the law has it otherwise. For when you sell a share for, say, $500, if the certificate you hand your purchaser is the one you received on January 1st for $100, you are taxed on $400, but if it's the one you received on January 2nd for $300, you are taxed on $200—whatever your intention.[10]

But suppose your broker has possession of your stock, and suppose you instruct him to sell a share without designating the particular certificate that represents it. If the date of purchase is known (of the particular certificate which the broker proceeds to deliver to your purchaser), that date will prevail for the purpose of determining the previous purchase price of what you are selling.[11]

But suppose your dealings with the broker have been such that the dates of purchase are *not* known (a situation which often obtains when the broker holds the stock on margin with power to repledge). Then the rule is: "first in, first out"; that is, it is conclusively presumed that the first certificate you bought is the first certificate you sell—and thereafter in consecutive order.[12]

But suppose that, under these conditions—i.e., when the certificates are not identifiable by date of purchase—you order the sale of whatever stock you bought on a given date (or, if necessary, on a given date at a given price). Then, no matter what

[9] Sec. 112 (b) (1).
[10] Cole v Helbrun, 4 F.S. 230, Mar. 24, 1933.
[11] Miller v Comm., 80 F 2nd 219 at 221 (dictum), Dec. 9, 1935 (CCA 2nd).
[12] 19.22 (a)—8. Helvering v Rankin, 295 U.S. 123, Apr. 29, 1935.

certificate your broker sells for you, the law treats it as representing the date and price named in your order to sell.[13] In other words, the rule of "first in, first out" is overridden.

Then the question arises: can such a specification by you (that is, by date and price) override the delivery by your broker of the *wrong* certificate when its date of purchase *is* known?

Answer: There is a Supreme Court case in which the mistake of the broker was held to override the will of the client, on principles of agency—under the special circumstances of that case;[14] and, on the strength of it, the Second Circuit Court of Appeals, having formerly held that the client's instruction prevailed over a broker's actual delivery, changed its mind, using the words, "as we understand the law at present."[15] Thus, when a certificate is actually identifiable by date of purchase, it may be open to doubt whether the will of the client is more important than the number of the certificate.

GAIN-CAPITAL-CONTINUITY VS. LOSS-CAPITAL-CONTINUITY— "WASH SALES"

On the stock market, if what you sell and, after a split second, repurchase, are "substantially identical securities" (whatever exactly that may mean), Congress has chosen to work it both ways. If the sale had resulted in a *gain*, the repurchase after a split second is *not* capital continuity and you must pay a tax on the gain; but if the sale had resulted in a *loss*, the repurchase after a split second *is* capital continuity, so that you cannot claim the loss.[16] This is called the "wash sales" provision and was doubtless enacted to prevent tax dodgers from record-

[13] Helvering v Rankin, 295 U.S. 123, Apr. 29, 1935; Miller v Comm., 80 F 2nd, 219, Dec. 9, 1935 (CCA 2nd); Curtis v Helvering, 101 F 2nd 40, Jan. 9, 1939 (CCA 2nd).
[14] Davidson v Comm., 305 U.S. 44, Nov. 7, 1938.
[15] Earlier case: Miller v Comm., 80 F 2nd, supra; later, Curtis v Helvering, 101 F 2nd, supra.
[16] Either after a split second or even within 30 days; i.e., 61 days counting day of sale and 30 days before and after. Sec. 118; 19.118-1.

ing trick losses! But the provision catches "innocent" people too. Moreover, Uncle Sam himself began it.

WHEN GAIN IS CAPITAL CONTINUITY AFTER ALL

But the present no-concept system keeps Congress hopping about to cure the hard-luck cases necessarily incident to a no-concept system; and, for some of these cases, Congress has provided for gain-capital continuity after all. For instance, this capital-continuity-in-spite-of-gain is allowed in carefully defined cases of reorganization. It is also allowed in certain involuntary cases, such as "eminent domain," provided the money received is "forthwith in good faith" reinvested in "related" property.[17]

And, as if all these contradictions and intricacies were not enough, cases arise which require allocation in order to determine how much *gain* is chargeable to one subdivisible transaction.[18] And these allocations are so difficult that, in the matter of wash sales, the legislators turned the allocation problem over to the Commissioner of Internal Revenue.[19]

POSTPONEMENT

In many cases of capital continuity allowed, the continuity merely postpones the pinning of the final gain or loss; that is, if property No. 2, received in a nontaxable way for property No. 1, is later transferred in a taxable way for property No. 3, the gain or loss is measured from the basis of property No. 1, not property No. 2.[20]

ULTERIOR EVILS

Aside from injustice and inconsistency—all *inherent* in the law—the capital gains tax has been a source of *ulterior* evils. Qualified authorities have condemned it as an unsatisfactory producer of revenue; as a cause of undue fluctuations in the

[17] Sec. 112 (f) ('39, Sec. 213).
[18] Sec. 112 (c).
[19] Sec. 118 (b) (c).
[20] Secs. 112 (b) etc. 113 (a) (6) etc. ('39 Secs. 213, 214).

revenue; as a chronic source of litigation; as costing Uncle Sam
more than it brings him; as reducing the revenue when the tax
rates were raised; as obstructing business enterprise.[21]

And certainly these capital-gain-and-loss provisions, as applied to the stock market, aggravate booms and depressions;
because, in a boom, the capital gains tax *punishes*, and so discourages, the selling which might moderate the undesirable *rise*
in prices; and in a depression the capital loss provision *rewards*,
and so encourages, the selling which aggravates the undesirable
fall in prices.

Supporters of this tax, however, argue that, if it were repealed, the professionals who make their living on the stock
market would escape the income tax.[22] Of course *mere* repeal,
leaving the rest of our no-concept law just as it is, might have
that effect; but not the yield tax; for the yield tax would enter
all cash ins and outs per year simply, not per transaction.

"Money Is as Money Does"[23]

The capital gains tax, like other tax evils, derives, in part,
from the modern confusion between money and reality—whether
real income or real capital. Money, though it is entitled to book
entries, is nothing in itself. What it is used for is all that counts.
In taxation, it should merely personify what it is used for.
Whatever its *origin*—whether wages or isolated capital gains—
the test should be its *destination*—its *purpose*—its *function*. So
far as it buys real income,[24] its flow should be entered on the
government books as income. So far as it buys capital[25] it
should be entered on the government books as capital. Thus, the
income tax would hit every spending and miss every investment.

[21] Elisha M. Friedman, New York *Times*, Feb. 16, 1938.
[22] Professor Haig, in Wall Street Journal, Mar. 23, 1937.
[23] An expression used by Francis Walker though not for precisely the
present purpose.
[24] Including for our practical purpose, "consumer goods."
[25] Other than money itself, which, as we have seen, is capital in the
"cash balance" snapshot.

Such is Yield.

Under the present law, however, if, at any time, "money is as money does," this is sheer accident.

WHEN DESTINATION DOES COUNT

But even under the present law, money received by a corporation as a subscription to its stock is not taxable to the corporation as income. The Treasury Regulations treat such money as not within the statutory definition of income.[26]

Presumably because it is dedicated to capital.

And there is another case.

The Cuban government[27] contributed cash subsidies for the construction of a railroad in Cuba by a New Jersey railroad corporation. The New Jersey corporation was, of course, taxable by the United States. The cash from Cuba was not a gift. It was paid to the New Jersey corporation under a contract for specific considerations, in addition to the general indirect benefit to Cuba.

The question would seem to be: was the subsidy inherently income or was it inherently capital—since it was earmarked for a capital *"purpose"*?

In the first place, the Court pointed out that certain physical properties of the railroad had also been contributed by the Cuban government—land, buildings and tools—and that our taxing authorities had not even made any attempt to tax these as income to the corporation. Whether these properties had a specific, contractual *quid pro quo* is not altogether clear; but, at any rate, the Court said that "such aids, gifts," etc., for public service are "not . . . mere gratuities." And, in explaining why these properties had not been taxed as income in the Cuba case, the Court pointed out that they were "used directly to complete the undertaking"; and then the Court denied that there was any more reason for sparing the physical properties than for sparing the cash (which had a very definite, contractual *quid pro quo*),

[26] 19.22 (a)—16, 17. See also 19.22 (a)—14.
[27] Edwards v Cuba R.R., 268 U.S. 628, June 8, 1925.

and the Court added: "the physical properties and the money subsidies were given for the same *purpose*" (italics ours), namely, (according to one phrase) "to reimburse . . . for capital expenditures" and (according to another phrase) as "contribution to capital assets."

The Court's conclusion was not only that the cash was not income, but that it was not income *within the meaning of the Sixteenth Amendment.*"

Now the word "purpose," when applied to an inanimate object, can hardly, we think, mean anything but "function."

In other words, cash received for a capital function *is* capital. In other words, "money is as money does."[28]

WHEN DESTINATION DOES NOT COUNT

But in our law, does money become capital whenever John Smith dedicates it to capital?—chooses capital for its destination?—its purpose and its function?—in other words, when John Smith makes an investment?

The answer is: absolutely not. Money received is conclusively treated as gross income when Smith receives it, and he cannot change it except so far as the statute authorizes deductions; and deductions are a matter of legislative grace;[29] and

[28] Sometimes contributions by Chambers of Commerce and the like are treated in the same way. Appeal of Liberty Light & Power Co., 4 BTA 155, 159 (June 21, 1926); Arkansas Compress Co. v Comm., 8 BTA 155, 158 (Sep. 22, 1927); Great Northern Ry Co. v Comm., 8 BTA 225, 247, 248, 271, 272 (Sep. 22, 1927) (affirmed 40 F 2nd 372 (CCA 8th), certiorari denied, 282 U.S. 855); Union Pacific Ry. Co. v Comm., 26 BTA 1126, 1128, Oct. 7, 1932 (reversed on other points in 69 F 2nd 67, CCA 2nd; 293 U.S. 282). Magill cites further cases, Taxable Income, pp. 344 ff. The Interstate Commerce Commission calls these items "donations" (Union Pacific case supra, p. 1128), though they seem to have at least an indirect quid pro quo, and the reasoning is not based on the gift idea. Public contributions for running expenses are treated conversely; see Helvering v Claiborne-Annapolis Ferry, 93 F 2nd 875 (CCA 4th), Jan. 4, 1938. In this case, the distinction argued was between income and gifts. See also Texas Ry. v U.S. 286 U.S. 285, May 16, 1932. Lykes Bros. v Comm. 126 F. 2nd 725, CCA 5th, Mar. 20, 1942.

[29] New Colonial Ice Co. v Helvering, 292 U.S. 435, 440, May 28, 1934; Helvering v Independent Life, 292 U.S. 371, 381, May 21, 1934; Stanton v

Congress has never had the grace to allow a deduction for an investment.

Or rather, Congress allows the deduction of an investment only in case the asset invested in is also sold, thus linking together the purchase and sale and calling their difference realized capital gain.

If this linking were abandoned and the costs of all investments indiscriminately (within the taxable year) were deducted, while the proceeds of all sales were still included, the result would, as we have seen, be Yield.

If, in addition, the existing "capital gain" were replaced by what we have called "capital-increase" (within the taxable year), the result would be Accretion.

Finally, if "capital gain" were simply abandoned, while the proceeds of all sales were still included, the result would be at least an approximation to the common man's mixture of Yield and Accretion.

But, as it now stands, our legal income is that mixture plus the capital gain excrescence, plus several other complications, not all of which have yet been mentioned.

Baltic Co., 240 U.S., 103, Feb. 21, 1916; Burnet v Harmel, 287 U.S. 103, Nov. 7, 1932. Congress apparently can tax gross income (capital gain being gross, per Doyle case).

CHAPTER 16

WHEN INCOME AND INCOME TAXES FAIL TO SYNCHRONIZE

ONE merit of the Yield system is that it lays the tax at a time when the wherewithal to pay it is in hand—or would be if not deliberately squandered by the taxpayer.

But under the present law, tax and wherewithal too often are not allowed to synchronize.

In the following cases, let us simplify by assuming there are no reinvestments, resavings, reloans, or reborrowings. If there were, the timing would be more complicated, but the Yield system would still be on the side of justice, for it would still account for every "in" when it comes in and every "out" (for other than consumer purposes) when it goes out, and arrive at the tax when the wherewithal is present and doing its good for consumer purposes.

BORROWING AND LENDING

As to interest on the loan, it would (in our simplified case) be treated the same by the Yield system as by the present law; that is, as income to the lender and deduction for the borrower.[1]

But the principal sum is simply ignored by the present law. What are the results?

Consider the three steps in a loan transaction, as simplified—three for each party.

[1] Secs. 22 (a), 23 (b).

153

THE BORROWER

1. Borrows $1,000 (and gets the good of it).
2. Earns and saves $1,000 for repayment (and does not get the good of it).
3. Repays $1,000 (and does not get the good of it).

The Yield system would cancel 2 and 3 and tax No. 1, the borrowing, which is when the borrower has the wherewithal and gets the good of it.

But the present law cancels 1 and 3 (by ignoring them) and taxes No. 2, the saving, which is when the borrower not only gets no good of it but is struggling to climb out of his debt.

THE LENDER

1. Earns and saves $1,000 to lend (and does not get the good of it).
2. Lends the $1,000 (and does not get the good of it).
3. Is repaid the $1,000 (and gets the good of it).

The Yield system would tax No. 3 and cancel 1 and 2; whereas the present law cancels 2 and 3 (by ignoring them) and taxes No. 1.

And what if the debt turns bad? Then, under the present law, the lender has a fourth *out*—that is, he is allowed to deduct the bad debt in some *future* year, to make up, in that *future* year, for having been taxed on the amount prematurely, before anyone knew whether it would do him any good or not.[2]

On the other hand, suppose a borrower negotiates a reduction of his debt. The present law, as judicially interpreted, treats such a debt reduction, say from $15,000 to $10,000, as a new positive taxable income item of $5,000 received by the borrower.[3]

Here again, the Yield system would arrive at the same eventual net, but by a different route; that is, the Yield system,

[2] For bad debts, see Sec. 23 (k).

[3] Individual via partnership negotiates a deduction: Walker v Comm., 88 F 2nd 170, Feb. 19, 1937 (CCA 5th), certiorari denied, 302 U.S. 692, Oct. 11, 1937. Corporation repurchasing its bonds at reduction: U.S. v Kirby Lumber Co., 284 U.S. 1, Nov. 2, 1931. See 19.22 (a)-14 & 18.

when deducting the repayments, would simply deduct $5,000 less, thus making the net come out $5,000 more.

And the idea that a debt reduction is a positive income item seems a very strange interpretation of "gain derived from capital, from labor, or from both combined."

Naturally the cases are not altogether consistent. For instance, when an American corporation, after World War I, paid off a debt to a German bank in depreciated German marks, the Court apparently refused to treat this diminution of outgo as "gain from capital and labor, or either of them."[4]

Somewhat similar to the bad timing of the tax in loan transactions is the bad timing in

BOUGHT ANNUITIES AND ENDOWMENT POLICIES

Again there are three factors:

1. Earning and saving
2. Investment (in Annuity or Endowment)
3. Receipts from the investment

In effect, the Yield system would cancel 1 and 2 and tax 3, whereas the law taxes 1, and cancels 3 and 2 (except the excess of 3 over 2, which is analogous to interest on a loan).

In this case, however, the statute does provide methods for mitigating this bad timing, but fails to cure it. The mitigations are as follows: if, at any given tax date, the untaxed proceeds received up to that date exceed the purchase payments made up to that date, the excess at once becomes taxable. Annuities, however, are taxable to the extent of 3 per cent of their cost,

[4] Bowers v Kerbaugh-Empire Co. (distinguished by the Kirby case supra) 271 U.S., 170, May 3, 1926. The Court started with the "question . . . whether the difference" of mark value "in dollars . . . was income"; and either there was no answer or the answer was negative. The final statement was that "diminution of loss . . . is not income." The lower courts have applied this to negotiated diminution. Dallas Transfer v Comm., 70 F. 2nd 95, Apr. 12, 1934 (CCA 5th); Transylvania R. v Comm., 99 F 2nd 69, Oct. 4, 1938 (CCA 4th); Hirsch v Comm., 115 F 2nd 656, Nov. 25, 1940 (CCA 7th); Sickles v U.S., 31 F. S. 654, Mar. 4, 1940 (Ct. of Cl.); Highland Farms v Comm., 42 BTA 1314, Nov. 27, 1940; Estate of Sherman v Comm., 44 BTA 853, July 3, 1941.

and the balance is excluded. After the total excluded equals the cost, then all subsequent receipts are taxable in full.[5]

INVENTORIES AND BOOK PROFITS[6]

Inventories are essential to the computation of "book profits," and therefore are extremely useful. They reveal and help to diagnose the condition of a business. By no means would we recommend that book profit accounting be abandoned. What we do recommend is that book profits be not used as the tax basis, because (for one thing) they frequently fail to correspond with wherewithal.

In the case of a corporation no difficulty would arise under the Yield system; for the tax would reach only so much of the book profits as reached the stockholders in the form of dividends.

But let us see the discrepancy between the two tax systems in the case of a private enterprise—the discrepancy between book profits and cash gain or wherewithal—in a word, Yield.

We still assume that there are no reinvestments, etc. Also, among business expenses, we shall consider only the direct costs—no "overhead."

Both Yield and the book profits start with the gross intake; but Yield deducts all costs actually incurred during the taxable year in order to arrive at the cash gain or wherewithal; whereas book profits deducts only the "net cost" of the "goods sold"; and this cost includes some costs of previous years which went into any inventory taken over on January 1st, and excludes some costs of the current year which go into any inventory handed over to next year on December 31st. Whether the book profit deductions are more or less than the Yield deductions de-

[5] Sec. 22 (b) (2); and see Lucas v Alexander, 279 U.S. 573, May 20, 1929. The law does not apply the word "annuity" to gifts or bequests of periodic income. And in these cases, each periodic receipt is taxed, Sec. 22 (b) (3); and see Irwin v Gavit, 268 U.S. 161 (Apr. 27, 1925).

[6] Form 1040, Schedule H (individuals); Form 1120, Schedules A and B (corporations); Sec. 22 (c)-(d) ('39, Sec. 219); Regs. 19.22 (c)-1, 2, etc.

pends on whether the inventory taken over from last year is more or less than the inventory carried over to next year. Thus:

Sales	$8,000	
Direct expenses	3,000	
Cash gain	$5,000	(*wherewithal*)
Inventory decrease (added to the deductions)	1,000	
	$4,000	(*book profit*)

or, in a converse case:

Sales	$12,000	
Direct expenses	7,000	
Cash gain	$5,000	(*wherewithal*)
Inventory increase (withdrawn from the deductions)	1,000	
	$6,000	(*book profit*)

Thus, under the present law, an inventory decrease decreases the taxable figure and an inventory increase increases the taxable figure.[7]

In the one case wherewithal exceeds, and in the other falls short of profits. In the end "wherewithal" and "profits" may approach equality; but meanwhile they do not synchronize.

We now come to the question of so-called

"OPERATING LOSSES"

Let us here consider a loss due to rising costs or excessive overhead or bad management or embezzlement—the same per present law as it would be per yield.

[7] Inventories, with the co-operation of the Commissioner, are in whatever form is recognized as most appropriate to the respective lines of business. For ordinary lines the most common form is the simplest—at cost (or else at either cost or market value, whichever is lower).

Logically, if a gain adds to a man's tax, a loss should subtract from it. If, in 1940, the taxpayer loses $5,000 and in 1941 nets $1,000, it would seem unfair in 1941 to tax the $1,000 after the $5,000 of accumulated loss. In Great Britain, this situation is met—or partly met—by allowing the taxpayer to carry over any year's business net loss for six years. In America there was formerly a carry-over provision, but this was dropped in 1933.[8] And now the principle has been revived (operative in and after 1940), by providing a carry-over of an "operating loss" for two subsequent years.[9]

The Yield system achieves the real purpose of loss carry-over by a different route. To one whose eye is on conventional book profits instead of wherewithal, the wherewithal system may seem severe in some cases; for even in case of an operating loss, if the taxpayer, by borrowing or otherwise, still has and employs wherewithal for consumer purposes beyond the taxable minimum, the Yield system would tax him on this borrowed income whereas the present law would spare him. But, on the other hand, when it comes to the repayment of the loan, the Yield system would allow it as a deduction, whereas the present law refuses this allowance when it is most needed. In a word, it taxes the debtor on $1,000 of business profit though he is paying $2,000 on his debt. Under the Yield system the citizen is taxed on what reaches him beneficially, even if there is no conventional *business* profit for the particular year. He is *not* taxed on what does *not* reach him beneficially, even if there *is* business profit in a mere bookkeeping sense. What reaches him is what counts in real life and what reaches him is what counts in the Yield system.

But suppose the taxpayer's losses continue so that he never becomes solvent. In that case, of course, his creditors have kept him alive and furnished the money out of which he paid his

[8] Magill, p. 167 note.

[9] 1939, Sec. 211 (a) to become Code Secs. 23 (s) and 122. "Operating loss" is a variation of regular gross less regular deductions, but is further varied to become "net operating loss carry-over" with further variations to make "net operating loss deduction."

taxes; but (under the Yield system), the creditors would not *also* have to pay a tax on what they lend; whereas, under the present law they do—and recover it afterwards by a bad-debt deduction.

OTHER CORRECTIONS

One other example of belated corrections under the book-profit system: When a single transaction involves many items and covers a number of years, the law usually treats each year separately (capital gains are an exception). Thus, the final year of the transaction may register a gain and be taxed, where the entire transaction for the whole period may be a loss. Is there a remedy for such a single transaction?

Yes, in a measure; for the law and the Commissioner have invented for this predicament a certain liberality in our book profit methods, including the entry of certain items contrary to the period of their actual occurrence. This requires the special permission of the Commissioner, requested by the taxpayer in his tax return.[10]

Doubtless even the Yield system could not entirely escape occasional small corrections; for instance, when a December check goes bad in January. But at any rate, under Yield, the initial picture would be of real income taken contemporaneously with its occurrence, as nearly as a monetary system allows. Under Yield, we need not concern ourselves with the taxpayer's mere book profits nor his bookkeeping methods. All we need to know is the cash excess which he spends no matter where his ability to spend came from nor whether he will have it next year.

[10] Secs. 41-44 [1941, Secs. 114 & 115]; 19.43—1; Burnet v Sanford, 282 U.S. 359, Jan. 5, 1931.

CHAPTER 17

DOUBLE TAXATION AND TAX EVASION

IN PART II we have justified one form of double taxation, namely, a tax on inheritance followed by taxes on the incomes derived from the inheritance by later generations who did not earn the capital.

Nor do we necessarily object to two taxes levied on one thing by two jurisdictions, or by one jurisdiction for two purposes; nor to double taxation as payment for double service furnished by the government.

But, in general, double taxation is regarded, and we believe rightly, as both unjust and destructive. We need not repeat the argument.[1]

BUT DOUBLE TAXATION IS CONSTITUTIONAL

According to a hopeful dictum of the Supreme Court, double taxation as a matter of general legislative policy ought to be avoided.[2] If a statute admits of two interpretations, one of which would involve double taxation, the other interpretation is to be preferred.[3]

Nevertheless, Justice Brandeis has said that the Fourteenth Amendment requiring "due process of law" (and this would apply to the Fifth) "does not prohibit double taxation";[4] and

[1] Chapters 8 and 9.
[2] Union Refrigerator Transit Co. v Kentucky, 199 U.S. 194, 203, Nov. 13, 1905.
[3] U.S. v Supplee-Biddle Hardware Co., 265 U.S. 189, May 26, 1924.
[4] Cream of Wheat Co. v County of Grand Forks, 253 U.S. 325, June 1, 1920. Fifth Amendment requires "due process" of United States; Fourteenth requires it of the states.

the Court has upheld various cases of double taxation. Some of them are mentioned in the footnote.[5]

Let us list the specific forms of double taxation imposed—consciously or unconsciously—by the present law.

CAPITAL AND ITS INCOME

("Successive" Double Taxation)

The following forms of capital acquired by any taxpayer are taxed when acquired, resulting in successive double taxation.

1. Savings
2. Investments
3. Money plowed back

—these three because deductions are a matter of legislative grace,[6] and Congress has not had the grace to allow deductions in these cases.

Also the following more obvious forms of capital are taxed as income:

4. Some stock dividends or quasi-dividends
5. Capital gains in the form of capital (or reinvested in capital)
6. Real-estate improvements made by a tenant and taken over by the landlord at the expiration of the lease.

[5] Cream of Wheat case, supra: state of incorporation taxing the corporate franchise as measured by the corporate property in another State, and said other State taxing said property. Hellmich v Hellman, 276 U.S. 233, 237-8, Feb. 20, 1928: taxing corporate profits and taxing the distribution of them to stockholders on dissolution. Curry v McCanless, 307 U.S. 357, May 29, 1939: taxing an intangible in one state and its transfer in another. Guaranty Trust Co. v Virginia, 305 U.S. 19, Nov. 7, 1938: taxing trustee on trust income in one state and a beneficiary receiving some of it in another state. New York ex rel Cohn v Graves, 300 U.S. 308, Mar. 1, 1937: taxing land in one state and income from it in another—but the Court denied this was double taxation (314). As to intangibles, See State Tax Comm. of Utah v Aldrich, 62 S. Ct. 1008, points 4 and 5, Apr. 27, 1942.

[6] New Colonial Ice Company v Helvering, 292 U.S. 435 at 440, May 28, 1934; Helvering v Independent Life, 292 U.S. 371, at 381, May 21, 1934 (and cases cited).

SUCCESSIVE DOUBLE EXEMPTION

Conversely, if a capital loss is deducted from any taxpayer's income, there is double deduction, because the current reduction of capital will entail future reduction of income, and the tax is reduced for both.

Under the present law, the following forms of capital loss are deducted from current income in figuring the current income tax.

1. Loss of uninsured capital
2. Capital loss on sale or conversion
3. Depletion
4. Depreciation—including
5. Obsolescence.[7]

Obsolescence is less than obsoleteness. According to the Supreme Court, it includes "diminution in value" caused by "changes in the art, shifting of business centers, loss of trade, inadequacy, supersession, prohibitory laws and other things . . . apart from physical deteriorations."[8]

All these forms of successive double taxation (and double exemption) apply to individuals and also to corporations.

"IDENTICAL" DOUBLE TAXATION

Partnerships and Trusts do not add any new form of double taxation.[9]

But Corporations do.

The corporation is taxed on its profits[10] and each stockholder is taxed on his share of those identical profits so far as they

[7] For cases 1, 3, 4, 5, see Sec. 23 (e) (f) (l) (m); for case 2, see Secs. 22, 23 (g), 111-118 ('39, Secs. 212-215 & 223) [2d '40, Sec. 501] ['41, Sec. 115 (b)].

[8] Real Estate Land Title & Trust Co. v U.S., 309 U.S. 13, Jan. 15, 1940, citing Regulations.

[9] Trusts: Secs. 161, etc., & fiduciary Form 1041. Partnerships: Secs. 181-188 and '39 Sec. 211 (d), now Code Sec. 189; Form 1065.

[10] There are various kinds of corporation "nets"; but for the present purpose, it will be enough to call them all "profits." Sec. 13 (1939, Sec. 201) [1941, Sec. 103].

become dividends.[11] The two taxes may even be paid on one day.

In England, this form of double taxation is avoided, since the corporation pays the normal tax and the stockholder only his surtax, if any. And this was formerly the practice in America,[12] but not now.

TWO CORPORATIONS AND A STOCKHOLDER—TRIPLE-IDENTICAL

Suppose John Smith is a stockholder in corporation B which is in turn a stockholder in corporation A. Corporation A pays a tax on *its* profits, and corporation B pays a tax on *its* profits which include its dividend (15 per cent of it taxable)[13] out of corporation A's profits, and finally, John Smith, already docked by these two corporate taxes, pays a third tax on that part of his dividend from corporation B which originated in corporation A; that is, he is triply taxed on that element in his dividend.

And, of course, the tax series can go on piling up as the succession of corporations lengthens.

UNDISTRIBUTED PROFITS AND QUINTUPLE IDENTICAL TAXATION

Before 1940, the triple tax above described could even be a quintuple tax without lengthening the succession of corporations beyond two; for (until 1940) the corporation itself was sometimes twice taxed on such of its profits as were not distributed in the year when earned.[14]

Corporations are subject to a miscellany of other taxes which amount to additional double taxations. For instance,

1. *"Declared Value Excess Profits" Tax*

This is levied on any excess of profits above 10 per cent of the

---

[11] Sec. 22 (1939 Secs. 215, 219), Secs. 11, 12 [1941, Secs. 101 & 102].

[12] Magill, p. 24 and footnote.

[13] Sec. 26 (b).

[14] See Sec. 13 before and after treatment by 1939, Sec. 201. Any stockholder who consented to pay an income tax on his share of the undistributed profits, just as if he had received it as a dividend, relieved the corporation of the extra tax so far as his share was concerned (Sec. 28).

capital value—that is, the *declared* capital value, the declaration being compulsory for the purpose of a capital-stock tax. If the capital-stock declaration turns out to be less than 10 times the profits, the resulting capital-stock tax is regarded as too low, and is made-up-for by the extra tax on the extra profits, now called the "declared value excess profits tax." There are two successive rates, not severe.[15]

2. *New Corporate Excess Profits Tax*

The second revenue act of 1940 has a brand new *additional* "excess profits tax" not derived from the capital-stock declaration. It is an extra tax on "normal-tax-net-income" with adjustments. There are two successive rates, severe and getting more so.[16]

3. *Corporate Surtax*

The law of 1941 also introduces a "surtax" on a certain corporate net: Two successive rates, not severe and not punitive.[17]

4. *A Restrictive "Surtax"*

In general, a surtax is simply a tax graded according to the size of the income. But here is a "surtax" for the purpose of preventing or penalizing the nondistribution of "earnings or profits" when the nondistribution is for the deliberate purpose of "preventing" the imposition of surtax on the shareholders. Intent is of the essence. The tax is levied on a special "net" bearing the title "undistributed section 102 net." Two successive rates, severe and getting more so.[18]

"Personal holdings companies" have a similar tax on certain nondistributions of still another special net, bearing the title

[15] Capital stock declaration Secs. 1200 and 1202 ('39 Sec. 301); declared value excess profits tax, Sec. 600 etc. [and see '41 Secs. 202 (h) (i), 301, 302]. The present name is assigned by the 2nd 1940 Act, Title V, Sec. 506. The declared value excess profits tax is reported in the income return—not so the capital-stock tax: Form 1120.

[16] [New Secs. 710 etc. added by 2nd 1940 Act, Sec. 201, Title II; amended by Act of '41, Sec. 201, etc.—also by act entitled "Excess Profits Tax Amendments of 1941."]

[17] [Act of '41, Sec. 104.]

[18] Secs. 102 (a) (b) (c) (d) (1939 Sec. 211 (f)) [1941, Sec. 103, (d) & 202 (b)].

"undistributed sub-chapter A net." Two successive rates, very severe and getting more so.[19]

Naturally all these restrictive and quasi-punitive corporate taxes increase the double-tax burden of the stockholder.

PROPERTY EXCHANGED FOR STOCK

Professor Magill points out that a form of double taxation sometimes arises when property is transferred to a corporation which is to be controlled by the transferor.[20] The capital-gain or straddle tax, in such case, as we saw in Chapter 15, is allowed to skip over one transaction,[21] but if later the individual sells what he got from the corporation, the straddle tax comes to life and gets *him*:—tax number one. Likewise, if the corporation sells what it got from the grantor, the tax gets the *corporation*:—tax number two, starting with the grantor's basis, prior to the corporate ownership.[22]

A MIXED TRIPLE TAXATION AVOIDED

(Capital Twice and Income Once)

When a stock dividend is sold, what is its "basis" for "capital-gain" purposes?

If, as in the *Macomber* case, it is not a *taxable* stock dividend, its basis is whatever value it has inherited from the original stock. For instance, if the value of the original stock had automatically risen from three quarters of a million to a million, and if the untaxable stock dividend merely represents that quarter-million gain, its basis, when sold, will be a quarter-million.

But what if the stock dividend is a *taxable* stock dividend, as in the case of common on preferred or preferred on common?

[19] Secs. 500 [1941, Sec. 110 (a)], 504 ('39, Sec. 228 (a)).
[20] Magill, pp. 145-152 at 151.
[21] Sec. 112 (b) (5).
[22] As to the grantor, Sec. 113 (a) (6). As to the corporation, Sec. 113 (a) (8).

In that case, the basis of the dividend stock is not a quarter-million but zero.[23]

And would not this tax seem to confront us with *triple* taxation?

First, a tax on the stock dividend—*full value* above zero.

Second, a tax on the cash dividends borne by the stock dividend.

Third, a capital gain tax on the same stock when sold—*full value* above zero.

But no. By some logical sleight of hand, departmental practice avoids thus using the basis of zero twice. The practice is as follows: if a taxable stock dividend has *not* in fact been taxed as a stock dividend, the basis for its capital gain when sold is zero; but if the taxable stock dividend *has* in fact been taxed as a stock dividend (of course on a basis of zero), the basis jumps (for purposes of sale) from zero to what the basis would have been if the stock dividend had not been taxable—that is, if it had taken over a proportionate share of the basis of the original stock as in the *Macomber* case.

TAX EVASION

The law is so complex and so self-contradictory that opportunities for dodging it are a daily invitation.

On the other hand, the law is so unjust, especially in the capital gains tax which punishes a man for merely changing the identity of his capital, that the grievance to be dodged is sometimes more flagrant than the dodging—and perfectly decent citizens dodge with gusto.

In fact, even when there is no grievance, it is often perfectly respectable to make a choice between two equally lawful provisions of the same law. Even in a case which went against the taxpayer, Judge Learned Hand said that it is neither unpatriotic

---

[23] Helvering v Gowran, 302 U.S. 238 (Dec. 6, 1937); Koshland v Helvering, 298 U.S. 441 (May 18, 1936). Sale of original stock, Koshland case (common on preferred). Sale of dividend stock, Gowran case (preferred on common).

nor discreditable to try to reduce your tax by altering the "pattern" in which you "choose to arrange your affairs."[24]

There will always be tax dodgers; but under a juster and simpler law—a law with fewer patterns—a law, in fact, with essentially only one pattern—under such a law, evasions will become less respectable and less successful; and the attempts, less frequent.

Not that we are taking sides with the tax dodgers, respectable or otherwise. The injustice (and unprofitableness) are hard on the government, too, as we have shown.[25]

[24] Helvering v Gregory, 69 F 2d 809, Mar. 19, 1934 (though case went against taxpayer). Affirmed (Gregory v H.), 293 U.S. 465, Jan. 7, 1935.
[25] Chapters 10 and 11.

CHAPTER 18

COMPLEXITIES

PERHAPS no law can escape complexities and debates. The Yield system, as applied to a monetary world, has some cloudy regions. We have touched upon them in the Appendix to Part I.

But the present law, having started without any genuine economic concept, has passed far beyond the understanding of layman, lawyer and accountant. Instead of being a simple, straightforward application of a definite rule, it has become a congeries of special expedients, forever undergoing correction by other special expedients, each more tangled than the last.

Let us take a very short look, first, at the profusion of "either-or."

FIRST SET OF EITHER-ORS

One taxpayer ought to have only one actual income, not two experimental and arbitrary incomes with complicated rules of choice between them. Yet one of the statutory efforts to mitigate the straddle tax results in such an "either-or."

That is, what is called, in the taxpayer's return, the "total" tax is only a provisional total tax. Before the taxpayer starts deducting from it his foreign taxes, if any (and taxes paid at the source, if any), he has to re-examine his total and make sure it will stand. In the individual tax return, the total is line 28; but, if "long-term capital gains or losses" are involved, the taxpayer is instructed to go to Schedule F and derive from it a line 29. Line 28 is the *either*; line 29 is the *or*; and they are figured as follows:[1]

[1] Form 1040. Sec. 117 (c).

Line 28: The taxpayer figures a tax on everything in the regular way.

Line 29: The taxpayer figures another tax in two parts: (*a*) the regular way on all but the long-term capital gain or loss, (*b*) 30 per cent on the long-term capital gain or loss (adding *b* to *a* if *b* is figured on a gain and subtracting *b* from *a* if *b* is figured on a loss). The result is line 29.

Then comes a choice between lines 28 and 29; and the rule is: if the said long-term capital item was a *gain*, choose the *smaller* tax: if the said long-term capital item was a *loss*, choose the larger tax.

In 1941 this either-or is not requisitioned unless the surtax-net (figured without long-term loss if any) exceeds $12,000. Below that figure any computation would be thrown away, since line 28 would be sure to win anyhow. The gamble begins after $12,000. This does not appear in the law. The Commissioner apparently discovered it and put it in the tax form.

EITHER-ORS IN THE "BASIS"

But the said capital gain or loss itself has some *inside* "either-ors" to be applied *before* the taxpayer is ready for the final either-or of tax computation.

First, each capital gain starts from an initial valuation called the "basis."[2] In a simple case, the basis is, of course, the price originally paid for the property.[3] But suppose the seller inherited the property or got it as a gift. And if he got it as a gift, suppose the gift came before 1921. Suppose it came in 1921 or after. Suppose the transferror to the seller originally got it as a gift. Suppose the transferror to the giver to the seller got it as a gift. Suppose the seller got it, no matter how, before March 1, 1913. For each case a special rule, and sometimes with an either-or!

[2] Secs. 111, 112, 113, 117 ('39 Secs. 212-215 & 223) ['41, Sec. 115 (b)]; 118.

[3] Sec. 113 (a).

Bases for Depletion and Depreciation

Allowances for depletion and depreciation also require "bases." In general, these are worked out under the rules prescribed for capital gain or loss.[4]

Inventory "Basis"—Either-Or

The Commissioner, in 2,000 words, has treated inventories to a double dose of either-or. On the one hand it is *either* and on the other hand it is *either-or*. That is, the taxpayer chooses either *cost* or *cost-or-market-whichever-is-lower*.[5]

Exemptions

There is a potpourri of exemptions and partial exemptions, some of them called "exclusions" (1,500 words), some, "credits" (3,000 words), and some, "deductions" (1,500 words—and 1940 makes it 4,500), with a special list of nondeductibles (over 600 words).[6] In some cases the exemption is for both normal tax and surtax; in some, only for normal tax; in some only part of the item is exempt.[7]

Over 20 Totals and Nets

There are at least 17 kinds or degrees of total or net income (not counting the new defense provisions) some of which are taxable for normal or abnormal purposes, and some of which are points of departure on the road to the taxable figures.

For individuals we have four regulars: total; net; normal tax net; surtax net.[8]

For corporations we have five regulars: gross; declared value

[4] Sec. 114.
[5] 19.22 (c)-2, authorized by Sec. 22 (c).
[6] Secs. 22 (b) ('39, Sec. 215 (a)); 116; 25 [1941, Secs. 111 (a), 113]; 23 ('39, Secs. 211, 224) [2nd of 1940, Sec. 301] ['41, Sec. 202 (a)].
[7] Instruction G for Form 1040, and preceding footnote. Also 19.22 (b) (1).
[8] Form 1040 and Code Secs. 11, 12 ['41, Secs. 101 & 102]; Sec. 21 et seq (amendments immaterial).

excess profits net; net; adjusted net; normal tax net;[9] and for various special purposes and types of corporation, there are other nets. Such are: sub-chapter A net; undistributed sub-chapter A net;[10] sec. 102 net; undistributed section 102 net;[11] supplement P net; undistributed supplement P net;[12] supplement Q net [and 1941 adds "supplement Q surtax net"];[13] also there is foreign-life-insurance company net,[14] though without a special name.

And the new 1939 carry-over provision for "operating losses" involves still another net for operating loss.[15]

And the Second Revenue Act of 1940 introduces what amounts to an amortization net [2,500 words];[16] also two alternative excess-profits nets for corporations, one of which is again varied according to whether the corporation is foreign or domestic. (The whole topic consumes 10,000 words.)[17] Also the law of 1941 introduces a net for a new, two-rate corporate surtax.[18]

Thus there are more than 20 totals and nets, of which 17 or more preceded the war emergency.

SPLITS OF SOME ITEMS

Besides different net incomes, there are different percentages of certain gross income items, to be taken into account in applying the tax. We refer to capital gains and losses: 100 per cent, 66⅔ per cent, 50 per cent,[19] which include complicated

[9] Form 1120 and Code Sec. 13 ('39, Sec. 201) ['41, Sec. 103]; Sec. 21 et seq (amendments immaterial).
[10] Secs. 505 & 504 ('39 Secs. 211 & 212; 228).
[11] Sec. 102 (d) (1) (2) ('39, Sec. 211 (f)) ['41 Secs. 103 (d) and 202 (b)].
[12] Sec. 336 (1939, Secs. 211 (g), 212 (c)); and Sec. 335.
[13] Sec. 362 ('39 Secs. 211 (h) and 209) ['41 Secs. 103 (e) and 104 (b)].
[14] Sec. 201 (b) (2) ('39 Sec. 203).
[15] '39 Sec. 211 (b), creating Code Sec. 122.
[16] Title III.
[17] Title II.
[18] [1941, Sec. 104 (a)].
[19] Sec. 117 (b).

"carry-over" items,[20] *not* meaning the new 1939 operating-loss carry-over.

RATES

Connected with this profusion of nets is a profusion of tax rates[21] for individuals and for corporations.

For the individual, the rates are 4 per cent normal and 31 rates of surtax (the top rate applying above 5 million).

[And the law of 1941 introduces an either-or list of 90 rates.[22]]

Of course, the grading of tax rates is desirable, but not a new either-or.

Also, under the law of '41, the surtax applies to so low a net that you may have to pay a surtax *without paying a normal tax at all*, since the earned income credit, if any, is allowed in figuring the net for normal tax and *not* allowed in figuring the net for surtax![23]

CORPORATION GRADES

Business corporations are divided into richer, less rich and betwixt-and-between—the betwixt-and-between being the lower ranks of the richer. The richer now have one rate. The less rich have the richer method or a flat sum on part of the income plus a percentage on the rest—and choose the lesser.

The division line between richer and less rich is at the *fourth* net.

Betwixt-and-between in 1941 runs from $25,000 to $38,461.54. This figure does not appear in the law. Apparently the Commissioner discovered it and put it in the tax form.[24] The practical effect is that there are not now three classes of corporations—except in name. There

---

[20] Sec. 117 (e) ('39, Sec. 212 (b)).

[21] For individuals, Secs. 11, 12; for business corporations, Secs. 13, 14 ('39, Sec. 201) [1941, Sec. 101 (individuals); 103 (corporations)].

[22] [1941, Sec. 102, Form 1040-A].

[23] Secs. 111, 112, 113, 117 ('39 Secs. 212-215 & 223) ['41, Sec. 115 (b)], (amendments immaterial).

[24] Form 1120. 1941, Sec. 103.

is really but one class, subject to progressive rates up to the $38,461.54, after which the rate suddenly drops from 37 per cent to 24 per cent.

In 1938 and 1939,[25] the richer corporations had only three nets, whereas the less rich had four; and the division line was at the *second*, but the tax for the richer was on the *third*, and for the less rich, on the *fourth*.

PUNITIVE AND QUASI-PUNITIVE RATES

The 1939 amendment (as noted in Chapter 17) abolished the undistributed profits tax: but there are still (as noted in Chapter 17), two rates on "declared value excess profits"; two for willful withholding of profits; two surtaxes on holding companies.

Also the law of '41 in its nonpunitive surtax on corporations has two.

And on nonresident foreign corporations, we have another variable tax—down to 5 per cent, by treaty.[26]

And the law recognizes 19 other carefully specified kinds of corporations as *un*taxable.[27]

MIXED DEFINITIONS

Identical words are defined different ways for different purposes including "surtax," "basic surtax credit,"[28] and "adjusted net income."[29]

"Stocks and securities" has a general definition; "securities" has a special definition for a special purpose; "security" has another special definition for another special purpose.[30]

[25] Code Secs. 13 and 14 unamended.

[26] Sec. 231 (a) ['41 Sec. 106].

[27] Sec. 101 (enlarged by '39, Sec. 217).

[28] Sec. 27 (b); Sec. 102 (d) (2). Surtax Secs. 12 & 102 (a).

[29] Sec. 13 (a) ('39, Sec. 201); and see '39, Sec. 228 amending Sec. 504 (a).

[30] Sec. 373 (f); 23 (g) (3); and see '39, Sec. 401 (b) (2) amending 3672 (b) (2).

In one case, the assumption of a liability is "considered as money."[31]

In some cases, assumption of a liability is "considered as stock or securities"![32]

EXCEPTIONS TO EXCEPTIONS

Naturally the law is full of exceptions, including a case of what amounts practically to an exception, to an exception, to an exception, to an exception, to the initial rule.

Initial Rule: in a sale or exchange of property, gain shall be recognized for tax purposes;[33] *except* that the gain shall be exempt if the consideration received is any one of five certain specified kinds;[34] *except* (or *but*) if there are additional kinds of consideration, the exemption shall be partial;[35] *except* (or *but*) the exemption shall be entire if the additional kind of consideration is a certain kind of additional kind;[36] *except* that, if the last named exception is invoked in bad faith, it shall not apply.[37]

AMENDMENTS TO AMENDMENTS

Amendments pile in so fast that some provisions never take effect. The Act of 1939 amended the corporation tax, amendment to take effect for the 1940 returns; the first Revenue Act of 1940, by a second amendment, amended this first amendment before said first amendment could begin to operate; and the second Act of 1940, by a third amendment, amended this second amendment before said second amendment could begin to operate.[38]

---

[31] '39 Sec. 213 (d) amending Sec. 113 (a) (6).
[32] '39, Sec. 213 (c) amending Sec. 112 (b) (5).
[33] Sec. 112 (a).
[34] Ibid. (b) 1-5 ('39, 213 (c)).
[35] Ibid. (c) (1).
[36] 1939 Sec. 213 (a) adding "k" to Sec. 112 (applying to two cases).
[37] Ibid., after "except."
[38] 1939, Sec. 201 (Sec. 229 for date of operation); [first Act of 1940, Sec. 3 (Sec. 9 for date); second Act of 1940, Sec. 101 (subsection (e) for date)].

Puzzling Phraseology

The phraseology grows more and more difficult to understand. For instance, "For the purposes of this chapter, 'supplement Q net income' means the adjusted net income, computed without the net operating loss deduction provided in section 23 (s), minus the basic surtax credit computed under section 27 (b) without the application of paragraphs (2) and (3)."[39]

In the law of 1938 there was a provision whereby certain kinds of stockholders in certain kinds of liquidations of certain kinds of corporations could elect or renounce the recognition of a certain kind of gain. That provision (though not all in one sentence) contained 762 words, with 14 numbered or lettered paragraphs and subparagraphs, 10 date references, 7 explanatory parentheses, and 6 lettered references forwards and backwards; and one of these referring letters was in a referring parenthesis.[40]

Forty Million Words

Counting the code, there have been (down to 1942) 21 revenue acts in 29 years, six of them in the three years 1939-1941. The single topic of "straddle" in 1939 consumed almost as many words as the entire income law consumed in 1913.

Let us attempt a very rough count. On the statutory side we consider only the code and the current forms, current instructions, and current treasury regulations. On the judicial and quasi-judicial side, however, we go back to the beginning, since a lawyer, even to interpret the present law, must sometimes consult cases dating back to the Corporation Law of 1909 and even cases on the laws of 1894 and 1864. We find forty three million words, as shown below.

To read these is to read the Old Testament more than 60 times or to read the New Testament more than 200 times.

[39] '39, Sec. 211 (h) amending Sec. 362 (a).
[40] Sec. 112 (b) (7), as in '38.

I. The Income sections of the code plus the net increases by the Acts of 39–41 plus the regulations (including excess profits) plus the 6 most essential forms with their "instructions" (ignoring 50 others)	395,700 words
II. To Jan. 1, 1942, Federal decisions,[41] promulgations of BTA, Treasury Decisions, Cumulative Bulletin (ignoring 16 other kinds of official memoranda)	42,735,000 words
	43,130,700 words

Even practicing attorneys, according to a headline of the New York *Times*,[42] have to "brush up on taxes at school."

Yet the man in the street has been offered all this as an explanation of what *he* meant by "income."

[41] American Federal Tax Reports, West Publishing Co.
[42] July 18, 1939.

CHAPTER 19

LESSONS FROM BRITISH EXPERIENCE

AN EXCELLENT epitome of the British income tax is contained in *A Summary of The British Tax System with Special Reference to its Administration,*[1] by Roswell Magill, L. H. Parker, and Eldon P. King. This is a very illuminating document, put together in a remarkably short time, being "researches in England covering approximately two months." It was prepared with the assistance of some thirty British tax officials and a number of British taxpayers.

Like the American concept, the British concept of income for income tax purposes (so far as any concept can be discovered) is evidently a mixture of the Yield and the Accretion concepts. But, either because of a hundred years' experience or for some other reason, the British income tax comes much nearer to the Yield concept than does the American. There are several features which evidence this fact. First and foremost:

CAPITAL GAINS AND LOSSES

We quote:

"The British do not consider income to arise in the case of gains arising from the sale of capital assets, unless the taxpayer makes transactions in such assets his trade or business.

[1] A Summary of The British Tax System with Special Reference to its Administration, by Roswell Magill, L. H. Parker, and Eldon P. King. Printed for the use of the Joint Committee on Internal Revenue Taxation Pursuant to Sec. 1203 (b) (6), Revenue Act of 1926. United States Government Printing Office, Washington, 1935. For sale by the Superintendent of Documents, Washington, D.C.

Inasmuch as they do not tax capital gains, they do not allow capital losses to be deducted from income.

"Except where the buying and selling of investments forms part of the business of the taxpayer (in which case, of course, the investments are really stock in trade), any gain made on the realization of an investment would not be income in the eyes of the British. The nature of the British concept is shown by the terms of the general charge under Schedule D, which imposes tax in respect of the '*annual* profits and gains arising and accruing from trade, etc., . . . and in respect of all interest of money annuities and other *annual* profits and gains' but although *prima facie* the word 'annual' to some extent connotes recurrence it is settled law that the charge extends to casual or isolated transactions if the casual or isolated transaction is of the nature of a trading transaction or consists of the rendering of services. . . ."

What is the reason, if any, that the British law taxes the professional dealer on regular deals exactly like the isolated deals on which the British layman is not taxed at all?

The American system, in this matter of capital gains, seems more self-consistent. It spares no one. And yet the British system is much more nearly coincident with what, in this book, are considered sound principles. Although characteristically the British method is not explicitly logical, it has, apparently, by empirical trial and error, hit on a practical scheme by which net cash yield, and therefore real income, are closely approximated.

In the first place, by distinguishing between regular and isolated capital gains, the British method comes nearer to "money is as money does" than the American method; because regular gains more often go into real income (and are taxed in Britain) whereas isolated capital gains more often go back into capital (and are not taxed in Britain). Not that the discrimination is perfect even in Britain; for, of course, irregular gains sometimes go into real income, and regular gains sometimes go into capital.

In the second place, as to the straddle over the years: although the purchase and sale of any single item may straddle the years, yet the aggregate of such transactions, when conducted daily by a professional dealer, constitute a reasonably even flow. Thus, if a dealer sells a block of stock for $5,000 in the present taxable year, having bought it two years earlier for $4,000, the $1,000 profit does, it is true, straddle the two-year interval between purchase and sale; but the dealer may well have a $4,000 purchase every year and a $5,000 sale every year so that a $1,000 profit will be recorded every year, even though each profit is nominally a straddle, reckoned between successive years instead of crosswise in a given year.

To take the most extreme case of such similarity, suppose he regularly buys some stock for $4,000 every day of every year, and two years after each purchase sells for $5,000. His capital gain is $1,000 every day. This straddles over a two-year period, but is exactly the same as his net cash yield found by subtracting each day's outgo of $4,000 from the same day's intake of $5,000.

Evidently the more "regular" the dealer's transactions are, the more nearly will the straddling capital gain tax approximate the nonstraddling net cash yield tax; and, therefore, the less harmful will be the consequences of the straddling.

It follows that, by taxing only regular dealers on their capital gains, the British system produces a minimum of the ill effects of the straddle tax and, at the same time, approximates the sound effects of a net cash yield tax.

Only in the borderline cases is any appreciable harm done. A dealer who merely takes an occasional "plunge in the waters of trade" sometimes suffers injustice, which probably explains why such cases get into the courts. Reversely, anyone who succeeds in not being classified as a dealer but who nevertheless operates with some regularity may conceivably achieve considerable tax avoidance, with corresponding injustice to the government.

The one way to prevent both injustices is, of course, to replace the capital gain tax by the net cash yield tax. This would accomplish everything now accomplished by the British system and much more, and at the same time, it would be self-consistent and logical instead of merely empirical.

ANNUITIES

The second example of the British approximation to the Yield tax system concerns life annuities.

The report states:

". . . In the ordinary case of annuities payable for life, the whole of the annuity is regarded as income and the tax is collected at the source. But where an annuity certain is purchased, which is payable for a fixed term of years independent of any contingency, only that part of the annuity which represents interest is taxable as income."[2]

Why should life annuities be treated as "income" as they are in England? Because, we venture to say, the recipients may reasonably be presumed to spend their annuities—to live on them. That is, life annuities are nearly identical with spendings,[3] with net cash yield, and with real income.

And why, on the other hand, is an "annuity certain" treated in England differently from life annuities? Presumably, because this rarer device ("annuity certain") is more likely to be thought of as *not* for daily spending but rather as a series of installment payments for a capital good.

DEPLETION, ETC.

The third example of the English approximation to the Yield system concerns depreciation, depletion, and obsolescence. In America, allowances for these are always made in conformity

[2] Ibid., p. 56.
[3] See Magill, p. 374.

to the Accretion concept; that is, the allowance is calculated relatively to a constant unimpaired capital.

But not so in England. The report states:

"In Great Britain, since capital gains and losses are not taken into account in computing income, profits are often taxed in their entirety even though the earning of these profits involves a wastage of capital. For instance, the owner of an apartment house [in Britain] must pay tax on the gross rent, less taxes and repairs, without being able to recoup his capital by depreciation deductions as in the United States. Likewise [in Britain], there is no depletion deduction on account of the exhaustion of natural resources, such as mines. It is true, depreciation is allowed on machinery and equipment, but no obsolescence is allowed unless and until such machinery is actually replaced.[4] . . .

"No depreciation is allowed on buildings."[5]

Evidently all these provisions are much more in tune with the net cash Yield tax than is the American system, which, in this respect, is more in tune with the Accretion concept. In America the owner of such an apartment house as cited in the above quotation is allowed deduction for depreciation even if he "milks" the property dry, getting meanwhile a big net cash yield, without sharing it fully with the government. In England, such a man is taxed, as he should be. Only when and if he actually goes to the expense of making repairs is his tax reduced accordingly. No mere bookkeeping reductions are allowed.

In the same way, if a mineowner exhausts his property, meanwhile taking out big gross profits in cash, he is, in England, taxed while the taxing is good. No mere bookkeeping obsolescence of machinery is allowed. But if the owner actually *pays* for replacements, he is allowed deductions for such actual expense. This comes close to being a deduction for a reinvestment —the key principle of the Yield system.

Yet, while all these British practices are more in tune with

[4] British Tax System, supra, pp. 20-21.
[5] Ibid., p. 20.

a net cash Yield tax than are our American practices, the British system does not follow through completely and consistently. Suppose the owner of the apartment house, mine, or obsolescent machinery purposely lets these properties run down to exhaustion, but fully makes up for this by reinvestment of part of his temporarily big returns in some entirely *different* direction. This reinvestment *should* be deductible, just as truly as if he had put the reinvestment into repairs of the apartment house, extension of the mine, or replacement of the machine. But such reinvestments are not deductible either in England or in America.

RENT AND OWNER-OCCUPANCY

There is one other important respect in which the English system, contrary to the American, approximates a true Yield tax, although, in this case the yield involved is not cash yield.

We quote from the report:

". . . The British conceive income to arise from all occupied real property, whether or not such income is actually received in the form of money or money's worth. If the property is occupied even by the owner, income is computed on the basis of the average rental value. This is entirely different from the conception in the United States. In the latter country, if a man owns and occupies a $10,000 house, which might normally rent for $1,000 per year, he is considered to receive no income from the house; on the other hand, in England, in a like case, he will be assessed on the annual value; that is, he will include $1,000 in his schedule A income.[6]

"The British law, of course, is final as to what constitutes income. On the other hand, our Federal income tax laws are subject to the limitations of the Constitution.

"In both Great Britain and in the United States the rent received from a house is income; but if the owner occupies the house instead of renting it, the rental value of the house is still income in Great Britain, but not in the United States. Under

[6] Ibid., p. 17.

the Constitution it is probable that we cannot tax the theoretical income arising from the occupation of a house by its owner.[7] As between taxpayers, however, the British system appears more equitable."[8]

As the title of the report indicates, it is mainly concerned with the problem of administering the law, not of reforming it. The report makes it clear that the English administration is better than ours, and the law perhaps simpler, certainly causing fewer complaints and less delay.

[7] See Helvering v Independent Life Insurance Company, 292 U.S. 371.
[8] British Tax System, supra, p. 20.

Chapter 20

CONSTITUTIONALITY

Does the Constitution stand in the way of Yield as a tax base?
Does it stand in the way of Accretion as a tax base?
Does it stand in the way of a simple spendings tax?

The Macomber and Pollock Cases

The two great judicial cornerstones hitherto have been the *Macomber* case and the *Pollock* case.[1] But it is now rumored that both have been buried, though the Supreme Court has held no funeral ceremony.

The gist of the *Macomber* case is:

(a) income under the Sixteenth Amendment is what the Common Man thinks it is;

(b) the Common Man thinks that capital appreciation is not income;

(c) the Common Man thinks that nothing is income until it is realized.

The gist of the *Pollock* case is:

(a) Taxes on the most important forms of income—namely, on incomes produced by property, real or personal—are direct taxes;

(b) thereupon, in order to free such taxes from the obnoxious apportionment rule of the Constitution, a Sixteenth Amendment seemed to be required.

First, has anything happened to the *Macomber* case? In 1936, Professor Magill said there was "little doubt that Con-

[1] Eisner v Macomber, 252 U.S. 189, Mar. 9, 1920; Pollock v U.S., 157 U.S. 429, reargued 158 U.S. 601, both in 1895.

gress could not compel the return as income of *unrealized* appreciation" (italics ours).[2] But then in 1940 came the *Bruun* case,[3] which softened realization, but did not abolish the requirement of it. And later in 1940 came the *Horst* case which not only records another softening of realization but has a dictum to the effect that the requirement of realization is a mere postponement of the tax for purposes of "administrative convenience."[4] Stanley S. Surrey, formerly assistant legislative counsel of the treasury, infers from this that realization is no longer a constitutional requirement of income.[5]

However, we are not convinced that the Court's meaning would include such an accretion as a silent growth in the value of a corner lot.

Next, has anything happened to the *Pollock* case? In 1936, Professor Magill said that "notwithstanding the *Pollock* case, it is likely that the Court today would accept the view that an income tax is an excise tax," thus requiring no Sixteenth Amendment. We take it that Professor Magill meant—if the Court had it all to do over again.

In 1937, occurred two cases which Mr. Surrey regards as, in effect, doing it all over again—that is, as extinguishing the *Pollock* case.[6] Both of these 1937 cases involved questions of state taxation—*not* the federal income tax. Nevertheless, both involved references to the *Pollock* case and in both the Court flatly denied that a tax on income is a tax on its source. However, the Court also denied that the *Pollock* case had ever said so. Nominally the *Pollock* case still lives.

At any rate, the deaths of *Macomber* and *Pollock* are still

[2] Taxable Income, p. 103.

[3] Helvering v Bruun, 309 U.S. 461, Mar. 25, 1940, discussed in Chap. 14.

[4] Helvering v Horst, 311 U.S. 112 at 116, Nov. 25, 1940. See also Helvering v Eubank, 311 U.S. 122, Nov. 25, 1940.

[5] "The Supreme Court & the Federal Income Tax," Illinois Law Review, March, 1941 (Vol. XXXV, No. 7, p. 779), Northwestern University.

[6] People of New York ex rel. Cohn v Graves, 300 U.S. 308, at 314-316, Mar. 1, 1937 (see also Graves v People of New York ex rel Keefe, 306 U.S. 466 at 480, Mar. 27, 1939). Hale v Iowa State Board, 302 U.S. 95, Nov. 8, 1937.

CONSTITUTIONALITY

speculative, and we feel that we must treat at least the *Pollock* case as still alive along with its Sixteenth Amendment, and that we must figure the chances of either a spendings tax or a yield tax.

Spendings Tax

There would seem to be no constitutional difficulty about an explicit spendings tax, substantially like the one prepared by Ogden Mills. It can hardly be called a direct tax. It seems to be covered by the expression "duties, imposts and excises" in Article I, Section 8, Clause 1 of the Constitution which the Supreme Court interprets as covering *all* indirect taxes.[7]

And, so far as we know, the only taxes which the Supreme Court has classified as direct (besides capitation taxes) are those on property, real and personal, and those on the income produced by such property. It is true that in these *Pollock* cases[8] there are dicta and English citations which mention not only directness to the property but directness to the person—a direct tax in this sense being an unshiftable tax; but the *Pollock* cases themselves impliedly treat several unshiftable taxes (for instance, a tax on salary) as not direct taxes within the apportionment rule.[9]

Moreover, the Court has since treated as indirect a number of other taxes which quite obviously cannot be shifted.

The Court describes as indirect, taxes on "business transactions"[10] or on "the happening of an event or an exchange" (citing French law),[11] including taxes on sales on a Board of Trade;[12] on sales of stock;[13] on gifts;[14] on inheritance (de-

[7] Thomas v U.S., 192 U.S. 363 (Feb. 23, 1904), citing Pollock v Farmers Loan & Trust Co., 157 U.S. 429, 557 (1895).
[8] Pollock v Farmers Loan & Trust Co., per last footnote & as re-argued 158 U.S. 601 (1895).
[9] See Justice White of the minority, 158 U.S. (page 710, 14th Point).
[10] Thomas v U.S. 192 U.S. 363, Feb. 23, 1904.
[11] Knowlton v Moore, 178 U.S. 41 at 47, May 14, 1900.
[12] Nicol v Ames, 173 U.S. 509, Apr. 3, 1899.
[13] Thomas case, supra.
[14] Bromley v McCaughn, 280 U.S. 124, Nov. 25, 1929.

scribed by the Court as "transmission from the dead to the living," the tax being not on the property but on its descent).[15] Also the famous corporation tax of 1909 was an "excise" tax, a tax on the *privilege* of operating as a corporation.[16]

All that the Constitution requires of "duties, imposts and excises" is that they be "uniform throughout the United States"; and the Court interprets uniformity to mean simply that the tax must have everywhere "the same plan and the same method."[17] For instance, the Court held that an inheritance tax was thus uniform, in spite of the fact that its rates were progressive.[18]

Examples of Unshiftable: inheritance tax and corporation tax; *example of progressive rates:* inheritance tax; *example of annual computation and payment:* corporation tax.

Finally, the *Pollock* case itself seemed to accept the view that "all taxes on expenses or consumption"—in other words, spendings—"are indirect taxes."[19]

It seems hardly open to question, therefore, that a spendings tax would fall securely under this category as an "indirect tax."

Nor do we think a spendings tax could be attacked as an improper subterfuge for a tax on income as income, any more than could the so-called excise tax of 1909 on corporations. That tax was quite clearly a tax on income masquerading as an "excise,"

[15] Knowlton case, supra.
[16] Stratton's Independence v Howbert, 231 U.S. 399, Dec. 1, 1913.
[17] Knowlton case, supra. Also Edye v Robertson, 112 U.S. 580, Dec. 8, 1884; Nicol v Ames, supra; Brushaber v Union Pacific, 240 U.S. 1, Jan. 24, 1916; Patton v Brady, 184 U.S. 608, Mar. 17, 1902.
[18] Knowlton case, supra.
[19] The Court quotes this (158 U.S. at 627) from Justice Paterson in an earlier case and merely denies the applicability of such a rule to a tax on carriages, as approved by Paterson. The Court also denies that income from property (as interpreted by Pitt in England) can be considered to have "lost all connection" with the property so as to make a tax on it merely "an assessment . . . on account of . . . money-spending power" (629). Finally, the Court said there was no occasion to consider whether a direct income tax "would enable the government to diminish taxes on consumption and duties on imports" by way of a "reform of its fiscal . . . system" (634).

and thereby (as the Supreme Court expressed it) "avoiding the difficulty"—i.e., the difficulty presented by the Constitution prior to the Sixteenth Amendment.[20]

Under a spendings tax, the source of the money spent would be of no moment, any more than in the case of a sales tax.

On the other hand, could a spendings tax take the sources of the spending money into consideration in such a way as to grant an exemption on part of it, corresponding with what is now called an "earned income credit"?

We should think so. If earners can be taxed less and bachelors more on *income*, why cannot the law thus consider the status of a taxpayer when levying *any* kind of tax—income tax, spendings tax, gift tax?

YIELD TAX AS SUCH

But it would be in the interest of clear thinking to call our spendings tax an income tax. Moreover, if it should seem desirable to tax items of real income, a spendings tax would be unavailable for that purpose, and an explicit yield tax would be necessary. Would a yield tax be constitutional?

A yield tax would, of course, depart from the present law in two ways. *First*, it would exempt some items now taxed; *second*, it would tax some items now exempt.

Exemptions would seem to present no difficulty, since Congress is not compelled to tax all the kinds of income that it has the power to tax.[21] But when it comes to taxing several kinds of income which the present law exempts difficulties do arise. Such items now exempt fall under the following heads:

> Alimony;
> Borrowings;
> Gifts;
>
> Compensatory payments, i.e., for { hurt feelings / hurt body / death / hurt property;
>
> Proceeds of capital sold;
> "Real Income."

[20] Stratton's Independence v Howbert, 231 U.S. 399, Dec. 1, 1913.
[21] Brushaber v Union Pacific, 240 U.S. 1, Jan. 24, 1916.

Some of these are exempt expressly, and some are exempt by being ignored. The yield system would enter all of them in the gross, offsetting them, of course, with appropriate deductions.

The question is: Would the Supreme Court recognize them as "gain from capital or labor"?

We consider the pros and cons in a very brief appendix,* on the assumption that the *Pollock* and *Macomber* cases still stand.

Two Problems

We pause here to mention only two of the problems. The first is a subdivision of the "real income" problem. This is the case of an individual occupying his own dwelling. Under the present decisions, if two such men live in their own houses, each house having a rental value of $5,000 per year, the taxable income allowed by the Sixteenth Amendment is zero. But, if each man decides to become a tenant of the other, the taxable income allowed by the Sixteenth Amendment instantly jumps to $10,000 with no change in the economic condition of either man.

Second, perhaps the most difficult problem derives, paradoxically, from a case relative to a law preceding the Sixteenth Amendment. In many situations, this pre-sixteenth Amendment decision now seems to make it actually unconstitutional in some cases to tax a spendthrift.

One Basic Difficulty

A misconception which gives rise to some of the puzzles discussed in the Appendix is the failure of Congress and the Court to distinguish properly between capital and income—or rather their attempt to identify improperly these two basic items.

"Money is as money does." No one, not even the Supreme Court, can tell whether a given $1,000 gained or acquired by John Smith will, in the end, add $1,000 to his capital or to his income or partly to one and partly to the other. John Smith will attend to that. And even he, in order to know the final result

* See Appendix to (this) Chapter 20.

for a taxable year, must wait not only for the disposition of this particular thousand dollars, but for the effect of all his transactions combined.

At the end of the year, and not before, with the help of that thousand dollars and of all other receipts and disbursements, he can calculate *exactly* how much he has added to his capital and how much he has spent as income. And that is all we need to know, whatever be our tax base—Yield or Accretion.

As long as we insist on labeling each dollar at the outset as "capital" or as "income," our courts can only continue to wander in the wilderness. If the Yield system were adopted, no such questions would ever reach the Supreme Court or any other court. For, under that system, all receipts are treated alike— as gross Yield. Some *disbursements* might still be debatable— as to whether they are genuine investments and so deductible.

MITIGATIONS—SOLUTION

Nevertheless, as to these and the other difficulties discussed in the Appendix, and even on the assumption that the *Pollock* and *Macomber* cases still stand, we derive considerable hope for the Yield system—hope for some items and makeshifts for others. In the case of the owner-occupancy of a dwelling, the makeshift is even preferable, in some ways, to a tax on the real income.

But is there not a way to cut at one stroke, completely and without makeshift, *all* the Gordian knots?

Of course, to set Congress free, we could go through the prolonged agony of a constitutional amendment: either defining income (but a once-for-all definition would be dangerous); or limiting the apportionment rule to capitation taxes and Congressional representation; or merely requiring of the court a 6-to-3 vote to invalidate any act of Congress.

But let us look at Mr. Surrey's conjecture that already the Supreme Court is disposed to accept any Congressional income tax which is "sensible" and not contrary to "due process."

We venture three beliefs about Court and Common Man.

First, that the Court really favors conceptual flexibility in the economic field—and more so in recent years; *second,* that the Court is flexible in its professed loyalty to the common man; *third,* that the common man himself is flexible and not in the habit of refusing expert help on his interpretations of the phenomena by which he is surrounded, and probably took such help for granted when he accepted the Sixteenth Amendment with its word "income." We consider these three in order.

1. JUDICIAL FLEXIBILITY

Justice Clarke once scouted "the refinements of lexicographers and economists"[22] as too cramping. Justice Holmes, on the same ground, scouted even the "judicial definitions"[23] which had dodged the lexicographers and the economists; he declared the word "income" to be "not a crystal," but a concept free to vary with time and circumstance.[24] And Member Sternberger of the Board of Tax Appeals, citing the Court's words "not a crystal," concluded that the Court was opposed to "defining words abstractly" and suggested that we are not "forever to be limited by a judicial definition" anyhow.[25]

2. THE COURT'S FLEXIBLE FIDELITY TO MAN-IN-STREET

In 1921 the Court said that "income" in the Sixteenth Amendment means what it meant in common speech at the time when the Sixteenth Amendment was adopted.[26]

Yet Justice Holmes, as we have seen, had said in 1918 that the meaning has never been crystallized and should vary with the time and circumstance.

The Court has said that the proceeds of life insurance are "not usually regarded" as income (which is plain English for "not according to common speech"); yet the Court expressly

[22] Merchants Loan & Trust v Smietanka, 255 U.S. 509 at 519, Mar. 28, 1921. (See also Weiss v Weiner, 279 U.S. 333, 335, Apr. 22, 1929.)
[23] U.S. v Kirby Lumber, 284 U.S. 1 at 3, Nov. 2, 1931.
[24] Towne v Eisner, 245 U.S. 418 at 425, Jan. 7, 1918.
[25] Hawkins v Comm. 6 BTA 1023, Apr. 25, 1927.
[26] Merchants Loan v Smietanka, supra.

left open the question whether this "usual" view was the correct view.[27]

Again, the Court said that the common man regards periodicity as an attribute of income;[28] yet elsewhere the Court held that, if the law did not tax "isolated" capital gains, the purpose of the Sixteenth Amendment would be largely defeated,[29] meaning, of course, the common man's purpose.

Finally, in 1936, by the pen of Justice Cardozo, the Court rather surprises us with a qualified version of the common man, holding him infallible *"with few exceptions if any."*[30]

3. THE COMMON MAN FLEXIBLE TOO, AND PRESUPPOSES AUTHORITY

Suppose that Congress and the Court could capture a composite of the common man, and convince him that, in 1913, he had really written the Sixteenth Amendment.

Question: "Do you know precisely what you meant by income?"

Answer: "In a general way. I'm no expert."

"But, sir, we couldn't construct a law in a general way. It *has* to be expert."

Answer: "Well, then, consult the experts."

"Do you mean that, by the word 'income,' you meant whatever the experts mean?"

Answer: "The other day a schoolmaster told me the meaning of 'gravitation.' I don't even remember the formula, much less understand it. I did know it makes apples fall—and I know *now* (because the schoolmaster told me) that it helps balloons to rise—much to my amazement. Well, if I'd put the word 'gravitation' into the Sixteenth Amendment, I'd be meaning whatever Isaac Newton meant."

"But there *is* no Isaac Newton in economics. The economists

[27] U.S. v Supplee-Biddle Hardware Co., 265 U.S. 189, May 26, 1924.
[28] Ibid.
[29] Merchants Loan v Smietanka, supra.
[30] U.S. v Safety Car Heating Co., 297 U.S. 88 at 99, Jan. 6, 1936.

themselves don't claim an exact science. They haven't crystallized a concept—if Justice Holmes is right."

Answer: "Well, anyhow, consult them. Of course, if one of them claims that his concept is the conclusive crystal, don't make all the other concepts unconstitutional—anyhow, not until there's impressive agreement as to just what an economic crystal is. So long as the experts disagree, for the love o' Mike don't bar any of them. That's my common-man verdict. Take it or leave it."

A PROPOSAL

Of course, we think that Yield is the crystal; but, in a world of un-unanimous votes, perhaps the Supreme Court could compromise thus:

"1. All concepts of income have at least a subconscious reference to real income.

"2. The concept embodied in the collective mind of the writers (or adopters) of the Constitution was extremely vague.

"3. Any Congressional concept that reasonably resembles that vague, popular concept shall be constitutional."

CHAPTER 21

CONCLUSIONS

SUMMARY

Certainly, for tax-base purposes, the Yield system is right: (1) because it conforms with the principles of discounting and so relates income to capital by an exact law; (2) because it avoids double taxation; (3) because thereby it rescues from compound destruction the country's future capital and the products thereof—which are real income.

(4) And above all, the yield tax is right because it is, in effect, a tax on real income.

The Accretion system, on the other hand (aside from its implications that we can eat and drink on an income of less than zero), is wrong for tax-base purposes: (1) because it violates the principles of discounting and so does *not* relate income to capital with any consistency whatever; (2) because it double-taxes—takes both the tree and its fruits; (3) because thereby it destroys at a compound rate—a very high rate in the case of important new inventions—the country's future capital and thereby the country's future real income, or standard of living, and thereby the Treasury's future revenue; (4) because, conversely, it allows double *exemption*—all four of which are both unjust and unprofitable.

As to the present law; partly by mixing with the Accretion system and partly by not adhering to either the one concept or the other, it raises the wrongs to the nth power: (a) it does not relate income to capital with any consistency whatever; (b) it causes double taxation—not only tandem but abreast; (c) by

194

taxing one corporation many ways plus another corporation many ways plus the stockholders, it involves even triple and other multiple taxations; (d) it destroys future enterprise at a compound rate; (e) it is not consistently annual but frequently straddles the years; (f) it hits some "patterns" of income harder than it hits others of the same amount (regardless of which pattern is owned by the rich and which by the poor); (g) it allows the clever taxpayer to escape by changing his pattern; (h) it taxes items which have no "wherewithal," so that sometimes the tax has to be financed; (i) it spares the spendthrift of capital and penalizes the thrifty; (j) it is a congeries of special expedients with exceptions to exceptions—a second provision superseding a first before the first can take effect, and a third superseding the second before either the first or the second can take effect—leading on and on through more and more words, less and less understandable, until lawyers go to school about it and members of Congress throw up their hands and call their own 19th elaborate alteration in 28 years a "mess" and a "monstrosity."

As to the social aspect it is far better that all of us should grow richer than that we should reduce the inequalities at the cost of making us all poorer. In America, though distribution is not by any means perfect, the total goods distributable, and therefore the standard of living of practically all of us, even of the poor, is, in this generation, higher than anywhere else in the world at any time in history; and it is worth noting that this American total was mostly built before the misnamed income tax became severe.

To "soak the rich" in the sense of savings would be to soak the poor in the sense of real income. Plutocratic aristocracy never springs from the builders of wealth who are big savers. It springs from inheritors who often are big spenders and not savers at all. Our plan, by means of yield-plus-succession-taxes, would be: (a) to limit big inheritance; (b) to "soak" big spendings; (c) to encourage the saver no matter who he is;

(d) thereby to increase the chances of all of us to rise in the economic scale according to ability.

Bigger factories, smaller palaces—such is the philosophy of the Yield tax.

Of course all taxes should mutually articulate: death duties, income taxes, gift taxes, and all the rest.

And plenty of other measures are needed for better social justice. Some of them have already been sponsored by the present administration and Congress. We do not propose our tax reform as a panacea.

But it is sorely needed. In fact, the tax on savings may well defeat the other social-justice expedients.

WAR

Private savings are not less essential in wartime. They are more essential.

In wartime, so far as concerns the task of co-ordination, private industry needs the command of government; but in the job of efficient production, as commanded, private industry, in most directions, is far more efficient than government industry.

And even if the government could manage *everything* better, there is no time, in the hurry of war, to make such a drastic change successfully. Practical exigencies require that we employ a mixed system and mixed motives. We must beware of the doctrinaire who capitalizes our difficulties in order to put over his favorite theories, not tested by experience.

In wartime, the patriotic motive should take first place and the profit motive (so far as it hinders instead of helping the war effort) should be relegated to the rear. But we must depend largely on private initiative and on private management. Nor can we expect businessmen as a group to be so patriotic as to risk big losses with little chance of gain.

What is especially necessary in wartime is not to put more taxes on savings. Rather should we take off those already on. And yet we now calmly discourage savings by imposing a new and drastic excess profits tax, which does not even discriminate between those profits which are distributed and those profits which are plowed back. And after thus discouraging by taxation the very expansion we ought most to encourage, we turn around and try to undo this harm by offering these same industries special government loans—virtually lending them back the very taxes taken from them.

What is most needed is to remove the initial handicap—the tax on the savings that build the plants.

Some of those who, a short time ago, were condemning so-called oversavings are now advocating compulsory savings for "the duration." The plan proposed in this book would accomplish almost the same end but by voluntary means. It should, we submit, be utilized first. It would automatically promote the purchase of government bonds both by releasing, for that purpose, the funds which formerly went into taxes and by generating and encouraging the creation of more.

Later on, compulsory plans could be tried in addition. And we might begin such compulsion by requiring that a part of undistributed profits be invested in government bonds.

Savings, moreover, have the virtue of retarding inflation.

AFTER THE WAR, RECOVERY?

Even in peace, reform is always blocked by inertia and by fear of the untried. At best, we do not expect to see the Yield system instituted at one stroke. Some sorts of capital gain with their several contributions to double taxation will doubtless have to be endured for some time. But the first step, and the most essential one, would be to emancipate savings: not to tax the individual on what he saves and not to tax the corporation on what it plows back.

The present excess profits tax leaves little or no reserve. When the war stops many corporations will be almost wholly dependent on the Government.

The very fact that war destroys our collective savings makes all the more urgent the immediate emancipation of individual savings and the preservation of past accumulations as embodied in our national capital equipment.

Let us not be improvident in war lest, after the war, we slump to the present standard of living of unhappy Europe, or perhaps that of more unhappy Asia.

We must not raze to the ground our capital equipment. Our wheat-growing Mississippi Valley would be just as fertile; but, without savings as embodied in farm machinery to plant, reap, thresh, and market the wheat, little could ever be made into bread—the ill fed would be worse fed.

Our cotton fields would be just as fertile as ever; but, without the savings embodied in the cotton gin, the spinning jenny and the loom, little could be made into clothes—the ill clothed would be worse clothed.

The forests, mines, and quarries would still be there; but, without the necessary machinery, little of the wood, ore or stone would be turned into dwellings—the ill housed would be worse housed.

APPENDICES

To Part I

To Chapter 7

To Chapter 8

To Chapter 9

To Chapter 12

To Chapter 20

APPENDIX TO PART I

SUBSIDIARY PROBLEMS

WE SHALL now list briefly some of the subsidiary problems which would confront the Yield system in practice.

I. DEDUCTIBLES

Insurance Premiums (*Fire and Other Damage*) (*line 20*). Deduct those that insure business or capital, not those that insure consumer goods. In short, the expense of such insurance is deductible or nondeductible according as the expense insured against is deductible or nondeductible.

All life insurance premiums would be deductible, whether the beneficiary were a personal dependent or a business enterprise. When the premiums are paid by a business enterprise on the life of an executive, they would be a business expense. Even the insurance of employees, for their families and not on behalf of the business, would be a business expense, like a bonus.

Premiums on life insurance for a relative or dependent or friend should (within reasonable limits) be deductible as a matter of public policy.

The insurance money in any of these cases would, of course, be gross income, whoever received it.

Taxes. In the tax return set forth in Chapter 1, *all* taxes were, for simplicity, made deductible.

As to the deductibility of the income tax itself (paid last year), there are arguments both for and against. On the whole, and contrary to the tax return illustrated in Chapter 1, we slightly prefer nondeductibility, as under present laws.

The two taxes are, of course, only nominally different. Either may be translated into the other with appropriately different rates. The rate on one of them, best called "net cash yield before taxes," is lower

201

than the equivalent rate on the other, best called "spendings after taxes." The former rate could not exceed 100 per cent, the equivalent to which in the latter would be an infinite rate.

But a detailed study is needed to discover the most equitable scheme for the deductibility or nondeductibility of various taxes. Probably no perfect equitability is attainable. The present law, as is almost universally admitted, is not equitable. The person who drives his own car may deduct gasoline taxes, but he who travels by bus cannot deduct the gasoline taxes included in the fare he pays. Probably neither deduction should be allowed.

So also a tenant may not deduct any part of the rent he pays, though part of it goes for taxes like what a homeowner may deduct. Probably neither should be allowed.

Nor should a tax on theater tickets, since it is the total price, including the tax, which the playgoer really spends.

Gifts. Exemption on gifts should be duly limited. The limitations on charitable gifts could be made substantially as now, by making the limit a fixed percentage of spendings-plus-savings. Or a new system could be devised such as a fixed percentage of the savings alone.

Credit for personally earned income. Such a credit is now fixed only by rule of thumb. Even under such a rule it could be improved upon. One proposal is that of William Vickrey. He would allow such credit to all those with personally earned income large enough to justify the presumption of full-time employment. If the earned income were less than this, only part-time employment would be presumed and the credit would be correspondingly reduced. In no case would any tax be payable unless the unearned income exceeded, say, the minimum exemption or the combined income exceeded double that.

Alimony. Whether the tax on alimony is paid by ex-wife or ex-husband should be a question of public policy. But if A contributes to B's income and is taxed on the contribution, A should have all the deductions which B would have if taxed—or a proper part of them.

II. INSTALLMENTS ON A DEBT INCURRED FOR A PURCHASE

In case of consumer goods bought with borrowed money, (for instance, a dwelling house bought on mortgage) the installments paid on the loan should be treated as installments on the purchase price. This could be accomplished by allowing the taxpayer to omit this particular kind of loan transaction from line 7, while requiring him to fill out an informative schedule on an inner page.

III. WHEN USER SELLS OR SELLER USES

Sometimes the private purchaser of a durable consumption good decides to sell it "secondhand." In that case, if what he receives is entered as income (line 10) it could be deductible (line 26), since he was already taxed on the unused life of the good when he purchased it.

In the reverse case, when a dealer decides to make personal use of an article out of his own stock, he might well be required to go through the bookkeeping motions of selling the article to himself, at the price he first paid.

However, these seller-user deals are unimportant and, in many cases, require no bookkeeping motions—for instance, when a secondhand car is "traded in" as part of the price of a new one.

IV. SPENDING AND INVESTING COMBINED

Sometimes, part of a house is occupied by the purchaser for dwelling purposes and part used for business purposes; or a car is used for both business and pleasure. In such cases, the allocation of purchase price and of upkeep including insurance could be delegated to the regulations and the Commissioner.

V. DATE DISCREPANCIES

The payer of a check might well enter it when mailed, and the payee, when received. The discrepancy might in rare cases be important; for instance, if a bank fails too late for a correction to be made in a tax return before filing it.

In such cases, the law should allow subsequent correction, and the Commissioner should devise appropriate forms.

VI. DISCREPANCIES BETWEEN CONSUMPTION AND SPENDINGS

Some enjoyments in year 2 were paid for in year 1 and some will be paid for in year 3—and the tax is on the year's payments. Ordinarily the discrepancies at the two ends will practically balance—at any rate, in the long run; and, even if not precisely, no provision need be made for correcting them.[1]

[1] See the writer's Income in Theory and Income Taxation in Practice (*In* Econometrica, January, 1937); also: A Practical Income Tax Schedule (*In* The Tax Magazine [now Taxes], July, 1937).

VII. ALLOCATIONS

The detailed solutions of certain problems would have to be worked out with the help of experts under present practice. We suggest only the outlines.

Certain inquisitorial powers would, as now, be delegated to the Commissioner.[2]

The taxable year would be the same for all returns including informative.[3]

In the case of a fractional year, the proposed law, like the present, would reckon a surtax under the hypothesis that the full year's income would be at the same rate.[4] This scheme would also be applied to years interrupted by death.[5]

If exempt or special-rate income were 1/10th of the gross, the exemption or special rate would be applied to 1/10th of the net.[6]

In the case of income derived from both American and foreign sources, the American taxpayer (also, in some cases, alien resident and American resident abroad) would be taxed on so much of his net as came from America.[7] Such business deductions as could not be ascribed to America or to "abroad" would be ascribed to both, in proportion to their respective contributions to the gross.

In case the foreign taxable year overlapped the American, there might be provisions for estimating the foreign expected tax and correcting the allocation later.[8]

As to foreigners resident in America, the present rules would be paralleled, including that for withholding at the source.[9]

[2] Code: subtitle E, Chap. 39, Sec. 3900; and Secs. 54, 62, 146.

[3] Sec. 164.

[4] Sec. 47 (c); **19**.47.

[5] Disregarding Sec. 42; and see Cumulative Bulletin, 1925, IV 1-p. 120.

[6] In some cases, there might be a constitutional question. Helvering v Gerhardt, 304 U.S. 405, May 23, 1938.

[7] Present law; Sec. 116 (a); Sec. 119; Sec. 23 (c) (2) ['41 Sec. 202 (a)]. **19**.131; Sec. 131 ('39 Sec. 216).

[8] Sec. 131 ('39, Sec. 216); Sec. 322; 19.131-3, last paragraph; Treasury Decisions 5056, June 28, 1941; U.S. v Anderson, 269 U.S. 422, Jan. 4, 1926; U.S. v Mitchell, 271 U.S. 9, Apr. 12, 1926.

[9] Sec. 119; Sec. 211 (a) (b) (c) ['41, Secs. 105, 109]; Secs. 212, 213; Sec. 143 (b) ['41, Secs. 107, 109].

This would apply to some foreign corporations;[10] and the tax might have to be corporate.

But probably not in the case of an American corporation or a foreign corporation operating in America. Such a corporation would function as our collector from its foreign stockholders; while, to each American stockholder, it would always deliver two dividend checks— one for his share of the American income and one for his share of the foreign, accompanying the latter with a memorandum of the foreign tax withheld from it.

Certain apportionments would be conditioned on foreign reciprocation;[11] and some taxes would perhaps be hybrid because of conflicting definitions.

VIII. Exemptions, Progressions, Etc.

The following five closely associated problems have to be faced in constructing any income tax:

1. Shall joint returns of husband and wife be allowed or required and on what basis?
2. What minimum exemptions for them shall be allowed?
3. What exemptions for dependents?
4. What credits for personally earned income?
5. What scales of progression?

These problems have been solved variously—always by rule of thumb.

To take an example, when a man and woman marry, they obtain under the present federal income tax, $2\frac{1}{2}$ times the exemption that each had before marriage. But this ratio has not always been employed. From 1913 through 1916 the exemption for a married couple was $4,000 as compared with $3,000 for a single person—making a ratio of only 1 1/3; from 1917 through 1920 they were $2,000 and $1,000 respectively—a ratio of 2; since then the ratio has always been above 2. "At present, of the 33 local jurisdictions having income taxes, in 8 the ratio is less than 2, in 15 it is exactly 2, and in only 10 is it

---

[10] Secs. 251-2 ('39 Sec. 207) ['41, Secs. 104 (e) & 111 (c)]; Sec. 131 (a) (b) ('39 Sec. 216); Sec. 14 (c) ('39 Sec. 201) ['41 Sec. 103 (c)]; Sec. 231 (b) (c) ('39 Sec. 206) ['41 Sec. 104]; Sec. 231 (a) (c) ['41 Sec. 106, 109 (a)]; Sec. 144 ['41 Sec. 107 (a), 109 (a)].

[11] Sec. 131 (a) (3) ('39 Sec. 216).

greater than 2. In 8 of these 10 the exemptions are exactly the same
as those of the Federal tax from 1932 to 1939."[12]

Another example: "Dependent exemptions in various states range
from 20 per cent to 50 per cent of the single person exemption, and
from 8 per cent to 25 per cent of the family exemption."[13]

This is not the place to discuss these five problems and their inter-
relations.

The following rough solutions are offered, more as constituting a
target to shoot at than as wholly satisfactory. Their chief merit is
their simplicity:

(1) Unless husband and wife agree to make separate returns and
agree on which dependents each shall include, require them
to make a joint return.

(2) Allow $500 exemption for each and the same for a single
person.[14]

(3) Allow $250 for each dependent.

(4) Allow an exemption (or "credit") of 50 per cent on all income
earned personally up to $1,000 for each person (husband,
wife, dependent) included in the return. Allow 20 per cent on
$1,001 to $2,000. Allow 10 per cent on $2,001 to $10,000.
Allow nothing thereafter.

(5) (a) Start the progression scale (which we here assume is
expressed in terms of spendings) after the foregoing exemptions and credits have been deducted (as well, of course, as
the regular deductible items).

(b) Begin with a 10 per cent rate for the first bracket.

Make it 20 per cent for the second bracket
30 per cent for the third bracket
40 per cent for the fourth bracket
*   *   *   *   *   *
*   *   *   *   *   *
100 per cent for the tenth and last.

[12] Tax Systems of the World, 8th ed., pp. 189-195. Tax Research Founda-
tion.
[13] Ibid.
[14] But if, as proposed by Professor Lutz, a system consisting of a flat
withholding tax were adopted (as we would approve, if not too high), all
exemption limits might well be increased rather than decreased. The
result of such a combination might be much greater revenue with far less
cost of administration, because of the lessened number of tax returns.

(c) Increase the bracket ranges for a married couple (with no children) making a joint return to *twice* the range for a single person. With such a set-up a joint return will result in a lower tax than two separate returns. Count each dependent as equivalent to *half* an adult so that, for instance, a couple with two children will have its bracket range three times that for a single person.

The basic set of ranges for a single person should be fixed according to circumstances.

In wartime the bracket ranges should be shorter than in peacetime. If in times of peace and prosperity (such as 1925-1928) each range was $10,000 (so that up to $10,000 the tax was 10 per cent; and, up to $20,000 it was 20 per cent; up to $30,000, 30 per cent; etc.), then in such times as 1942, the scale might well be

10 per cent up to $1,000
20 per cent on $1,001 to $2,000
* * * *
100 per cent on $9,001 to $10,000 and over.

The ascent could be even steeper and need not stop at 100 per cent. Nor need the successive ranges all be equal. As already indicated, we have purposely oversimplified. A scientific solution, if such is ever possible, should be expressed according to a mathematical formula, ascending smoothly, not by steps, and geometrically or logarithmically rather than arithmetically as above. The ideal ascent may even be more complicated and should be definitely related to the law of diminishing marginal desirability of money with increasing income or spendings, when, if ever, that law can be reduced to dependable statistics.[15]

IX. INCOME IN KIND

The yield tax as proposed in Chapter 1 is on income in cash not income in kind. This should be limited to avoid evasion. Ogden Mills,

[15] See Ragnar Frisch: New Methods of Measuring Marginal Utility, 1932, Verlag Von J. C. B. Mohr (Paul Siebeck), Tübingen. 142 pp.

Irving Fisher: A Statistical Method for Measuring "Marginal Utility" and Testing the Justice of a Progressive Income Tax (in Economic Essays Contributed in honor of John Bates Clark. Macmillan Co., 1927).

Also an article on the subject (not yet published) by Dr. Hans Staehle of Harvard University.

Also Elmer B. Fagan: Recent and Contemporary Theories of Progressive Taxation, Journal of Political Economy, August, 1938, pp. 452-498. See also Chapter 11 Supra.

in his bill, had the phrase money *or money's worth*. Collusive wage payments in form of consumer goods such as garden truck or the use of a dwelling might occur. This dodge could seldom be important, but real income might be made exempt only below a certain figure and also (for the protection of the taxpayer) below a certain percentage of his total net.

(Capital, such as stocks or bonds, paid for services would, of course, not be taxed as income. Their fruit—dividends, interest, etc., would be taxed instead).

X. Ogden L. Mills's Proposed Spendings Tax

Mr. Mills's spendings tax bill (H.R. 7867) was introduced July 20, 1921, when he was a congressman. Hearings were held at which he appeared and the bill was discussed in Congress[16] (by Frear, Stevenson, London, Green, Layton, Fordney and Mills himself). Mr. Mills also wrote an article in favor of his bill.[17]

Later[18] in answer to a question Mills said, "I was very wrong" and "I now think that, on the whole, that is uneconomic," showing that he had receded from his 1921 attitude.

He was presumably influenced by the prevalent opinion in the depression (the bottom of which was 1932-1933) that spending (at that time at least) should be encouraged and that saving (then often mere hoarding) should be discouraged. Some persons, at that time even advocated taxing only savings and not spendings.

This temporary renunciation by Mills, as shown by the hearings of 1932, was unknown to the author until he began in 1941 to construct the bibliography now at the end of this book. Its discovery gives significance to a remark which had been made to the author by Mr. Mills at our meeting in 1937 referred to below. This was to the effect that "the time is now ripe again for a spendings tax." It may also explain why he never, apparently, when Secretary of the Treasury, proposed anew a spendings tax.

In 1936 he commended an article on this subject by the author, and on August 24, 1937, had the author at lunch to talk it over. When asked if he still favored a spendings tax to supplant our existing

---

[16] Congressional Record, pp. 5138-5139, on Aug. 17, 1921.

[17] The Spendings Tax, in Bulletin of the National Tax Association, October, 1921, pp. 18-20.

[18] In 1932 at the Hearings (on) Revenue Revision, p. 25.

income taxes, he stated that he did. As to his bill of 1921 he said it had been prepared by the late Professor Thomas S. Adams,[19] subsequently of Yale. As to the author's new proposal, he said that he especially liked its simplicity. A few days later he wrote the author a letter to the same effect. This was only a few weeks before his death, which occurred October 11, 1937.

[19] It now appears that the idea of the bill was suggested to Professor Adams by Chester A. Jordan, accountant. The author also recalls that Professor Adams spoke to him of the bill when in preparation as embodying the principles of the author's The Nature of Capital and Income.

APPENDIX TO CHAPTER 7

THE FIVE NECESSARY CONDITIONS

FIVE conditions or attributes of income—four as to yield-income and one more as to accretion-income—have been implicitly assumed in Chapters 6 and 7. Let us now make them explicit.

CONDITIONS DEFINING YIELD-INCOME

1. It must consist of *services* (payments being one species of services);
2. It must flow through *a period of time*;
3. It must flow from some *source* or sources;
4. It must belong to some *person* or persons.

For example; let us consider a certain income of $1,000. (1) It consists of certain *payments* of dividends. (2) It arrives during a certain *year*. (3) It comes from one thousand shares of a certain *stock*. (4) It belongs to *John Smith*. This is John Smith's yield-income from that stock in that time. (It may not, of course, be his whole income).

FIFTH CONDITION NEEDED FOR ACCRETION-INCOME

5. The accretion-income must include the yield, as just defined, and also any increase (or decrease) in the value of the source of that yield.

This capital-increase, in turn, implies the following:

5a. *A future expected yield;*
5b. *Chances* as to the size of said future expected yield and its distribution in time;
5c. A *rate of interest* by which that future expected yield is discounted.

It is by means of this apparatus (5a, 5b, 5c) that the future yield is translated into present values, (1) at the beginning and (2) at the end of the taxable year, the difference between them being the capital-increase or decrease.

210

NEGLECT OF THE FIVE CONDITIONS

That the foregoing four and five conditions respectively should be fulfilled, in order to constitute income in the two senses, may strike the reader as too obvious to require such meticulous formulation. But, astonishing as it may seem, in the voluminous literature on this subject, some, if not all, of these conditions have at times been violated and, oftener, overlooked.

First, consider these violations or oversights in respect to the four conditions defining yield-income.

THE STUFF THAT YIELD-INCOME IS MADE OF

There are many who do not think of income as necessarily conforming to the first of the four conditions—the condition that it must consist solely of services.

It is often said that income consists of "goods and services." In a practical sense this is admittedly true. As noted in several connections already, we must, in practice, often accept the value of goods as approximately *measuring* the value of their services, because the services are not customarily valued separately in the markets. For instance, we must accept the price of bread as measuring the value of the use of the bread. The same is substantially true of clothes. Only occasionally does the use of clothes, as distinct from the clothes themselves, get registered in a money transaction. That is, ordinarily clothes are sold, not rented. In fact, very few so-called "consumer goods" are commonly rented, except buildings and (much less often) their furnishings—pianos more often than most.

A case in which it is desirable to insist on fine distinctions is that of net cash yield. We were careful to observe that by "cash" yielded by a cash balance is meant *payments* of cash, i.e., the services rendered by that cash balance—not the cash balance itself, which is a commodity, or capital.

The payment of a dividend to John Smith is an event occurring in time, and, to him, a desirable event. It is definitely a *service* rendered by his stock, just as the use of his house is a service rendered by his house. But the money received is not itself income. Money is not even an event. So also wages consist of the *payment* of money to the worker, not the *money* itself.

CLASSIFICATORY DEFINITIONS

Much of the discussion of what is income has missed the point and become a futile effort to classify concrete wealth into capital and income, instead of distinguishing between capital and income qualitatively—the one as concrete things and the other as abstract events occurring by means of those concrete things.

Most of the attempts to distinguish capital and income on the basis of mere classification are now historical curiosities. But, when, in 1897, the present writer began to protest against this practice, it was the prevailing vogue for textbooks on economics to try to formulate which wealth is capital and which wealth is income, the two being regarded as parts of one whole.

For instance, wealth was classified into "wealth to produce more wealth" (such, typically, as a machine to weave cloth) and on the other hand, wealth *not* so used (such, typically, as food and clothing). The former was called capital and the latter income.

We conclude, therefore, that it is important in our thinking to recognize services as the stuff, and the only stuff, out of which yield-income is made.

INCOME, A FLOW, NOT A STOCK OR FUND

That income is a flow during a period of time would, even more, seem to go without saying. Yet Malthus, in his *Definitions in Political Economy*, wrote: "Revenue: That portion of the stock or wealth, which the possessor may annually consume without injury to his permanent resources."[1]

In the same way, the classical economists would speak of the "wage fund," though wages must necessarily be not a fund but a flow. A "wage fund" is a contradiction in terms. Yet it took a generation to make this clear.

YIELD MUST HAVE A SOURCE

It has been seen that, according to the yield concept, every item of income—that is, services or uses, including payments—must come from some source and logically be credited to that source—that is, some asset or person; and, except the final consumption, every such

[1] Personal Income Taxation, H. C. Simons, University of Chicago Press, 1938, p. 630.

service (usually a payment), being an "interaction," must be debited to some interacting asset or person.

In almost all of the discussions of income, however, this important double entry is completely overlooked. Too often the question is asked about any item: "Is it income?" This question by itself is meaningless. It implies that an income item is absolute, instead of being always and necessarily relative to some source; and it overlooks the fact that the item in question can be, and usually is, both income relative to some source A, and outgo (negative income) relative to some other source B.

By this simple procedure, many of the supposed "riddles" of income are easily resolved.

Income Must Belong to Somebody

Since yield-income consists of services and services are desirable events, there must be some person or persons to experience the desire and the satisfaction of the desire. He is the beneficiary or owner.

Preservation of the Source

We come now to the fifth condition, peculiar to accretion-income.

It means that income (in the accretion sense) must include any increase in value of the source. It also means that, reversely, if the source is decreasing in value, the accretion-income from it is only that part of the yield which remains over and above the decrease; the value of the source must be preserved before there is any income.

This condition has often been called the condition—or test, or criterion—of the "preservation of the source."

This fifth condition, unlike most of the four preceding, is widely recognized and emphasized, though sometimes confusedly. For instance, some writers, when they call for "preservation" of the source confuse physical preservation with the preservation of value. The two are sometimes very far apart, particularly in the case of obsolescence.

The Necessary Conditions Are Also Sufficient

In the extensive economic literature on income concepts we find numerous alleged characteristics of income which have proved to be erroneous or superfluous.

The chief among these are:

"Income must be periodic, recurrent, or regular" like wages, salaries, interest, rent, dividends.

"Income must be produced by the recipient," not a gift.

"Income must be realized in cash."

"Income must be 'disposable.' "

"Income must be detached or severed from capital."

But we all know that some incomes are extremely *ir*regular; some are donated; some are in kind. Some accretion-income (e.g., undistributed profits) is not disposable by the owner (e.g., stockholder). Some accretion-income (such as accrued interest) is not detached from capital.

Those who assert that such characteristics are necessary confuse what is necessary with what happens to be *usual*. Income is usually regular, usually produced, usually in cash, usually disposable, usually detached—but not necessarily.

No one has ever shown any conditions to be necessary in addition to the four and five above specified, respectively, for the two senses of income.

APPENDIX TO CHAPTER 8

THE DUPLICATION QUESTIONED

THE only writers known to us as on record in opposition to the main thesis of Chapter 8, namely, that to tax both savings and their fruit is virtually to tax the same thing twice, are the following: Adolph Held (1872); Winthrop M. Daniels (1908); Frank A. Fetter (1908); A. W. Flux (1908); N. G. Pierson (1912); Edwin Cannan (1921); Umberto Ricci (1927); Ettore Lolini (1928); Donald V. Weaver (1932); C. W. Guillebaud (1935); Sir Josiah Stamp (1936); Viti de Marco (1936); Guglielmo Masci (1937); Clyde H. Graves (1937); Hugo C. W. Bordewijk (1939); William L. Crum (1939); Richard A. Musgrave (1939); W. W. Hewett (1941); H. S. Benjamin (1941).

Their writings on the subject are cited in the bibliography at the end of this volume as are our answers to some of them, namely: Graves (1939); Hewett (1941); Benjamin (1941); Crum (1942); Musgrave (1942).

The arguments of the others are, in general, similar to those thus answered. In the original manuscript prepared for this book they were answered individually and specifically, the idea then being to leave unanswered no argument of any sort. This part of the unused manuscript is being mimeographed in order to make it available to any reader of the book who may ask us for it.

ALLEGED OBJECTIONS

In some cases the argument alleged is clearly, if not avowedly, a replica of that employed by a former writer. For instance, in Italy Masci blindly follows Ricci and in Holland Bordewijk blindly follows Pierson.

Many of the objections alleged seem primarily verbal. Such are those of Daniels, Fetter, Flux, and Weaver.

Some of the views expressed are recognized by us as entirely correct

215

but are based on misunderstandings of our own contentions. Such are those of Graves and Crum and part of those of Stamp.

One writer, Cannan, merely expresses casually his adverse opinion—a sentence in a review of Pigou. Yet he was afterward cited by Guillebaud as the leading opponent in England. That a thinker, usually so clearheaded as Cannan, should be found on record against the double taxation or double counting thesis must, we believe, be due to inadvertence, or failure to give the subject his careful attention.

It is probably true that most people, however able, at first make mistakes when entering this field so full of pitfalls and paradoxes. Some of the arguments, like those of Pierson, represent demonstrable mental confusion, yet difficult, at first, to unravel.

Some of the opponents can be entirely acquitted of any such confusion even to the point of frankly accepting the double taxation thesis, but belittling it. For instance, Guillebaud, quite contrary to Pierson, even goes so far as to say that the double taxation proposition is so evidently true as to be a truism—"tautological"—if "income" be restricted to its "narrow" sense. But if, he says, we broaden its meaning so as to include a sense of security, power, pride of ownership, and other intangibles, savings may be legitimately taxed as affording current satisfactions rather than exempted as representing abstinence from them. Therefore, his article, while purporting to deny the double taxation, may rather be considered an apology for it.

Lolini, on the other hand, complains of the double taxation-proposition on the ground that it takes too much account of intangibles instead of too little as Guillebaud would have it. Lolini says "Fisher is perfectly right from the mathematical and accounting point of view [just as Guillebaud admits], but not from the financial and fiscal standpoint [unlike Guillebaud]."

Other inconsistencies among the dozen objectors could be cited. If we analyze the various arguments they offer we can find no valid objection but many misunderstandings. Graves, for instance, fully admits existence of the double taxation but makes the mistake of thinking we meant by that phrase exactly "twice the tax" and not simply "twice taxed." With Crum's conclusions we find no fault except that he imagines they are inconsistent with our own and that he seems to think his conclusions apply not only to the hypothetical cases which he constructs but also to the world as it is. Hewett admits an "additional burden" but doesn't like to call it double taxation. Stamp does the same. But he agrees that saving should be encouraged in some separate way. Benjamin explicitly admits that it is yield, not accretion, which makes market value. This, of course, is the basic principle involved from which the double taxation of savings necessarily follows.

The other writers seem not to admit the main point; but, in all cases, this failure is due to misunderstanding, which would, were it corrected, compel an admission. Thus Ricci, Masci, and Guillebaud allege an effect of the tax on the rate of interest which, even if it were correct,[1] would be irrelevant. Musgrave admits that taxing savings handicaps the saver relatively to the spender but argues that this is the same as saying that taking off such taxes would handicap the spender relatively to the saver, not noticing that if the two are measured in terms of a third, only the former statement is correct.

The most typical confusion is that of Pierson and his follower, Bordewijk. Probably the majority of objectors, of whom there must be many not on record, have made this slip. While they think of income as "accretion" or earnings rather than as "yield," they imagine that capital value is discounted earnings instead of, as it is (see Chapter 7), discounted yield. In doing this, they oversimplify the income series which they think they are discounting. They imagine the series to be simple perpetual annuities and do not realize that the very process of savings disturbs such imagined simplicity.

In view of the trifling character of these differences of opinion, in view of their wide variety (for almost no two writers make the same objection), and in view of the fact that strong feelings are evidenced in favor of taxing savings, it seems probable that the many ingenious arguments represent primarily the rationalization of a strong wish to tax savings, whether or not there is double taxation.

At any rate, such a wish clearly exists; and those who feel it think that self-evidently more revenue can be raised by taxing spendings plus savings than by taxing spendings only. That this is untrue is shown in Chapter 9.

[1] But it is incorrect. Under the yield tax proposed in this book, while it is quite true that a $5 return on $100 invested would be reduced to $4.50 by a 10 per cent tax, this would be exactly offset by the deductibility (see line 6 of the tax return in Chap. 1) of the $100 invested. A man saving and investing $100, rather than spending it, would perceive that he was really sacrificing only $90. The net return ($4.50 a year) is, therefore, not 4½ per cent but 5 per cent on his net sacrifice ($90).

Those in Favor

It seems to us quite certain that, even if we could concede any validity and strength in the objections just cited, the great weight of authority is on our side. This is asserted in spite of the high standing of many, in fact most, of those cited against us above.

At any rate, there are on our side authorities of the very highest standing, including John Stuart Mill, Alfred Marshall, A. C. Pigou, and F. C. Benham among English economists, and Luigi Einaudi, Guiseppe Prato, Mauro Fasiani, and Marco Fanno among those in Italy—where a lively controversy went on after the publication of *The Nature of Capital and Income*—and Fred Rogers Fairchild of Yale.

In Germany, a follower of John Stuart Mill, Eduard Pfeiffer, wrote the largest treatise on the subject, in two volumes. This was called to our attention, and parts of it translated for us, by Hans Cohrssen, after most of the present book had been written.

John Stuart Mill was apparently the first to call attention to the double taxation involved in taxing savings and their fruit. As stated elsewhere, his advocacy was not known to us until Professor Seligman mentioned it in 1938.

Mill stated the principle clearly and crisply in the following words:

If, indeed, reliance could be placed on the conscience of the contributors, or sufficient security taken for the correctness of their statements by collateral precautions, the proper mode of assessing an income-tax would be to tax only the part of income devoted to expenditure, exempting that which is saved. For when saved and invested (and all savings, speaking generally, are invested) it thenceforth pays income-tax on the interest or profit which it brings, notwithstanding that it has already been taxed on the principal. Unless, therefore, savings are exempted from income-tax, the contributors are twice taxed on what they save, and only once on what they spend. To tax the sum invested, and afterward tax also the proceeds of the investment, is to tax the same portion of the contributor's means twice over.[2]

Mill also appeared before a Parliamentary Committee[3] to champion the exemption of savings, saying:

. . . But what I should lay down as a perfectly unexceptionable and just principle of income tax, if it were capable of being practically realized, would be to exempt all savings; . . .

[2] Principles of Political Economy (edited by Laughlin), Book V, Chapter I, Sec. 4, p. 543. Appleton & Co., New York, 1884.

[3] Parliamentary Papers, Vol. VII, 1861.

Though his testimony and argument occupied many pages, he repeatedly expressed doubt about the practicability of applying his recommendation, as later did Pigou and others.

A chief feature of the present book is the method by which a spendings tax may be made practicable without trusting to direct records of the spendings.

Appendix A to Chapter 9

THE DESTRUCTIVENESS ANALYZED

For the astonishing destructiveness which we have found in taxes on savings levied annually, instead of one tax at death, there are three separate reasons.

The first is the lapse of time between the tax in any year and the end of the life of our taxpayer, Henry Forward.

The second is the repetition of the tax every year (for forty years in the examples in the text).

The third is the assumption that the rate at which the taxpayer would accumulate without a tax is high—that it at least exceeds the rate of interest at which the Government can borrow.

Let us consider these three reasons separately. Suppose, for simplicity, the tax rate to be 50 per cent and the growth rate, 40 per cent, the period of accumulation 40 years (1900-1940), and consider only the first year.

In that year the capital grows from $1,000 to $1,400, and a 50 per cent tax on the $400 growth reduces the capital to $1,200, or by one-seventh.

If this one year's tax were the only tax, there being none in the remaining 39 years, the result would evidently be to reduce the final $700,500,000 by the same one-seventh, or by about $100,000,000. That is, the taking from Henry Forward of $200 in 1901 deprives him in 1940 of $100,000,000.

In the same way we may suppose a 50 per cent tax on any other one year's capital-increase, say that of 1921, there being no tax either before or after 1921. Under these conditions, the fortune would increase in that year from $1,000,000 to $1,400,000. A 50 per cent tax on the increase of $400,000 is $200,000 which again is a one-seventh reduction of the capital and which again spells a one-seventh reduction in the end. That is, the taking in 1921 from Henry Forward of $200,000 deprives him in 1940 of $100,000,000.

The same one-seventh could be applied to any other one year, likewise reducing the final fortune by one-seventh.

Evidently the longer the lapse of time between such a solitary tax and the end of the saving period, the greater the destructive effect. In the time elapsing between 1901 and 1940 the magnification is from $200 to $100,000,000, or 500,000-fold; while, in the time elapsing between 1921 and 1940 the magnification is from $200,000 to $100,000,000, or only 500-fold.

When such one-seventh is taken out forty times in succession, naturally the effect is far greater. One-seventh of the final $700,500,000 is sliced off by the tax of 1901, shrinking that huge sum nearly to $600,000,000. A seventh of this remainder is then sliced off by the tax of 1902, reducing it to about $514,000,000. A seventh of this remainder is cut away by the 1903 tax, and so on. After forty successive destructions, each removing one-seventh of what is left, the final estate surviving out of the potential $700,500,000 is $1,470,000.

The effect on the estate is the same as if, instead of slicing off the one-seventh year by year, the same slicing was done all at once at the end, the estate being subject to a levy of one-seventh forty times over. This would seem fantastic. But a year by year tax on savings ought to be regarded as equally fantastic.

The third reason why the tax is so destructive is the relatively high rate of capital-increase assumed. We have seen that if Henry Forward can make his capital grow 40 per cent per annum while the government can borrow at 2 per cent interest, it is "good business" to borrow so as to let Henry Forward amass a big taxable estate.

If we wish to be realistic, we must acknowledge that this condition practically always exists so that there is practically always a disadvantage—and usually an enormous disadvantage in taxing annual accumulations in life instead of a final fortune at death. This enormous disadvantage, the "destructiveness" of an annual tax, is then magnified by the two other conditions, repetition and lapse of time.

APPENDIX B TO CHAPTER 9

THE RELATION OF DOUBLE TAXATION TO DESTRUCTIVENESS

THE two effects, duplication and destruction, are inseparable. Every tax on savings involves both. But the higher the tax the greater its destructiveness and the less (relatively) is its duplication.

This inverse relationship may be clearly seen as a definite mathematical relationship if, for simplicity, we make abstraction of the "discouragement" element, as was done in most of Chapter 9.

Assuming, then, that the tax on savings does not discourage savings, we note that a 100 per cent tax is 100 per cent destructive but not at all duplicative. Since a 100 per cent tax on capital-increase entirely destroys that capital-increase, there is nothing left to bear fruit for a later tax.

If now we reduce the tax to 90 per cent, it will destroy (absorb) 90 per cent of each item of capital-increase, leaving 10 per cent to bear taxable fruit. That is, in this case, 10 per cent of the savings is taxed twice. For instance, if the capital-increase is $100, the first tax is $90 and the present worth of the second tax (90 per cent of the yield of $10), is $9, so that the total tax burden is $99.

If the tax is 10 per cent, it destroys $10 and leaves 90 per cent to bear fruit to be taxed 10 per cent so that its present worth is $9, making a $19 tax burden in all.

If the tax is 1 per cent it destroys only $1 and leaves $99, the fruit of which is to be taxed 1 per cent later, making an additional tax burden of 99 cents, or $1.99 in all—practically doubling the burden.

The factor of discouragement adds, in every case, to the destructiveness and subtracts from the duplication.

The result is, especially under modern taxes, which are far higher than previously, that destructiveness rather than duplication is the dominating factor.

APPENDIX C TO CHAPTER 9

SOME "REALISTIC" COMMENTS

SOME of our critics have complained because the examples given in Chapter 9 are oversimplified. Of course this was done for purposes of easy exposition.

In real life the rate of capital-increase is never a constant as we assumed, nor is the tax a flat tax, the same for forty years of growth.

Seldom does a business grow exclusively through reinvestment from an initial nest egg; its growth is usually accelerated by the adding of other "eggs" annually. Usually these additions come, in the early stages, out of savings from personally earned income and, in the later stages, from outside financing—borrowing or sale of stock.

And when there is reinvestment, it is not usual to plow back *all* the earnings; some are usually spent.

Of course also the government borrowing which, in some of our calculations, we supposed to tide over a lifelong period of saving by our Henry Forward, implies (in normal cases at least) that each dollar so borrowed by government was drained out of the savings of individuals—those buying the government bonds.

Of course also the 40 per cent rate of capital-increase which we have supposed in some of our illustrations, is extraordinarily high. In reality the rates range from well above 40 per cent down to zero and below.

Some of these deviations from reality in our illustrations work in one direction; some in the other. But whether the net effect is one way or the other, the principles presented remain unaffected.

HENRY FORD AND HENRY FORWARD COMPARED

Moreover, our imaginary examples are not very far from real ones which could be cited. For instance, our imaginary Henry For'd and the real Henry Ford are certainly not very far apart, in most significant respects. The varying rates of growth of the Ford Company, whatever they have been, have been consistent with an enormous expansion in less than forty years, quite comparable with that supposed for Henry Forward. That expansion was, or is generally believed to have been, almost exclusively through reinvestment and comparatively little has been taken out of Ford's business to be spent.

The supposed 40 per cent growth rate without any tax on savings cannot be called unreasonable; it is presumably less than the Ford rate even with taxes. Had there been no tax on capital-increase throughout the whole history of the Ford Company, there can be no reasonable doubt that its growth would have been still greater.

After the text was in type the following factual data came to hand.

The Ford Company, in its 33 years through 1937, had sold 24 million units of all types (pleasure cars, trucks, tractors, etc.) for 13.2 billion dollars. Of this sum 89.2 per cent went for wages and materials and 4.4 per cent for taxes, while 6.4 per cent (or 845 million dollars or $35 per unit) went for "improvement, expansion and profit" —nearly all for plants and machinery.

These illuminating facts are contained in the "Ford Home Almanac and Facts Book" for 1937. (On inquiry, we are informed that, since then, the 6.4 per cent has shrunk).

That is, a mere 6.4 per cent of the price sufficed to account for the rapid expansion of the company. Whether this 6.4 per cent translated into a rate of expansion of capital amounts to a little more or a little less than the 40 per cent compounded which we have assumed for our imaginary Henry Forward, we do not know.

We note that the average tax through the 33 years was 4.4 per cent of the sales or two-thirds as much as the 6.4 per cent "profits." Since 1937, of course, it must have become far greater. Its effect on expansion depends, of course, on whether it is levied on, and so discourages, that expension. At least this would be true of companies whose stockholders desire to spend. As long as the profits are reinvested—that is, are undistributed—they will mean *nothing but growth*, by which the titular owner, so far as he is benefited in the form of spendings, may be benefited little more than the consumer.

If the government, instead of taxing the Ford expansion, had borrowed if need be the same sums from others, there would necessarily have been a wide disparity, comparable with our illustrative figures, between this trifling loan and the vastly greater revenue thereby obtainable from the Ford estate. Therefore the drain which this interim borrowing would require on the savings of others would be correspondingly trifling. It would simply mean that, in order to permit a phenomenally rapid growth of the automobile industry, the government had added a trifle to the investment opportunities of the ordinary saver.

It is true, of course, that some of these savers might have invested directly with our Henry Forward had the government taxed him instead of borrowing of them, though investors in government bonds are often the sort of people who would not invest directly with Henry Forward. It seems a fair assumption, therefore, that such a man's capital-increase would not seriously interfere with ordinary savings. It adds, not subtracts. His capital-increase is of the kind which creates new capital by invention and innovation, not merely saves it by abstaining from consuming a pre-existing income.

FAILURES VS. SUCCESSES

Our next question is: May not our taxes on capital-increase, while, as we have seen, they retard our few Henry Forwards and so do harm, retard also our many investing overenthusiasts and their exploiters, often unscrupulous promoters, and so do some good? If so, the removal of such taxes and the substitution of a simple spendings tax would clearly do some harm along with the good.

We do not doubt that some such harm might, in individual cases, result. But that it could be preponderant or even substantial seems to us, at least, very unlikely.

For one reason (to be realistic as here we should) no tax on capital-increase applies until some capital-increase exists; and, in most cases, when for a new enterprise, capital-increase once comes into existence, it is good evidence that the enterprise was worth starting.

We infer that, in the second place, the wastage or loss of capital from the failures is probably, all put together, small anyway, as compared with the opposite gain of capital from the really successful inventions. The get-rich-quick enterprises are usually "quick" in reverse. They are snuffed out soon after they start, for lack of outside capital. "Capital is timid" and not much of it is lured into enterprises not offering at least a good chance of success.

Some evidence has been offered that the failures fully offset the successes so that the "average" investor in risky enterprises gets little or nothing. But, this scarcely meets the case. We are not primarily concerned with the generation of the early investors. Granted that Ford was one success out of many failures and that even his gains were at first no more than their losses (which may have been true) or granted that his gains even up to date are no more than their losses (which seems preposterous) it seems certain that the net result, a successful cheap Ford car, not to mention its indirect consequences in the successful Chevrolet, Plymouth, Willys, etc., has not cost more than it was worth but has added greatly to the net welfare of the people of the United States.

At any rate, few would have the hardihood to contend that the effort to produce and develop useful inventions has ever set any country back. If, in the end, the wastage from the failures had equaled the progress from the successes, the net progress would have been nil. This, being contrary to the facts, is a *reductio ad absurdum*.

In the third place, the taxes are usually low at the crucial time when the enterprise begins to grow. The assumption made, for simplicity, in Chapter 9 that the tax is a flat rate through forty years is, of course, far from realistic. Actually the rate starts at near zero and ends at near 100 per cent. Consequently its effect in retarding Henry Forward through forty years is very great, but the effect in retarding the get-rich-quickers through only a few years is very small.

In the fourth place, the latter species of investors are, almost by hypothesis, so constituted as not to be greatly retarded by sober facts or calculations—not at least in advance. Confessedly they are gamblers, trusting to luck, some of them gullible, the sort who "invest" in the "Sweepstakes." The little wastage of which they are guilty will go on, little affected by any tax system.

These four answers are in addition to the fundamental point stressed in the text of Chapter 9, namely that, where compound rates are concerned, big rates dominate, not average rates.

We conclude that any harm which could possibly be done by introducing our proposed tax system through helping waste the capital of get-rich-quicks would not go far in offsetting the good done through genuine technological progress.

"A Spendings Tax Cuts Down Savings as Well as Spendings"

It is true that a spendings tax of $50 would not simply reduce the spendings by $50. It would reduce it by less, say by $40, and reduce the savings by $10. It would act like a wedge driven between spendings and savings.

The present tax does not simply reduce the savings. It too is a wedge. Yet a tax explicitly on spendings would, of course, discourage spendings more than a tax on spendings plus savings.

In short, the same principles apply realistically as applied to our imaginary Henry Forward, whether as strikingly or not.

The abolition of all taxes on capital-increase through the adoption of our spendings tax would operate on the real Henry Fords very much as described in Chapter 9 for our imaginary Henry Forward.

But these are cases of giant creators of capital through new inventions. Among the rank and file of people, who are not creators of anything but are simply spenders with a small margin of savings, there would be comparatively little difference between a tax on an income, say of $1,000, including $100 saved, and a tax on the $900 spent.

The really important points of this book relate only slightly to the taxation of the ordinary man. He is near the bottom of the economic ladder and ordinarily does not move many rungs up or down. Our points relate to the taxation of those who are ascending and descending that ladder.

Is Capital-increase Desirable?

But when all is said and done, do we want capital-increase? Hitherto this has been assumed. It is generally assumed. As a matter of fact, however, there are exceptions. Even some of the most creative inventions really do great harm and may do more harm than good.

Until we get a world government or other effective machinery for keeping the peace, every invention which can destroy human life, bombs and bombing planes, for instance, are harmful for mankind. Yet, paradoxically, they are necessary for any one nation's survival in an anarchic world. Any proposal, therefore, to tax their creation, now at least, would be absurd.

Again, inventions tending to increase the use of habit-forming drugs including those most in common use—alcohol and tobacco especially—are degenerative not regenerative. Special taxes on them have always found favor. Therefore a tax on capital-increase in these industries could not be said to be harmful. In this case we have to admit a genuine exception to our rule. Yet such a tax is not necessary. Quite other methods of repression can be and usually have been used.

Again, it is now known that most refined foods, such as white bread and white sugar, by eliminating much of the original mineral content, are a chief reason for our bad teeth.

Thus capital-increase is a two-edged sword, and not a universal good. But an indiscriminate tax on capital-increase is clearly no solution.

The only rational solution must involve discrimination between what capital-increase is good and what is bad. But discriminatory taxes on the "bad" capital-increases and not on the "good" is scarcely feasible. Nor is it necessary.

In wartime the discrimination is through priorities. In peacetime, if discriminatory taxation is to be resorted to, it need not be on capital-increase. And if resorted to, it could claim justification only on the ground that its destructiveness is, in this case, a virtue.

There seems, therefore, no reason, under any circumstances to tax capital-increase.

"Oversaving"

Our next problem comes from another direction although it is on the same problem of injurious saving. There are those who are predisposed toward taxing savings because of theories of "oversaving" as the cause or *a* cause of depressions.

While we do not attribute the same importance to this factor as do some prominent writers, we agree that there is at least a grain of truth in the theory,[1] especially under our existing monetary system.

But there is no need of introducing here any discussion of this controversy. For, even if the utmost claims of this theory were correct, they would need consideration only under very exceptional circumstances, and at these exceptional times the appropriate remedies are mainly monetary. At any rate, they certainly do not include the taxation of *investments*.

We have elsewhere[2] favored special antihoarding taxes in a depression. As we write, however, we are confronted by the opposite situation, inflation, when even hoarding is beneficial.

The idea that thrift in general should be curbed is supposed to be based on the theories of John Maynard Keynes. He, however, quite consistently, would not curb thrift now; but is now advocating one or more forms of *compulsory* savings.

[1] For a general and well-balanced discussion of the various aspects of this theory see Joseph A. Schumpeter's Business Cycles, especially pp. 820-827. McGraw-Hill Book Co., New York, 1939.
[2] See our Stamp Scrip, Adelphi Co., New York, 1933. 117 pp.

The truth seems to be not so much that Keynes has influenced economic thought on this subject on its merits as that he has unwittingly become a convenient instrument for the rationalization of projects of powerful political interests. Keynes's supposed hostility to savings was hailed by many "New Dealers" who want State Socialism and saw in his theories some help. For an obvious way for the government to take over private capital is to tax capital-increase. Whether intentional or not this is exactly where we are now headed because of our taxes on capital-increase.

The most extreme form of such taxation yet attempted was the ill-fated law of 1936 imposing a special tax on corporate savings.

Businessmen were so harassed by this corporate undistributed profits tax that they accomplished its repeal. In doing so, they had to dispel the naïve but prevalent idea that undistributed profits are held in cash!

Less specifically, *any* tax on corporate income includes a tax on corporate savings and the higher the tax—as in the excess profits tax —the more nearly the reversion toward the 1936 law.

It seems significant that, though Keynes properly adjusted his attitude when the depression gave way to a boom, his followers still use his theories as if applicable generally.

In the nonpolitical world, antisaving theories and projects are, we think, fading out, and a reaction against them is setting in. The present economic situation, especially in America, is bound to produce such a reaction and to bring us back to the thrift ideas of Benjamin Franklin and Adam Smith. For a decade, we have been living largely on our capital. If we are not to become impoverished as a nation, we must soon reverse this process. We must be emphasizing production not consumption, saving not spending.

CORPORATIONS ARE MADE WASTEFUL

As this is being written, information comes that numerous corporations are deliberately and wastefully adding to various expenses such as salaries, directors' fees, advertising, and other items, far beyond what these items would have been but for the huge normal-plus-excess-profits taxes on gains plowed back. A plowed-back gain of $1,000 could often be cut 70 per cent by these taxes, or $700. Very well, instead of plowing back $1,000, say on the laboratory, let us *spend* $1,000, say

on salaries. Since this $1,000 is deductible as an expense it saves $700
of tax. The government then "pays $700 out of the $1,000."

Thus the law encourages waste and discourages expansion and
progress.

DEVIATIONS FROM REALISM

We shall continue to assume that capital-increase is, in general, of
benefit and not injury to the vast majority of our people.

On this assumption let us now attempt to pass judgment on the
various deviations from realism of our Henry Forward illustrations.

In each case we shall try to indicate in which direction the deviation
points—whether toward strengthening or toward weakening the force
of our Henry Forward calculations.

(1) The inconstancy of the rate of capital-increase would seem at
first to weaken that force. For it requires that, in order to have a full
equivalent of a constant 40 per cent rate, rates above 40 per cent
must often appear. Is this realistic?

In the case of Henry Ford, apparently yes—as we have seen. We
are unable to furnish any figures. We can only state our strong impression that each generation can furnish many examples of what is
equivalent to 40 per cent and over.

(2) The fact that a business seldom, if ever, reinvests all its earnings also weakens the force of our argument. It confines it to a smaller
area than in our imaginary example. But the real area is large. According to the Cowles *Monograph on Common-Stock Indexes*,[3] over
one-third of the earnings of corporations (those listed on the New
York Stock Exchange) for the period 1871-1935 were undistributed.
And recent estimates indicate that a much larger fraction, over 50
per cent, of personal incomes over $20,000 is usually saved.[4]

(3) The fact that most business is aided by outside capital
strengthens our argument. It makes the rate of growth of the net
worth more rapid. Government aid, through the RFC or otherwise,
works in the same direction.

[3] Common-Stock Indexes 1871-1937, by Alfred Cowles, 3rd and Asso-
ciates. Cowles Commission for Research in Economics, Monograph No. 3,
Principia Press, 1938.
[4] Since the above was written, this 50% estimate (of N.R.C. and
T.N.E.C.) has been cut in two by Rufus Tucker (In *Review of Economic
Statistics*. Feb. 1942).

(4) The fact that existing tax rates as a whole are so high works toward strengthening our case.

In our Henry Forward illustration we found that a mere 20 per cent tax from start to finish was exceedingly destructive. But, in actual fact, the rates on corporations now start higher than that and run up to three or four times as high. Their destructiveness is thereby greatly increased.

On the whole, while data are lacking for any sure judgment, we are convinced that the use of our Henry Forward illustration does not greatly, if at all, exaggerate the destructiveness of our present taxation of savings as it actually applies to many corporations and individuals.

We did not, of course, intend to present that picture as representing an average condition. It was confessedly a picture of exceptional cases. But we stressed the fact that, if only a few such exceptional cases exist, they would in a generation or two dominate the growth of capital. It seems fair to say that more than a few such exceptional cases do in actual fact exist.

WORLD WAR II

From all this, it results that, in our "excess-profits" taxes, so far as they are undistributed and unspent, we are making a great mistake, just as we did in World War I. During that war, Secretaries of the Treasury Houston and Glass were led to protest against this harmful, though well-intentioned, legislation; and likewise today, as we write, similar protests are being heard, and they come from those best qualified to observe what is really happening. On the one hand, the country clamors for the most rapid plant expansion possible and, on the other hand, it clamors for big taxes to be clamped down on that expansion.

If our reasoning is correct, the country is already, and even irrespective of the new excess profits law, missing billions upon billions of possible revenue and many times as much in national income, all because of the short sighted policy of taxing the seed corn which might have made crops.

"INCOME" ACCORDING TO EXPERTS

ECONOMISTS

ECONOMISTS have usually assumed that only one valid income concept could exist.

The only clear cut ones offered have been yield and accretion, usually the latter.

Among those economists who have stressed the importance of the Yield concept, though not always under that name, are Alfred Marshall,[1] Raymond T. Bye,[2] Fairchild, Furniss and Buck[3] and several Italian writers.[4]

Among the leading users of accretion have been Georg Schanz,[5] Robert M. Haig,[6] and Henry C. Simons.[7]

As we have tried to show, the Accretion concept is unsuitable for a tax base.

All other proposed concepts, we believe, turn out on examination, to reduce to yield or accretion or a mixture of both, often vague and confused. The studies of Wueller[8] seem to confirm this.

[1] Principles of Economics, Macmillan, London, 1907, Vol. I, p. 77-79.

[2] Principles of Economics, New York, Knopf, 1924, p. 26-27.

[3] Elementary Economics, Macmillan, 1930 Vol. 1 Revised Ed., p. 17-18.

[4] P. H. Wueller, Concepts of Taxable Income, III. The Italian Contribution. (In Political Science Quarterly, December, 1939).

[5] P. H. Wueller, Concepts of Taxable Income, I. The German Contribution. (In Political Science Quarterly, March 1938, p. 104-106).

[6] The Concept of Income—Economic and Legal Aspects. Chapter 1. (In Federal Income Tax. A series of Lectures delivered at Columbia University in December 1920. Edited by Robert Murray Haig. New York, Columbia University Press, 1921, p. 128).

[7] Personal Income Taxation, University of Chicago Press. 1938, p. 50.

[8] P. H. Wueller, Concepts of Taxable Income. (In Political Science Quarterly, March 1938, December 1938, December 1939).

ACCOUNTANTS

The accountants employ, and rightly *for business purposes*, the Accretion concept, though they usually leave it undefined or ill-defined. Among those who have given special attention to its definition and to its relation to the Yield concept are Professor John B. Canning[9] and Dr. C. A. LeDeuc.[10]

STATISTICIANS

Statisticians are, as it were, accountants for a nation, and naturally, though usually unconsciously, employ the Accretion concept, though they often separate this accretion-income into national savings and national consumption (real income or yield).

Among the special students in this field are Lord Stamp[11] and Dr. Simon Kuznets.[12]

EXPERTS LARGELY IGNORED

But "Income" according to Law—the subject matter of Part III, has not paid much attention to any of the experts above named, though much more to accountants than to economists or statisticians. Allegedly it follows common usage; but, as we have shown in Chapter 12, it has developed a separate statutory determination of income quite different from common usage as formulated in the dictionaries, something much more definite yet quite as illogical in mixing the two valid concepts.

[9] Economics of Accountancy, Ronald Press, 1929.

[10] As presented before the Retail Controllers Association of Los Angeles by C. A. LeDeuc, Ph.D., Controller, Co-author of Hadley's Pathfinder Course in Executive Accounting.

[11] The Fundamental Principles of Taxation in the Light of Modern Developments by Sir Josiah Charles Stamp. London, Macmillan, 1929, new and revised edition, 1936.

[12] National Income (*In* Encyclopaedia of the Social Sciences, Macmillan, 1933, p. 205-224).

APPENDIX TO CHAPTER 20

MISCELLANEOUS CONSTITUTIONAL
PROBLEMS

ASSUMING that the *Pollock* and *Macomber* cases still live:
1. *Must income be periodic in order to be constitutional?*
We think not.

Chief Justice Taft recognized periodicity as a popular notion of income, and used it as a last straw in the interpretation of a statute;[1] but there is no periodicity to capital gains, nor to a negotiated reduction of debt.

2. *Must the capital and labor be those of the taxpayer?*

The Supreme Court has held that the "dominant purpose of the revenue laws" is to tax income to "those who earn or otherwise create the right to receive it,"[2] but this does not make such purpose a constitutional requirement.

A Circuit Court of Appeals did deny the status of income to an item partly because it was "not derived from the taxpayer's capital or labor," and cited the *Macomber* case.[3] But the Supreme Court itself seems not to be committed to this view. It has held, for instance, that the tax hits the recipient of a bequest of income made through a trustee; that the statutory exemption of gifts and bequests (clearly applicable to capital) did not apply to this income; and that the *Macomber* case was not inconsistent with this view. Justice Holmes added that, in his opinion, (1) the recipient need not be the owner of the capital; but (2) "if it were material, a gift of the income . . . ordinarily is treated by equity as creating an interest in the fund."[4]

[1] U. S. v Supplee-Biddle Co., 265 U.S. 189, May 26, 1924.
[2] Helvering v Horst, 311 U.S. 112, Nov. 25, 1940.
[3] Central R. Co. v Comm., 79 F 2d 697 (CCA 3d) Sep. 24, 1935. Case condemned, but not necessarily on this point: Lyeth v Hoey, 96 F 2d 141; Sterling v Comm., 93 F 2d 304; both CCA 2d. Certiorari denied in latter, 303 U.S. 663; former reversed, 305 U.S. 188.
[4] Irwin v Gavit, 268 U.S. 161, Apr. 27, 1925.

234

However, this second ground makes the first ground a dictum, and the second is the one cited in subsequent cases.[5]

In another case, Justice Holmes acknowledged "a very forcible argument . . . that the statute seeks to tax only income beneficially received."[6] Yet the beneficial recipient (of assigned earnings) escaped in that case on statutory grounds. So this, too, was dictum.

In another case, a woman with no claim to an estate, received a share of its price when sold—this merely in order to satisfy unfounded misgivings of a title company. A Circuit Court of Appeals confirmed a tax on her entire receipts. The Court treated them as a capital gain with basis zero. Certainly zero represented the capital and labor furnished by the woman. Was it not really a windfall? (Certiorari denied, without opinion).[7]

Again the Supreme Court in treating an ex-wife as exempt from any income tax on her alimony, used arguments so meticulously statutory as to suggest that Congress could have taxed the alimony. Nor was there any capital in the wife, either legal or equitable. It was a simple case of monthly payments out of the husband's pocketbook.[8]

And in a 1942 alimony case taxing the wife (whose husband had bought her an annuity), the Court said it relied on precedent "in the absence of a different statutory formula."[9]

Even in trust estates, the question of who pays the tax appears to be statutory. The beneficiary pays unless the trust is controlled by the trust-maker or (in alimony) by the Court.[10]

On a somewhat analogous question as to which of two parties was

[5] Blair v Comm., 300 U.S. 5, Feb. 1, 1937.
[6] Lucas v Earle, 281 U.S. 111, Mar. 17, 1930.
[7] Sterling v Comm., 93 F 2d 304, CCA 2d, Dec. 6, 1937 (Certiorari denied, 303 U.S. 663).
[8] Gould v Gould, 245 U.S. 151, Nov. 19, 1917.
[9] Pearce v Comm., 62 S.Ct. 754, Mar. 9, 1942.
[10] Alimony: Helvering v Fuller, 310 U.S. 69, Apr. 22, 1940; Helvering v Fitch, 309 U.S. 149, Jan. 29, 1940; Douglas v Willcuts, 296 U.S. 1, Nov. 11, 1935. As to a trust to avoid tax otherwise due under a statute, Burnet v Wells, 289 U.S. 670, May 29, 1933. Other trusts: Corliss v Bowers, 281 U.S. 376, Apr. 28, 1930; Helvering v Clifford, 309 U.S. 331, Feb. 26, 1940. See also Helvering v Horst, 311 U.S. 112, Nov. 25, 1940; Helvering v Eubank, 311 U.S. 122 (same date); Harrison v Schaffner, 312 U.S. 579, Mar. 31, 1941.

taxable, Judge Learned Hand said, "the difference is conventional . . . the distinction is historical, not rational."[11]

Sometimes the owner or earner of income makes himself a conduit of it to another party. In some of these cases, the Court evidently suspects the conduit of trying to dodge surtaxes, and lays down the law that the "satisfaction" of being a conduit is an "economic benefit" comparable with the "satisfaction" of buying groceries—though the beneficiary really buys the groceries and is *not* taxed! Anyhow the argument is still statutory.[12]

On the whole, from Justice Holmes' dicta we are hopeful that, so far as the Constitution is concerned, it does not matter who owns the capital or performs the labor.

In fact, how otherwise explain the tax on a negotiated debt reduction?

Also, very recently, Circuit Courts of Appeals have held sweepstakes winnings and embezzled money to be taxable income.[13] It would be far-fetched to ascribe these to the taxpayer's capital or labor.

3. *Borrowing, Lending and Annuities.*

In Chapter 16 we showed that these are essentially cases of timing, the question being which two items of three should cancel. We see no difficulty as to annuities. As to borrowed money, we are not sure the common man could see it as income, but if the reshuffle of the 3 items were explained to him, he would doubtless approve of applying the tax at a more convenient stage. And if Congress should perform the reshuffle, we think the Court would try hard not to allow the taxpayer to escape through a mere change of dates. According to Professor Magill, the Court is quite willing to stretch a point in order to prevent the escape of what the statute really means to tax.[14] According to Justice Cardozo, the Constitution should not be interpreted so "narrowly and pedantically" as to allow a taxpayer to escape the usual tax by putting a certain item through the hands of a trustee.[15] According to Justice Oliver Wendell Holmes, a statutory exemption

[11] Comm. v Field, 42 F 2d, 820, CCA 2d, July 7, 1930.
[12] Helvering v Clifford, 309 U.S. 331, Feb. 26, 1940; Helvering v Horst, 311 U.S. 112, Nov. 25, 1940; Helvering v. Eubank, 311 U.S. 122, Nov. 25, 1940.
[13] Riebe v Comm. 41 BTA 935, affirmed, 124 F 2d 399, CCA 6th, Dec. 11, 1941; Kurrle v Helvering (embezzled), 126 F 2d 723, CCA 8th, Mar. 14, 1942. (But see Addendum p. 246.)
[14] Taxable Income, p. 399.
[15] Burnet v Wells, 289 U.S. 670, at pp. 677-8, May 29, 1933.

should not be allowed to make the statute "miss" what its initial definitions really meant to "hit."[16]

4. *Gifts (including bequest, devise and inheritance).*

These are expressly exempt by the code.[17] The law of 1894 (prior to the Sixteenth Amendment) included gifts as income.[18] The law of 1913, after the amendment, exempted gifts to individuals, but the Treasury ruled that gifts to corporations were taxable.[19] Magill derives from this a "slight inference" that Congress could tax gifts as income.[20] A District Court apparently barred an inheritance from the very definition of income, but the Supreme Court, in affirming the *result*, reasoned the case all over again and put its decision expressly on the statutory ground.[21]

But even if gifts shall never achieve the status of "income," still a tax on gifts is already held to be indirect, as we have seen in Chapter 20;[22] and no objection seems to have been raised to the statutory provision which makes the donee personally liable if the donor fails to pay.[23] We cannot see any constitutional objection to splicing a recipient's gift tax into his income tax, since both gift taxes and income taxes now enjoy the same immunity from the obnoxious apportionment rule.

OMNIBUS CLAUSE

The statute, after specifying many kinds of income, has an omnibus provision to include "gains or profits or income from any source whatever." This might suggest that any item of Yield which is now exempt in practice without any statutory explanation is exempt because it is not constitutionally taxable. And the Court at least once invoked this omnibus phrase as justifying a tax not explicitly imposed by the statute.[24]

At all events the omnibus phrase could hardly be invoked to justify

---

[16] Irwin v Gavit, 268 U.S. 161, April 27, 1925.
[17] Sec. 22 (b) (3).
[18] 28 Stats. 1894, Ch. 349, Sec. 28, p. 553.
[19] 16 Treas. Dec. (Internal Rev.) 259 at 267 and 280, Dec. 14, 1914.
[20] Taxable Income, pp. 357-358.
[21] Lyeth v Hoey, 20 F.S. 619, July 22, 1937; 305 U.S. 188, Dec. 5, 1938.
[22] Bromley v McCaughn, 280 U.S. 124, Nov. 25, 1929.
[23] Sec. 1009.
[24] Gain over cost from an endowment policy under an earlier law; Lucas v Alexander, 279 U.S. 573, May 20, 1929.

exacting a tax from B on income already taxed to A;[25] and, by the same token, we think, the failure of the law to tax B after it has taxed A is no proof that what B receives is not income. We suggest, as sound economics, a general application of Justice Holmes's words: "The money was income in the hands of the trustee and we know of nothing in the law that prevents its being paid and received as income by the donee."[26]

5. *Compensation for Injury (Nonphysical: Defamation, Breach of Promise, Alienation).*[27]

Here the statute is silent. The Internal Revenue Department once treated such items as income; but later the department and the Board of Tax Appeals reached the opposite view, at first citing the Macomber definition as to the inherent nature of income, but later saying in effect: "at any rate not income until the statute expressly says so." As to inherent considerations, it was suggested that such injuries are not susceptible of measurement (but we suggest that the thing to be measured is the money); and in 1935 a Circuit Court of Appeals suggested (in dictum): "the thought is that" such items are "compensatory" for "injuries sustained" (but this begs the question).[28]

PUNITIVE OR EXEMPLARY DAMAGES

The Board at first left this question open—in a defamation case[29]— as if such damages could be "gain," over and above restitution. But in 1940 it denied punitive items the status of income,[30] citing a Circuit Court of Appeals as to a "penalty."[31] Both the citing case and the case cited involved only business penalties, but both were again dealing with the inherent nature of income, though without referring directly to the Constitution.

The Circuit Court case also called the "penalty" a "windfall." It was brought about by the misconduct of a fiduciary.

But again we prefer the case of the woman who was taxed on her

---

[25] Lucas v Earle, 281 U.S. 111, Mar. 17, 1930.
[26] Irwin v Gavit, 268 U.S. 161, Apr. 27, 1925.
[27] Cumulative Bulletin I—1, p. 92 (1922); Hawkins v Comm., 6 BTA 1023, Apr. 25, 1927; McDonald v Comm., 9 BTA 1340, Jan. 16, 1928; Cumulative Bulletin II—2, p. 66, 1923 (damage on annulment).
[28] Central R. Co. v Comm., 79 F 2d 697, supra.
[29] Hawkins v Comm., 6 BTA 1023.
[30] Highland Farms v Comm., 42 BTA 1314.
[31] Central R. v Comm., supra.

total receipts from an estate to which she had no claim (certiorari denied).[32]

BODILY INJURIES

The statute takes the trouble expressly to exempt the compensation for bodily injuries.[33] On the other hand, the statute provides no deductions for the medical and other expenses entailed by such injury.

The Yield system would both deduct the expenses and enter the compensation in the gross, and also give the damage-payer a deduction. This arrangement would, we submit, be more just, both to the victim and to the Treasury. When there is no compensation for the injury, the Yield system would favor the victim. When the expense and the compensation are equal, the two systems would be equal. When the compensation exceeds the expense, the Yield system would favor the government by recognizing an addition to the gross income. If the taxpayer's injury diminishes or destroys his future earning power, Yield would diminish or destroy the future tax accordingly. Anything more would be "up to" Social Security.

DEATH DAMAGES—LIFE INSURANCE

The proceeds of life insurance are explicitly exempt by statute; and departmental practice exempts damages for death—for instance, money received by a widow for the death of her husband—as not properly within the concept of income.[33a]

But under an earlier statute, a question arose as to whether a provision for the deduction of insurance receipts from gross income applied to corporations.[34] Chief Justice Taft held that it did apply, as a matter of statutory interpretation. The constitutional question was raised, but Taft refused to decide it. However, in interpreting the statute, he gave weight to the alleged popular concept of income, saying, "life insurance is, like . . . fire and marine insurance . . . a contract of indemnity . . . the benefit . . . has no periodicity. It is a substitution . . . for something permanently lost. . . . Assuming without deciding that Congress could call the proceeds of such indemnity income, and validly tax it as such, we think that, in view of the popular concep-

[32] Sterling v Comm., 93 F 2d 304 supra.
[33] Sec. 22 (b) (5).
[33a] Sec. 22 (b) (1); Cumulative Bulletin, VII—27—3788, 1928, citing the insurance case which follows.
[34] U.S. v Supplee-Biddle Hardware Co., 265 U.S. 189, May 26, 1924.

tion of the life insurance as resulting in a single addition of a total sum to the resources of the beneficiary, and not in a periodical return, such a purpose on its part should be express, as it certainly is not here."

It seems to us significant that Taft avoided constitutional grounds.

Moreover, ten and sixteen years later, in cases of corporation officials insured for their corporations, two Circuit Courts of Appeals found means of taxing the insurance money through another statutory provision, namely the dividend clause.[35] This clause was applied when there was an explicit arrangement whereby the insurance money was "promptly" converted into "a dividend" taxable to the stockholders. The insurance "premiums . . . were paid by the company."[36] Surely the stockholders *are* the company in equity. In fact, a somewhat similar argument was made in a dissenting opinion in the second of these cases, in which an actual trustee replaced the corporation on behalf of the stockholders.

If these two decisions are sound, it seems to us that life-insurance money can be income if Congress chooses.

SUMMARY

Assuming that the *Pollock* and *Macomber* cases still live, we conclude that the Court has at least left itself free to accept the following propositions if Congress should offer them.

(1) "Gain" is still "gain" when it flows through A to B.

(2) He who enjoys the good should suffer the tax.

(3) If the injury cannot be measured, the money can.

(4) If future income suffers, the future tax will "ease up" accordingly.

(5) Who shall pay the tax on alimony is a problem for public policy.

DAMAGES FOR PROPERTY IN GENERAL

The statute has a somewhat general provision for the deduction of "losses" (including property losses) "not compensated for by insurance or otherwise."[37] The compensation is not treated as income, but the Board of Tax Appeals has ranked as income any *excess* (of insur-

[35] Cummings v Comm., 73 F 2d 477, Nov. 10, 1934, CCA 1st; Golden v Comm., 113 F 2d 590, CCA 3d, June 29, 1940 (dissent).

[36] Quoted words are from the earlier case.

[37] Sec. 23 (e) (f); Regs. 19.23 (e) (f).

ance) above the compensation, unless the compensation is reinvested pursuant to a section of the capital gains law.[38]

So far as we know, the Supreme Court is not committed to the view that such compensation could never function as gross income if Congress chose—as to property other than capital.

CAPITAL IN PARTICULAR

But here comes the great trouble, regardless of whether the *Pollock* and *Macomber* cases still live. For the *Doyle*[39] case still lives (we fear), though based on a law preceding the Sixteenth Amendment. It dealt with the inherent nature of income and has been cited over a hundred times since the word got into the Constitution.

First, what is capital?

(1) So far as concerns the capital gains tax, Congress seems to be free to make its own definitions.[40]

(2) In cases where income has matured before the effective date of the Sixteenth Amendment, the Court exempts it and calls it capital. Apparently it is not exempt because it is capital but is capital because it is exempt.[41]

(3) However, in 1875, the Court defined capital[42] as "property or means" "set apart for, or invested in business"; and we think that substantially this definition is in mind when the question is whether compensation for an injury to capital is taxable as income.

We have seen in Chapter 15 that the *Doyle* case, in effect, treats compensation for capital *sold* as itself capital—up to the basis value; and this same Doyle idea seems to be applied to *damages* or *insurance* for capital. That is, such damage money or insurance is held *not* to be income, whereas damage money or insurance to compensate for loss of income is itself income, even if not used for income purposes.

We mention a few typical cases:

[38] Now Sec. 112 (f), to be read in connection with Sec. 23 (e) (f): Chickasha Cotton Oil Co. v Comm., 18 BTA 1144, Feb. 14, 1930.

[39] Doyle v Mitchell, 247 U.S. 179, May 20, 1918, on the corporation tax of 1909.

[40] Sec. 117 (a) (1).

[41] With fine distinctions as to what constitutes maturity; U.S. v Safety Car Heating Co., 297 U.S. 88, Jan. 6, 1936; Lynch v Hornby, 247 U.S. 339, June 3, 1918; Southern Pacific v Lowe, 247 U.S. 330, June 3, 1918; Lucas v Alexander, 279 U.S. 573, May 20, 1929. See also Old Colony R. R. v Comm., 284 U.S. 552, Feb. 15, 1932.

[42] Baily v Clark, 21 Wall. 284, 1875.

242 MISCELLANEOUS CONSTITUTIONAL PROBLEMS

(1) Fire-insurance receipts are taxable income when paid for loss of profits.[43]

(2) Recovery for defamation of a *business*, if it is measured by damage to "financial standing, credit, reputation, good-will, capital and other possible elements" (in contrast with profits) is not income and not taxable.[44]

(3) After the first World War, under the "Mixed Claims Commission," a recovery for property destroyed in Germany and not in excess of its value was held not taxable income.[45]

(4) If a trespasser on mine property extracts ore, the damage he pays for the ore is taxable income; not so the damage he pays for harm to the premises.[46]

(5) The American government, after a treaty with Russia about Alaskan waters, agreed to pay damages to seal hunters with whom it had interfered. A recovery of such damage was taxed as income. *Held* on appeal: If the Commissioner taxed the whole amount, presumably the whole amount was profits; and the taxpayer must overcome this presumption or pay.[47]

So far as we know, this rule (that compensation for damage to capital is not income), has not been ascribed to the Constitution. But in *U.S. v Safety Car Heating Co.*,[47a] the Supreme Court takes it for granted in a dictum; and the minority in that case (in full support of the same rule) also cites the *Doyle* case; and we fear that the Court may still regard all compensation for capital as *inherently*—and that means Constitutionally—not income.

LOOPHOLE?

Had there never been a *Doyle* case exempting the *price* of capital, perhaps there would never have been these cases exempting *compensation* for damage to capital; and perhaps there would never have been a *Doyle* case if Congress had (as Yield would do) exempted the

[43] Appeal of International Boiler Co., 3 BTA 283, Jan. 12, 1926.
[44] Farmers and Merchants Bank v Comm., 59 F 2nd, 912, June 27, 1932, CCA 6th.
[45] Helvering v Drier, 79 F 2nd, 501, CCA 4th, Oct. 8, 1935.
[46] Bankers Pocahontas Coal Co. v. Burnet 55 F 2nd, 626, CCA 4th, Jan. 25, 1932; affirmed in Supreme Court, but this point was not involved: 287 U.S. 308, Dec. 5, 1932 (and Strothers v Burnet, 287 U.S. 314).
[47] Liebes v Comm., 90 F 2nd, 932; CCA 9th, June 14, 1937.
[47a] 297 U.S. 88 at 93, 98, and the dissent, Jan. 6, 1936.

reinvestment of money received, whether compensatory or not compensatory. For, in the absence of such exemption, the Court was faced by the choice of either taxing the *entire* proceeds of the capital sold (even though those proceeds were all reinvested), or contriving a deduction which it could deem inherent in the very concept of income.

So the Court substituted one evil for another.

Suppose, then, that Congress should now adopt the rule that money is as money does and that therefore reinvestments are exempt. Would not this be another case of better timing, as in the case of borrow-and-lend?—but involving 2 items instead of 3:

Present Rule:

A. Tax $5,000 when invested,
B. exempt $5,000 when disinvested.

The Yield Rule:

A. Don't tax $5,000 when invested,
B. tax $5,000 (as gross income) when disinvested.

Of course, the two steps (invest and disinvest) might occur in two different generations; but, when justice is the question, the *total* exemption of investments and reinvestments in *all* generations is the only unqualified justice.

And, after all, the *Doyle* case was based on a law before the Sixteenth Amendment.

MAKESHIFT FOR THE DOYLE EMBARRASSMENT

If the Supreme Court felt itself really estopped from progress by the *Doyle* case, could Congress find a makeshift? Deductions are a matter of legislative grace, and this is held to include the power to grant deductions on condition.[48] Could not Congress grant a deduction of investments, reinvestments and savings on condition that the *Doyle* deduction (of "basis" or purchase price) be surrendered? True, in some cases, it would be to the advantage of the taxpayer to adhere to the *Doyle* deduction; and in some cases the problem might be too tangled for the proposed choice—for instance, when the purchase price is to be received in installments which can not be computed in advance.[49]

[48] Helvering v Independent Life, 292 U.S. 371, May 21, 1934 (though not to defeat a contract: National Life v U.S., 277 U.S. 508, June 4, 1928).

[49] Burnet v Logan, 283 U.S. 404, May 18, 1931.

6. Real Income.

The present statute has no such expressions as "real income," though it is well known to the common man.

The statute, as applied by the Commissioner, does tax income in kind (which is not always real income), but only when *paid* by A to B.[50] Garden truck consumed by the producer is not taxed.[51] So far as we know, the Supreme Court has not dealt with the question of real income except owner-occupancy of a building, and this, the Court says, is not income.[52] In Chapter 20, we have shown how this rule can raise two men's taxable income from zero to $10,000 with no change in the real income of either.

But the Court itself (in the same case) approves a statutory makeshift applicable to insurance corporations. By this makeshift the deduction of taxes and real-estate expenses are allowed only on condition that the occupant increase his gross income figure by an item amounting to rental value.

This same idea might perhaps be applied to apartment house owners living in their own apartments. As for owner-occupants of private dwellings, we have already discussed our own makeshift—taxing, in effect, the payments of the purchase price (or of the loan which furnished the purchase money).

INCOMPLETE ESCAPE

There may be other enjoyments and receipts not definable as income under the present law and yet taxable on the excise principle. In that case, possibly, an excise tax could be spliced with a tax on income under its present definition, in such a way as to produce the effects of a Yield tax. However, there may perhaps be items which the Court would neither regard as income under the Sixteenth Amendment nor as proper subjects for excise. For instance, if insurance receipts never achieve the status of income, they might be denied the privilege of an excise on the ground that any tax on such receipts is a direct tax, since the beneficiary is regarded as owning a property in the insurance policy.[53] That is, such a tax might not be able to escape the obnoxious rule of apportionment.

[50] 19.22 (a)—3, per Sec. 22.
[51] Treas. Decision 2665, Mar. 8, 1918.
[52] Helvering v Independent Life, 292 U.S. 371, May 21, 1934.
[53] Central Bank of Washington v Hume, 128 U.S. 195, Nov. 12, 1888.

Escape via Court

The Supreme Court is bound to respect its own decisions, but it has never consented to be helpless in the case of obvious injustice and impracticality. It has been known to change quite definitely, in order to forestall genuine evils which could not be taken care of by mere Congressional action. An example is the *Macomber* statement that, according to the *Pollock* case, taxes on income from property are "in effect" taxes on the property. This idea was invoked to prevent New York from taxing a New York citizen on income from bonds secured by New Jersey real estate. Thereupon the Supreme Court flatly repudiated the *Macomber* statement, observing that it "once won a qualified approval."[54]

And Professor Magill believes that, "notwithstanding the *Pollock* case, it is likely that the Court today would accept the view that an income tax is an excise tax."[55]

The Court and Periodicity

Professor Magill argued that annuities could be treated as simple income[56] because they are "periodical" and because probably the common man thinks of them as dedicated to "current expenditures." In a word, as we see it, destination—that is, real income—is the great subconscious test of the common man. Hence periodicity.

Yet, under the present congeries of special expedients, the common man's periodicity is trampled on at every turn.

Why?

Because the present practice is based, not on destination but on source.

Yield, on the other hand, goes entirely by destination. True, its gross may go by source, but not its net; and only its net is taxable; and its net equals the spendings; and the destination of the spendings

---

[54] People of N. Y. ex rel Cohn v Graves, 300 U.S. 308 at 314-316, Mar. 1, 1937; Graves et al v People of N. Y. ex rel Keefe, 306 U.S. 466 at 480, Mar. 27, 1939. But Court uses essentially the Macomber idea to effectuate express exemption of securities; National Life v U. S., 277 U.S. 508 at 521, June 4, 1928. But, under special circumstances under a state law, the Court allowed tax on income of such securities: Hale v Iowa State Board, 302 U.S. 95, Nov. 8, 1937.

[55] Taxable Income, p. 329.

[56] Taxable Income, p. 374.

is real income to which periodicity has a rough correspondence; so that, under Yield, this reasonable periodicity would never again have to be trampled on unless by the taxpayer's voluntary irregularity of life.

In this appendix we have assumed that the *Pollock, Macomber* and *Doyle* cases are still alive.

But has Mr. Surrey[57] guessed right: that hereafter any income tax will be safe from interference if it is "sensible" and not contrary to "due process"?

[57] See Chapter 20.

ADDENDUM TO NOTE 13, P. 236:

Comm. 127 F 2d 572, CCA 5th, Apr. 29, 1942, denies that embezzled money is taxable, but is not necessarily inconsistent with taxing stolen money not traceable to source.

BIBLIOGRAPHY

A. WRITINGS OF THE AUTHOR

B. WRITINGS OF OTHERS

BIBLIOGRAPHY

on

THE DOUBLE TAXATION OF SAVINGS

(and closely associated subjects)

A BIBLIOGRAPHY on income taxation, or even on the concepts of taxable income, would be too enormous to be of practical use. But the writings on that phase of the subject specially treated in this book are not numerous. So far as they have come to the author's attention they are all included below.

In fact, in the twilight zones surrounding the main theme, probably too many rather than too few items have been included, especially on income concepts, on the undistributed profits tax of 1936, on the stock-dividend controversy, and on capital gains taxation.

On the other hand, it is probable that some references in foreign languages have been overlooked.

A

WRITINGS OF THE AUTHOR (CHRONOLOGICAL)

What is Capital? (*In* Economic Journal. December 1896 p. 509-534. See especially p. 514)

Senses of "Capital." (*In* Economic Journal. June 1897 p. 199-213. See especially p. 202)

The Rôle of Capital in Economic Theory. (*In* Economic Journal. December 1897 p. 511-537. See especially p. 535 fn. 3 to p. 534)

The Nature of Capital and Income. New York, Macmillan, 1906. 427 p. (See especially p. 249-254)

Professor Fetter on Capital and Income. (*In* Journal of Political Economy. July 1907 p. 421-434)

Are Savings Income? (*In* Publications of the American Economic Association Third Series. April 1908 p. 21-58)

249

Comment on President Plehn's Address. (*In* American Economic Review. March 1924 p. 64-67)

The Income Concept in the Light of Experience. English reprint [address the author, New Haven, Conn.], 1927. (The original publication of this article was in German in Vol. III of the Wieser Festschrift, "Die Wirtschafttheorie der Gegenwart," Verlag von Julius Springer, Vienna, 1928 p. 22-45)

Economics of Accountancy. (*In* American Economic Review. December 1930 p. 603-618. Review of Canning's The Economics of Accountancy 1929)

Income. (In Encyclopaedia of the Social Sciences, 1932 Vol. 7 p. 622-625)

Income in Theory and Income Taxation in Practice. (*In* Econometrica. January 1937. See especially the numbered formulas)

A Practical Schedule for an Income Tax. (*In* The Tax Magazine—now Taxes. July 1937)

A General View of the Income Tax. (*In* Cornell Law Quarterly. December 1937 p. 39-44)

A Simplified Income Tax Schedule. (*In* Nation's Business. February 1938)

Double Taxation of Savings. (*In* American Economic Review. March 1939 p. 16-33)

The Concept of Income [A Rebuttal to Clyde Graves]. (*In* Econometrica. October 1939 p. 357-361)

Tax Bill Change Suggested. (*In* Letter to Editor of New York Times, New York Times, September 9, 1940)

A Fundamental Reason for Not Taxing Savings. (*In* The Tax Magazine—now Taxes. January 1941 p. 3-6, 52-54)

Rebuttal [to W. W. Hewett and H. S. Benjamin]. (*In* Taxes. May 1941 p. 276-279)

A Second Reason for Not Taxing Savings. (*In* Taxes. August 1941 p. 459-463, 488)

Testimony before House Ways and Means Committee. (*In* U. S. Congress. House. Committee on Ways and Means. Hearings . . . on Revenue Revision of 1941 V. 2, p. 1050-1067)

Testimony before Senate Finance Committee. (*In* U. S. Congress. Senate. Committee on Finance. Hearings . . . on H. R. 5417 [Revenue Act of 1941] p. 525-532)

Paradoxes in Taxing Savings. (*In* Econometrica. April 1942 p. 147-158)

A Rebuttal [to W. L. Crum and R. A. Musgrave]. (*In* American Economic Review. March 1942 p. 111-117)

Constructive Income Taxation. New York, Harper & Brothers, 1942 p. 275

Comments

In the first item in the above list (1896) on "What is Capital?" (written before the question "What is Income?" had been given equal attention) the idea was expressed in the second paragraph on page 514 that income differs from capital *solely* in its relation to time. This was soon seen to be erroneous and was explicitly withdrawn in the article "The Rôle of Capital" on page 535 (fn. 3 to page 534). The change of view was due in part to the criticisms of Cannan and Edgeworth and occurred long before Professor Fetter took the author to task.

The Nature of Capital and Income (1906) includes the substance of the three articles preceding (as well as of others not eligible for this bibliography). The conclusions of this book have not since been changed, though they have been elaborated, and their application to income taxation developed. The terminology, as given in full in the Glossary, p. 329-337, has later, in 1939, been modified by the use of the terms "enrichment-income" or "accretion-income," or simply "accretion" as synonymous with the "earned income" or earnings of *The Nature of Capital and Income*. That book contained the first statement (p. 249-254) of the author on the double taxation of savings.

The article "Are Savings Income?" contains many points not covered before and a few not recurred to later.

The *Econometrica* articles of 1937 and 1942 contain, in mathematical language, considerable material not published elsewhere.

The article of 1937 in the *Tax Magazine* (now *Taxes*) was the first effort, in nonmathematical terms, to show how what is here called a yield tax can be practically computed in a tax return.

Those writings of others which were answered by the author in the articles listed above are included in the bibliography of others which follows below—articles by Fetter, Plehn, Graves, Hewett, Benjamin, Crum, Musgrave.

Besides these seven there are twelve other objectors on record (as per Appendix to Chapter 8) whose objections have been answered only by implication in print.

Specified answers have, however, been prepared in all cases, ready to be sent in mimeographed form on request.

B
WRITINGS OF OTHERS (ALPHABETICAL)

Adams, T. S. Immediate Future of the Excess Profits Tax. (*In* American Economic Review. Supplement. March 1920 p. 15-18)

Alessio, Giulio. Saggio sul sistema tributario in Italia e sui suoi effetti economici e sociali. Turin, Fratelli Bocca.

Anderson, Benjamin M., Jr. Eating the Seed Corn. (*In* The Chase Economic Bulletin. May 12, 1936 p. 3-37)

Benham, F. C. Notes on the Pure Theory of Public Finance [Suggested by the Ottima Imposta of Professor Einaudi]. (*In* Economica. November 1934 p. 436-458)

Benjamin, Harold S. The Reasons for Taxing Savings. (*In* Taxes. May 1941 p. 271-275) [Rebuttal in same issue]

Bittel, Karl. Eduard Pfeiffer und die deutsche Konsumgenossenschaftsbewegung. Schriften des Vereins für Socialpolitik. Undersuchungen ueber Konsumvereine 151. Band. Monographien aus dem Konsumvereinswesen. Erster Teil. [München und Leipzig] Verlag von Duncker & Humblot, 1915

Bond, Henry H. A Practical Aspect of the Stock Dividend Question. (*In* Bulletin of the National Tax Association. June 1918 p. 237-240)

Bordewijk, Hugo C. W. De Theorie der Belastingen en het Nederlandsche Belastingwezen. 3rd ed., No. 10. (*Of* Het Nederlandsche Belastenrecht. Under Prof. J. Ph. Snyling, Swolle 1939)

Buehler, Alfred G. Some Phases of the Undistributed Profits Tax. (*In* National Tax Association Bulletin. November 1936 p. 46-54)

—— The Undistributed Profits Tax in the Fiscal System. (*In* Harvard Business Review. Autumn 1936 p. 29-43)

—— The Undistributed Profits Tax. New York and London, McGraw-Hill Book Company, Inc. 1937 281 p.

Burrows, John A. Suggestions for a New Income Tax Law. (*In* American Industries. August 1920 p. 29)

Cabiati, Attilio e Einaudi, Luigi. L'Italia e I Trattati Dei Commercio Milano, Uffici della Critica Sociale, Portici Galleria 23 1903 98 p.

Cabiati, Einaudi, Luigi; Fasciani, Mauro; Fubini, Renzo; Loria, Achille; and Ricci, Umberto. La Riforma Sociale. (*In* Rivista Critica Di Economia E Di Finanza. March-April, May-June, July-August 1928)

Cannan, Edwin. (*In* Review of The Economics of Welfare by A. C. Pigou. Economic Journal. June 1921 p. 213)

Canning, John B. Economics of Accountancy. Ronald Press 1929. 367 p.

―――― and Nelson, E. G. Relation of Budget Balancing to Economic Stabilization. (*In* American Economic Review. Vol. 24 p. 26-37)

Caverly, Harcourt R. Taxation of Corporate Income under the Revenue Act of 1936. (*In* Michigan State Bar Association Journal. February 1937 p. 90-100)

Cohen [now Coe], Jacques S. Stock Dividend as Income Discussed Again. (*In* The Annalist. April 1, 1918 p. 347)

Colm, Gerhard. The Revenue Act of 1938. (*In* Social Research. September 1938 p. 273-277)

――――. Full Employment through Tax Policy? (*In* Social Research No. 4 November 1940 p. 447-467)

Crum, William L. On the Alleged Double Taxation of Savings. (*In* American Economic Review. September 1939) [Rebuttal in March 1942 issue]

Daniels, Winthrop M. Discussion of Are Savings Income? (Address by Irving Fisher). (*In* Publications of the American Economic Association. Third Series. April 1908 p. 48-51)

Editor. The Corporate Undistributed Profits Tax. (*In* Columbia Law Review. December 1936 p. 1321-1354)

Editor. The Press Condemns Business Profits Tax. (*In* Industrial Canada. March 1920 p. 128. *From* Ottawa Journal, Dec. 4, 1919 and Montreal Gazette, Jan. 22, 1920)

Einaudi, Luigi. [See also Cabiati] Contributo alla Recerca della 'ottima' Imposta. (*In* Annali di Economia. July 1929 p. 9-244) Contains extensive bibliography

―――― Il Sistema Tributario Italiano. Quarta Edizone Rifatta Ed Ampliata Con La Collaborazione Di, Francesco A. Repaci, Professore Nella R. Universita Di Padova, Guilio Einaudi, Editore. Torino. 1939, XVII

Fagan, Elmer D. Recent and Contemporary Theories of Progressive Taxation. (*In* Journal of Political Economy. August 1938 p. 457-498)

Fairchild, Fred Rogers. The Economic Nature of the Stock Dividend. (*In* Bulletin National Tax Association. April 1918 p. 161-163)

———— The Stock Dividend—A Rejoinder. (*In* Bulletin of the National Tax Association (June 1918 p. 240-243)

———— The Stock Dividend Decision. (*In* National Tax Association Bulletin. April 1920 p. 208-211)

———— Federal Taxation of Income and Profits. (*In* American Economic Review. March 1921 p. 148-159)

———— Suggestions for Revision of the Federal Taxation of Income and Profits. (*In* Amer. Econ. Rev. December 1920 p. 785-799)

———— Forest Taxation in the United States. (*In* Report of the Forest Taxation Inquiry 1935)

Fanno, Marco. Scienza delle Finanze Le Imposte Dirette. La Litotipo, Editrice Universitaria. Padova 1925 280 p.

———— Lezioni Di Scienza delle Finanze e Diritto Finanziario. Parte generale. Padova, La Litotipo 1926 290 p.

Fasiani, Mauro. [See also Cabiati] Der Gegenwärtige Stand der Reinen Theorie der Finanzwissenschaft in Italien. Band III and IV of the Viennese Zeitschrift für Nationalökonomie

Fernald, Henry B. What Tax on Undistributed Earnings Would Mean to Corporations. (*In* Controller. June 1936 p. 130-135)

———— The Tax on Undistributed Profits Imposed by the Revenue Act of 1936. (*In* The New York Certified Public Accountant. October 1936 p. 22-45)

Fetter, Frank A. The Nature of Capital and Income. (*In* Jour. Polit. Econ. March 1907 p. 129-148) [Rebuttal in July issue]

———— Discussion of Are Savings Income? (Address by Irving Fisher). (*In* Publications of the American Economic Association. Third Series. April 1908 p. 51-55)

Flux, A. W. Irving Fisher on Capital and Interest. (*In* Quarterly Journal of Economics. February 1909)

———— Discussion of Are Savings Income? (Address by Irving Fisher). (*In* Publications of the American Economic Association. Third Series. April 1908 p. 55-56)

Friedman, Elisha M. The Capital Gains Tax. (*In* Memorandum prepared for American Taxpayers Association, Inc., Jan. 5, 1942)

Fubini, Renzo [see Cabiati]

———— Lezioni Di Scienza delle Finanze. Padova 1934 327 p.

Graham, Benjamin. The Undistributed Profits Tax and the Investor. (*In* Yale Law Journal. November 1936 p. 1-18)

Graves, Clyde H. The Concept of Income. (*In* Econometrica. October 1939 p. 349-356) [Rebuttal in same issue]

Graziani, Augusto. Instituzioni Di Scienza delle Finanze. Turin, Fratelli Bocca, 1911 2nd ed. rev. 785 p.

Great Britain. Report from the Select Committee on Income and Property Tax Together with the Proceedings of its Committee, Minutes of Evidence and Appendix. 1861 V. 7 Contains testimony of J. S. Mill and others. [See extensive index entries on p. 45]

—— Royal Commission on the Income Tax, Minutes of Evidence. 1919 p. 582-583, 1630-1688, 11, 796, 19, 813

Guillebaud, C. W. Income Tax and the Double Taxation of Savings. (*In* Economic Journal. September 1935 p. 484-492)

Guthmann, Harry G. The Effect of the Undistributed Tax upon the Distribution of Corporate Earnings; A Note. (*In* Econometrica. October 1940)

Haig, Robert Murray. The Taxation of Excess Profits in Great Britain. (*In* Amer. Econ. Rev. Supplement. December 1920)

—— The Concept of Income—Economic and Legal Aspects. Chapter 1. (*In* The Federal Income Tax. A series of Lectures delivered at Columbia University in December 1920. Edited by Robert Murray Haig. New York, Columbia University Press 1921 p. 128)

—— Taxation of Capital Gains. Series of 6 articles. (*In* Wall Street Journal, March 23, 25, 29, Apr. 2, 8, 13, 1937)

Hazelett, Clarence William. Incentive Taxation. 3rd Ed. New York, E. P. Dutton, 1939 p. 170-173

Held, Adolf. Die Einkommensteuer. Bonn, 1872

Hendricks, Homer. The Surtax of Undistributed Profits of Corporations (*In* Yale Law Journal. November 1936 p. 19-51)

Hewett, William Wallace. The Concept of Income in Federal Taxation. (*In* Journal of Political Economy. April 1925 p. 155)

—— The Definition of Income and Its Application in Federal Taxation. Philadelphia, Westbrook Publishing Co., 1925 Rev. ed. 91 p., p. 28-31

—— Professor Irving Fisher on Income, in the Light of Experience. (*In* American Economic Review. June 1929 p. 217-226)

—— Double Taxation of Savings as Income. (*In* Taxes. May 1941 p. 270, 275-276) [Rebuttal in same issue]

Jordan, Chester A. The Spendings Tax. Southworth Printing Co., 1921 79 p.

Jordan, Chester A. Spending Tax. (*In* Testimony before Senate Finance Committee in U. S. Congress. Senate. Committee on Finance. Internal Revenue Hearings . . . on the Proposed Revenue Act of 1921 p. 487-497)

—— Advantages of the Spendings Tax. (*In* Forum. March 1922 p. 264-270)

Jourolmon, Leon, Jr. Capital Gains as Measured by the Trend of Prices. (*In* Tennessee Law Review. June 1927 p. 197-218)

Knollenberg, Bernhard. Taxable Income Under the Sixteenth Amendment. (*In* The Tax Magazine. March 1931 p. 87-90)

Kracht, George V. Incidence of Business-Profits Taxes. (*In* Journal of Accountancy. October 1924 p. 241-253)

Kuznets, Simon. National Income. (*In* Encyclopaedia of Social Sciences. Macmillan, 1933, p. 204-224)

Lolini, Ettore. Un Sofisma Finanziario: La Doppia Imposizione del Reddito Risparmiato. (*In* Economica. November 1928 p. 403-419)

Loria, Achille. La Synthese economique; etude sur les lois du revenu. Paris, M. Giard & E. Briere, 1911

—— [See also Cabiati] The Economic Synthesis. Macmillan, 1914 368 p.

McCormick, Robert R. The Sacking of America. Chicago, The Tribune Company, 1932 57 p.

McIntyre, Francis. The Effect of the Undistributed Profits Tax: A Reply. (*In* Econometrica. October 1940)

Magill, Roswell F. Taxable Income. New York, Ronald Press, 1937 437 p

Malburn, William P. Is a Stock Dividend on Earnings Income? (*In* The Annalist. Feb. 11, 1918 p. 173-174)

Marschak, Jacob (in collaboration with Helen Makower). Assets, Prices and Monetary Theory. (*In* Economica. August 1938)

—— Money and the Theory of Assets (*In* Econometrica. October 1938)

Marshall, Alfred. Social Possibilities of Economic Chivalry. 1907. (*In* Memorials of Alfred Marshall. Ed. by A. C. Pigou. London, Macmillan, 1925 Part II p. 350-351)

—— National Taxation after the War. The Appropriate Distribution of its Burden. Limitations of the Scope of Taxes on Capital.

After-War Problems. New York, Macmillan Co., 1917 p. 322-324

Martin, John B., Jr. Taxation of Undistributed Corporate Profits. (*In* Michigan Law Review. November 1936 p. 44-72)

Masci, Guglielmo. Saggi Critici di Teoria e Metodologia Economica. Catania, Studio Editoriale Moderno, 1934 XII 336 p.

—— Corso di Scienza delle Finanze—diritto finanziario. Roma 1937 Vol. I 2nd ed. of the Foro Italiano

Mill, John Stuart. Testimony. (*In* Report of the Select Committee on Income and Property Tax. Parliamentary Papers. Vol VII 1861)

—— Principles of Political Economy. New York, D. Appleton & Co. (Laughlin Ed.) 1884, Book V, p. 543. Same 1883, Vol. II p. 428

—— Principles of Political Economy. Longman's Green & Co. (Ashley Ed.) 1920 p. 813-817, 831

Miller, Merle H. The 1936 Federal Corporate Surtax. (*In* Indiana Law Journal. October 1936 p. 19-46)

Mills, Ogden L. The Spendings Tax. (*In* Bulletin of the National Tax Association. October 1921 p. 18-20)

—— Speech in Congress. (*In* Congressional Record. August 17, 1921 p. 5138-5139)

—— Testimony before House Ways and Means Committee. (*In* U. S. Congress. House Committee on Ways and Means. Hearings on Revenue Revision 1932 p. 25)

Moir, Henry. Annuity Income Tax Situation. (*In* The Eastern Underwriter. March 23, 1934)

Mortara, Augusto. I Doveri della Proprieta Fondiaria, e la Questione Sociale. Milano, Napoli, Palmero, Roma, Torino, Unione Tipografico-Editrice Torinese 1912

Musgrave, Richard A. A Further Note on the Double Taxation of Savings. (*In* American Economic Review. September 1939) [Rebuttal in March 1942 issue]

Needham, Raymond. Income Tax. The Distinction between Capital and Income. (*In* The Accountant. June 6, 1925 p. 917-920)

Nelson, Godfrey N. Taxation of Capital Gains. (*In* Proceedings of Institute of Public Affairs. University of Virginia. July 1936 p. 309)

—— Capital Gains and Losses. (*In* The Tax Magazine. December 1936 p. 708-709)

Nelson, Godfrey N. Undistributed Corporate Profits Are Not Savings. (*In* Report Committee of National Tax Association. October 1939 p. 29)

—— The Case Against Taxation of Income from Capital Gains. (*In* publication of Symposium, Duke University Law School. 1940 p. 208)

Newmarch, Sir William. Testimony. (*In* Report from the Select Committee on Income and Property Tax. Together with the Proceedings of the Committee, Minutes of Evidence, and Appendix. April 23, 1861 p. 36)

New York Times. Reich to Reward Patient Savers. October 30, 1941 p. 10, c. 2

Patch, Buel W. Revision of Federal Tax on Capital Gains. (*In* Editorial Research Reports. Vol. II 1936, No. 22 December 1936 p. 437-453)

Pfeiffer, Eduard. Die Staatseinnahmen. Geschichte, Kritik, und Statistik. Stuttgart, 1866. Zwei Bände.

Pierson, N. G. Principles of Economics. (Translated from the Dutch by A. A. Wotzel), London, Macmillan & Co., Ltd., 1912 Vol. 2 p. 570-573

Pigou, A. C., Editor. Memorials of Alfred Marshall. London, Macmillan, 1925 (Part II, Selections from Alfred Marshall's Writings, Social Possibilities of Economic Chivalry, 1907 p. 350-351)

—— Report of the Royal Commission on the British Income Tax. (*In* Quarterly Journal of Economics. August 1920 p. 607-625)

—— The Economics of Welfare. Second Edition. London, Macmillan & Co., Ltd., 1924 p. 670-673

—— A Study in Public Finance. Macmillan & Co., Ltd., 1928 Part II, Ch. 10

Plehn, Carl C. Address. (*In* Proceedings of the National Industrial Tax Conference. May 1920 p. 23-45. On the subject of Substitutes for the Excess Profits Tax and the Higher Income Surtaxes)

—— Income, as Recurrent, Consumable Receipts. (*In* American Economic Review. March 1924 p. 1-12) [Reply in same issue]

Prato, Guiseppe. L'Impiego Dei Capitali, Guida Dei Risparmiatori-Unione Tipografico, Editrice Torinese, Torino, Tipografia Social Torinese, 1928

Ratchford, B. U. Fisher's Concept of Taxable Income. (*In* The Tax Magazine. November 1937 p. 647, 692)

Revans, John. A Percentage Tax on Domestic Expenditure to Supply the Whole of the Public Revenue. London, 1847. [Available at the Peabody Institute, Baltimore]

Review. (*In* Bibliografia. De la Revista de Economia y Estadistica. Ano I No. 2, 1939 p. 7-8 of Fisher, Irving. Double Taxation of Savings. (*In* American Economic Review. March 1939 p. 16-33)

Review. (*In* Bibliografia De la Revista de Economia y Estadistica. Ano I No. 2, 1939 p. 8-10, of Crum, W. L., Alleged Taxation of Savings. Musgrave, Abel., A Further Note on the Double Taxation of Savings. *In* American Economic Review. September 1939 p. 538-551)

Ricca-Salerno, Paolo. II Risparmio Nel Sistema Tributario 1928

Ricci, Umberto. [See also Cabiati] L'Imposta unica sui consumi non necessari. (*In* Giornale degli economisti. Rome 1914 [A criticism of Einaudi])

——— La Taxation de l'epargne. (*In* Revue d'economie politique. May-June 1927 [A criticism of Einaudi])

Rottschaefer, Henry. The Concept of Income in Federal Taxation. (*In* Minnesota Law Review. June 1929 p. 637-674)

Schanz, Georg. Der Einkommenbegriff und die Einkommensteurgesetze. (*In* Finanz Archiv. Vol. XIII 1896 p. 23. Also Finanz Archiv. Vol. XXXIX, 1921, p. 505-523)

Seligman, Edwin R. A. Are Stock Dividends Income? (*In* American Economic Review. September 1919 p. 517-536)

Sher, I. Herman. The New Corporation Income Tax. New York, Simon & Schuster, 1938 60 p.

Shoup, Carl. Distinction Between "Net" and "Gross" in Income Taxation. (*In* Vol. I, Studies in Income and Wealth. National Bureau of Economic Research. 1937 p. 251-281)

Simons, Henry C. Personal Income Taxation. University of Chicago Press, 1938 p. 238

Stamp, Sir Josiah Charles. The Fundamental Principles of Taxation, in the Light of Modern Developments. London, Macmillan & Co., Ltd., 1929, new and revised edition 1936 p. 57-61

Tremaine, Morris S. Capital Gains Tax: A Drag on Industry? (*In* United States News. March 22, 1937 p. 18 Newsgram 16)

Vickrey, William. Averaging of Income for Income Tax Purposes. (*In* Journal of Political Economy. June 1939 p. 381)

Viti de Marco, Antonio de. First Principles of Public Finance. Translated from the Italian by Edith Pavlo Marget. New York, Harcourt, Brace & Co., Inc., 1936 p. 225-233

Weaver, Donald. An Economic Fallacy: The Double Taxation of Saving. (*In* Economic Journal. September 1932 p. 494-498)

Whitaker, A. C. Stock Dividend Question. (*In* American Economic Review. March 1929 p. 20-42)

Wueller, Paul H. Concepts of Taxable Income I. The German Contribution. (*In* Political Science Quarterly. March 1938 p. 83-110)

—— Concepts of Taxable Income II. The American Contribution (*In* Political Science Quarterly. December 1938 p. 557-561)

—— Concepts of Taxable Income III. The Italian Contribution (*In* Political Science Quarterly. December 1939 p. 555-576)

INDEX OF LEGAL CASES

Arkansas Compress Co. v Comm.,
151n.

Baily v Clark, 241n.
Bankers Pocahontas Coal Co. v
Burnet, 242n.
Blair v Comm., 235n.
Bowers v Kerbaugh-Empire Co.,
142n., 155n.
Bromley v McCaughn, 186n., 237n.
Brushaber v Union Pacific, 138n.,
187n., 188n.
Bruun case, see Helvering v Bruun
Burnet v Harmel, 152n.
Burnet v Logan, 243n.
Burnet v Sanford & Brooks, 142n.,
143n., 159n.
Burnet v Wells, 235n., 236n.

Central Bank of Washington v
Hume, 244n.
Central R. Co. v Comm., 234n., 238
Chickasha Cotton Oil Co. v
Comm., 241n.
Cole v Helbrun, 146n.
Comm. v Field, 236n.
Comm. v Tillotson Mfg., 137
Corliss v Bowers, 235n.
Cream of Wheat Co. v County of
Grand Forks, 160n., 161n.
Cullinan v Walker, 131, 132, 135,
136, 138
Cummings v Comm., 240n.
Curry v McCanless, 161n.
Curtis v Helvering, 147n.

Dallas Transfer v Comm., 155n.
Davidson v Comm., 147

Douglas v Willcuts, 235n.
Doyle v Mitchell, 143, 241, 242,
243, 246
Dreyfuss v Manning, 137n.

Edwards v Cuba R.R., 150n.
Edye v Robertson, 187n.
Eisner v Macomber, 6n., 16n., 127n.,
128, 130, 131, 133-134, 137, 139,
140, 142, 143, 165, 166, 184, 189,
190, 234, 238, 240, 241, 245, 246
decision, 133, 139, 141
Estate of Sherman v Comm., 155n.

Farmers and Merchants Bank v
Comm., 242n.
Flint v Stone Tracy Co., 128n.

Golden v Comm., 240n.
Gould v Gould, 235n.
Gowran case, see Helvering v
Gowran
Graves v People of New York ex
rel Keefe, 185n., 245n.
Great Northern Ry. Co. v Comm.,
151n.
Guaranty Trust Co. v Virginia,
161n.

Hale v Iowa State Board, 185n.,
245n.
Harrison v Schaffner, 235n.
Hawkins v Comm., 16n., 238n.
Hellmich v Hellman, 161n.
Helvering v Bruun, 140, 141, 185
Helvering v Claiborne-Annapolis
Ferry, 151n.
Helvering v Clifford, 235n., 236n.
Helvering v Drier, 242n.

Helvering v Eubank, 185n., 235n., 236n.
Helvering v Fitch, 235n.
Helvering v Fuller, 235n.
Helvering v Gerhardt, 204n.
Helvering v Gowran, 134, 135, 136, 137, 166n.
Helvering v Gregory, 167n.
Helvering v Horst, 141, 185, 234n., 235n., 236n.
Helvering v Independent Life Insurance Company, 151n., 161n., 183n., 243n., 244n.
Helvering v National Grocery, 6n.
Helvering v Rankin, 146n., 147n.
Highland Farms v Comm., 155n., 238n.
Hirsch v Comm., 155n.
Horst case, see Helvering v Horst

International Boiler Co., appeal of, 242n.
Irwin v Gavit, 156n., 234n., 237n., 238n.

Knowlton v Moore, 126n., 186n., 187n.
Koshland v Helvering, 134, 135, 136, 137, 166n.
Kurrle v Helvering, 236n.

Liberty Light & Power Co., appeal of, 151n.
Liebes v Comm., 242n.
Lucas v Alexander, 156n., 237n., 241n.
Lucas v Earle, 235n., 238n.
Lyeth v Hoey, 234n., 237n.
Lykes Bros. v Comm., 151n.
Lynch v Hornby, 241n.

McCoach v Minehill, 128n.
McCulloch v Maryland, 61n.
McDonald v Comm., 238n.
Macomber case, see Eisner v Macomber
Marr v U.S., 131, 132, 133, 134, 135, 136, 138

Merchants Loan & Trust v Smietanka, 128n.
Miller v Comm., 146n., 147n.

National Life v U.S., 243n., 245n.
New Colonial Ice Co. v Helvering, 151n., 161n.
Nicol v Ames, 186n., 187n.

Old Colony R.R. v Comm., 241n.

Patton v Brady, 187n.
Pearce v Comm., 235n.
People of New York ex rel Cohn v Graves, 161n., 185n., 245n.
Phellis case, see U.S. v Phellis
Pollock v Farmers Loan and Trust Co., 39n., 127n., 186n.
Pollock v U.S., 184, 185-186, 187, 189, 190, 234, 240, 241, 245, 246

Real Estate Land Title & Trust Co. v U.S., 162n.
Riebe v Comm., 236n.
Rockefeller v U.S., 131, 132, 136, 138

Sickles v U.S., 155n.
Southern Pacific v Lowe, 241n.
Springer v U.S., 127n.
Sprouse v Comm., 137, 138
Stanton v Baltic Co., 151n., 152n.
State Tax Comm. of Utah v Aldrich, 161n.
Sterling v Comm., 234, 235n., 239n.
Strassberger v Comm., 137, 138
Stratton's Independence, Ltd. v Howbert, 128n., 187n., 188n.
Strothers v Burnet, 242n.

Texas Ry. v U.S., 151n.
Thomas v U.S., 186n.
Tillotson case, see Comm. v. Tillotson Mfg.
Transylvania R. v Comm., 155n.

Union Pacific Ry. Co. v Comm., 151n.

Union Refrigerator Transit Co. v
   Kentucky, 16n., 160n.
U.S. v Anderson, 204n.
U.S. v Kirby Lumber Co., 142n.,
   143n., 154n., 155n.
U.S. v Mitchell, 204n.
U.S. v Phellis, 131, 132, 133-135, 136,
   138
   decision, 133

U.S. v Safety Car Heating Co.,
   241n., 242
U.S. v Supplee-Biddle Hardware
   Co., 160n., 234n., 239n.
U.S. v Whiteridge, 128n.

Walker v Comm., 154n.
Weiss v Stern, 133, 138

GENERAL INDEX

Ability principle, 97-98, 101
Accountants, according to, 233
Accounting, 35, 42, 46
  accretion, 116
  book profit, 156-159
  double-entry, 18-23, 28, 139, 213
  examples of, 18-23
  income, 43
Accretion, 48-55
  to accountants and statisticians, 233
  defined, 49
  discounted, 51-55
    vs. discounted yield, 54-55
  judicial approaches to, 139-141
  questions to the layman on, 110-120
  regressive rates of taxation under, 102
  as tax base, 58-59, 75-77, 120, 194, 232
    effect of, 57
  and yield, mixture of, in American tax law, 109
Accretion-income, 48-55, 120,
  conditions needed for, 210, 213
  regressive rates in, 102
Accretion tax
  disadvantages of, 194
  revenue under, 194
  social effects of, 92-105
Adams, Thomas S., 209
Alimony
  exemption of, 188, 202
  tax on, 235
Allocations, 204-205
American Telephone and Telegraph Company, 86
Amortization, 171

Annuities, 155, 236, 245
  perpetual, 47, 57
  taxing of, in England, 59, 180
Antisaving theories, 228, 229
Apportionment rule, 186, 190, 237, 244
Appreciation of capital, 116, 184
Arkwright, Richard, 79, 86
Assets, 7, 142, 152
Automobile industry, 72

Balance, cash, 7, 211
Balances, method of, 20, 44
"Basis" in tax computation, 169-170
Bell, Alexander Graham, 79
Benefit principle, 95, 98
Benham, F. C., 218
Benjamin, Harold S., 75, 215, 217
Bequests, 11, 22-23, 57-58, 88-89, 93, 100, 156n., 234, 237-238
Beretvas, Andor, xii
Bissonnette, W. J., xiii
Bloodgood, William, xii
Book profits, 156-159
Bordewijk, Hugo C. W., 215, 217
Borrowing
  exemption of, 188
  for expansion, 82-84
  by the government, 72, 73, 74, 221, 223, 224
  and lending, 153-155, 202-203, 236
Brandeis, Justice, 130, 160
British corporation taxes, 30n., 163
British income taxes, 30n., 59-60, 177-183
  nearer to yield concept, 177
Brown, Harry G., xii

265

Bulletin of the National Tax Association, 208n.
Business
  dynamic, 86
  government management of, 90-91, 196
  static, 85
Business Cycles, by Schumpeter, 79n., 228n.
Business enterpriser, importance of, 80
Business Expansion
  benefit of, to public, 80
  borrowing for, 82-84
  high profits necessary to, 83, 85, 86
  influence of discouragement on, 71-72
  risks of, 80-81
  taxed, 32, 35, 61-74, 84, 230
Bye, Raymond T., 232

Cannan, Edwin, 215
Canning, John B., 233
Capital
  classes of, 41
  consumers' and producers', 41
  defined, 40
    by Supreme Court, 241
  as discounted yield, 46, 49
  outside, growth through, 82-84, 223, 230
  relation of, to yield-income, 40-41
  "venture," 83
Capital continuity, 145-148
Capital-decrease, 49, 59, 76, 116, 171
Capital gains tax, 11, 17, 35, 49-50, 142-152, 165, 166, 225, 241
  examples, 144
  in Great Britain, 178-180
  major premise of, 143
  mitigations of, 144-145, 168
  ulterior evils of, 148-149
  unsatisfactory as producer of revenue, 148-149

Capital-increase, 49, 51, 57, 58, 79, 81, 116, 171, 210, 213, 221, 225, 230 (*see also* Growth rate of capital *and* Savings)
  desirability of, 227-228
  exemption for, 89
  included in accretion, 75
  negative, *see* Capital decrease
  tax on, 3, 72-73, 132, 161
    destructiveness of, 61-74, 92, 195, 231, 220-221
Capital loss, forms of, deducted, 162
Capital sold, proceeds of, exempted, 188
Capital-stock tax, 164
Capitalism the Creator, by Snyder, 79n.
Capitalization principle, 46-55
Cardozo, Justice, 192, 236
Carnegie, Andrew, 89
Carry-over of losses, 158, 171
Cartwright, Edmund, 86
Cash
  bank savings as, 112
  capital income as, 116
  as concept of income, 116, 118
Cash balance, 211
  yield from, 7, 18, 19-20, 21
Cash yield, *see* Yield, cash
Catherwood, M. P., xii
Clark, Colin, 93
Clarke, Justice, 191
Class consciousness, growth of, 92
Credit, 18, 42, 46
Credits, *see* Exemptions
Crum, William L., 215, 216
Cohrssen, Hans, xiii, 218
Cole, George J., xii
Common man
  flexibility of, 192-193
  question to, 110-120
Compensation, workmen's, 96
Compensatory payments, exemption of, 188, 238-239
Compounding of taxes, 47, 48
Concepts of Taxable Income, by Wueller, 232n.

Congress
 deductions granted by, 151-152, 161, 243
 exemptions of dividends granted by, 139
 failure of, to distinguish between capital and income, 189-190
 powers of taxation granted to, 126, 142, 152n., 184-185, 190, 236
 and securities tax, 147-148
 tax decisions of, in reorganizations, 138
Congressional Record, 208n.
Constitution
 interpretation of, 236
 limitations of, on income tax laws, 182
 powers of taxation granted by, 126
 problems involving, 234-246
 and yield tax, 184-193
Constitutional problems, 234-246
Consumer goods, 25-27
Consumers' capital, 41
Consumption, 14, 26, 40
 an inept term, 24-25
 as net yield-income, 51
 services of, as real income, 43-44
 and spendings, discrepancies between, 203
Co-operatives, 84-85
Corporate identity, change in, 133, 136
Corporation
 as "artificial person," 28
 as association of real people, 28
 grades, 172-173
Corporation income taxes, 6, 17, 32, 84, 162-165, 205, 229 (*see also* Excess profits tax)
 and personal tax, 30
Corporation profits, 51, 73, 80, 82, 83, 118, 162-164, 171, 214, 230, 231
 double tax on, 34
Corporation tax of 1909, 187

Country Home Magazine, 90n.
Couples, method of, 20, 42, 44
Courts of Appeals, tax cases in, 137-138, 147, 234, 235, 236, 238, 240

Daniels, Winthrop M., 215
Date discrepancies, correction of, 203
Dealer
 nonprofessional, affected by capital gains tax, 143
 professional
  not affected by capital gains tax, 143
  taxed in Great Britain, 178-179
Death duties, 70, 71, 93, 94, 95, 196, 239
Debit, 18, 42, 46
Debt reduction, 154-155, 159, 236
Debts, 202-203
 bad, 154, 159
Deductions, 35, 59-60, 123-124, 168, 170, 190, 201-202 (*see also* Exemptions)
 double, 162
 for loan repayment, 158
 a matter of legislative grace, 151-152, 161, 243
 for reinvestment, 181-182
 under yield, 204, 239
Defamation, 238
 of a business, 242
Definition of Income, The, by Hewett, 138n.
Definitions in Political Economy, by Malthus, 212
DeForest, 80
De Marco, Viti, 215
Democracy, threat to, of accretion tax, 92-95
Dependents, exemptions for, 205-207
Depreciation, 7, 59, 116, 162, 170
 British treatment of, 180-182
Depression, antihoarding taxes in, 228

Destructiveness of present tax law
    on capital-increase, 92, 195,
    231
  analyzed, 220-221
  avoided by yield tax, 194
Discounting
  basis for, 47-48, 55, 59
  double, 56
Discounting principle, 46-55, 59, 194
Discouragement
  of business expansion, 71-72, 93-
    94
  of saving, 73, 84, 196
  of spendings, 227
  of waste, 84
Disservice, see Services, negative
Dividends
  as capital, 130, 131
  exemption of, 139
  as income, 130
  increased, 84
  limitation of, 80
  tax on, 29, 30-31, 32, 129, 130-141,
    161, 162-163, 208
    and accretion concept, 139
    "basis" of, 165-166
    Common on Common, 130-
      134, 137
    Common on Preferred and
      Preferred on Common, 134-
      138, 165, 166n.
  treated as cash yield, 10
Dorsey, Robert J., xii
Double-entry accounting, 18-23, 28,
    42, 139, 213
Double exemption, 3, 58-60, 92,
    162
Double taxation, 3, 56-60, 92, 120,
    129, 160-166
  avoided by yield tax, 194
  constitutionality of, 160-161
  controversy over, 215-219
  of corporate profits and stock-
    holders' dividends, 29, 34,
    165
  identical, 162-164
  involving more than one state,
    161n.
  remedy for, 30, 31-32

Double taxation—(Continued)
  successive, 161-162
  vs. destructiveness, 222
Due process of law, 160n.

Earned income
  to the accountant, 124
  credits for, 123-124, 202, 205, 206
  distinguished from earnings, 49n.
  to the Treasury, 124
  as yield from work, 6, 15, 19
Earnings (see also Accretion)
  contrasted with yield, 50-51
  distinguished from earned in-
    come, 49n.
Econometrica, xi, 62n., 69, 203n.
Economic Essays Contributed in
    Honor of John Bates Clark,
    102n., 207n.
Economics of Accountancy, by
    Canning, 233
Economists, income according to,
    232
Edgeworth, 102
Edison, Thomas, 79, 86
Einaudi, Luigi, xiii, 4, 218
Elementary Economics, by Furniss
    and Buck, 232n.
Eminent domain cases, 148
Encyclopaedia of the Social Sci-
    ences, 233n.
Endowment policies, 155
England
  carry-over of losses in, 158
  corporation taxes in, 30n., 163
  income taxes in, 30n., 59-60, 177-
    183
  primogeniture in, 93
Estate tax, 70, 71, 73, 87, 94, 235
Estates, motive for building, 88-89
Exceptions to exceptions in present
    law, 195
Excess profits tax, 163-164, 171, 173,
    196-197, 229, 231
"Exclusions," 170
Exemptions, 89, 123-124, 170, 202,
    205, 206, 234, 237
  of dividends, 139
  double, 3, 58-60, 162

Exemptions—(*Continued*)
  minimum, 5, 205-207
  of reinvestment, 242-243
  of securities, 34
  under yield tax, 188-189, 201-202, 204
Expansion, business
  benefit of, to public, 80
  borrowing for, 82-84
  high profits necessary for, 83, 85, 86
  influence of discouragement on, 71-72
  risks of, 80-81
  tax on, 32, 35, 61-74, 84, 230
Exploitation, commercial, necessity of, 85

Fagan, Elmer B., 207n.
  on progressive taxation, 103-104
Failures vs. successes, 225-226
Fairchild, Fred R., xii, 218, 232
Fanno, Marco, 218
Fasiani, Mauro, 218
Federal Income Tax, ed. by Haig, 232n.
Federal Tax Handbook, 125n.
Fetter, Frank A., 215
Fifth Amendment, 160
Figueroa, Asisclo A., xii
Firman, John E., xii, 110
Fleischer, Otto F., xii
Flux, A. W., 215
Ford, Edsel, 87
Ford, Henry, 62, 82, 87, 227, 230
  and Henry Forward, 223-225
Ford Company, 81-82, 223
  statistics on, 224
Ford Home Almanac and Facts Book, 224
Foreign reciprocation, 205
Forward, Henry
  career of (hypothetical case), 62-68, 71, 72, 74, 220-221, 226, 227, 230
  compared with Henry Ford, 223-225
Fourteenth Amendment, 160
Franklin, Benjamin, 229

Friedman, Elisha M., 149n.
Frisch, Ragnar, 102, 207n.
Fulton, Robert, 79, 86
Fundamental Principles of Taxation in the Light of Modern Developments, The, by Stamp, 233n.
Furniss and Buck, 232

Gifts, 100, 150, 156n., 169, 186, 188, 196, 234, 237-238
  limited exemption of, 202
  in tax return form, 10
Glass, Secretary of the Treasury, 231
Government
  aid from, 230
  borrowing by, 72, 73, 74, 221, 223, 224
  management by, 90-91, 196
Graves, Clyde H., 215, 216
Griswold, Erwin N., xiii
  on income concept, 122-123
Growth rate of capital, 68-69, 70, 71, 72, 81-83, 86, 220, 221, 223, 230
  maximum, significance of, 78-80
Guillebaud, C. W., 99, 215, 216, 217

Haig, Robert M., xii, 45, 49, 121, 144, 149n., 232
Hand, Judge Learned, 166, 236
Hargreaves, 79
Hazelett, C. W., xi
Held, Adolph, 215
Hereditary plutocracy, 93-94
Hewett, Wm. W., xii, 138n., 215, 216
Holding companies, 173
Holmes, Oliver Wendell, 121, 130, 191, 234, 235, 236, 238
Hong, E. N., xii
Houston, Secretary of the Treasury, 231
Howe, Elias, 79

Identical double taxation, 162-164
Illinois Law Review, 185

Income
    according to common usage, 109-
        120, 128-129, 130, 184, 233
    according to experts, 232-233
    accretion, see Accretion-income
    beneficiary of, 210, 213
    big, uses for, 89-90
    British concept of, 177-178, 182
    as cash yield, 116, 120
    commonest concept of, 116-120
    concepts of, x, 44-45, 48-50, 191,
        193, 212, 232-233, 234-246
    degrees of, for individuals and
        corporations, 170-171
    destination of, 245
    earned, see Earned income
    erroneous ideas of, 213-214
    gross, 123, 124
    in kind, 207-208, 244
    legal, 120-129, 152, 233, 234-246
    marginal utility of, 101-103
    national, 44-45, 104, 231
    need for scientific concept of,
        109-110
    personally earned, an example
        of yield, 49n.
    preservation of, 213
    property-earned, an example of
        accretion, 49n.
    psychic, 43n., 99-101
    real, see Real income
    social and individual, 44-45
    sources of, 18, 22, 26, 29, 188,
        210, 212-213
    spent, see Spendings
    Supreme Court's efforts to de-
        fine, 127-129, 130
    yield, see Yield-income
Income tax law, present
    administration of, 4
    complexities of, 168-176
        amendments to amendments,
            174
        degrees of total or net income,
            170-171
        depletion and depreciation, 170
        either-ors, 168-169, 170
        exceptions to exceptions, 174

Income tax law, present—(Con-
    tinued)
        exemptions, 170
        inventory basis, 170
        mixed definitions, 173-174
        puzzling phraseology and
            wordiness, 170, 175-176
        rates, 172, 173, 187
        splits of some gross income
            items, 171-172
    controversies under, xi, 34, 57
    discordant principles in, 97-98
    discouragement of saving by, 84,
        73, 196
    double taxation under, 3, 56-60,
        92, 120, 129, 160-166
    effect of, on business, ix
    effect of, on commercial re-
        search, 87
    encouragement of waste by, 229-
        230
    hardship items taxed, 35
    history of, 126-128
    income concepts used in, 121-129
    inconsistent on gains and losses,
        147-148
    loss of revenue under, 73
    a mixture of yield and accretion
        concepts, 109
    need for a new approach to, 3
    objections to, 3-4, 194-195
    revenue from, 75-77
    social consequences of, 92-105,
        195
    tax annually computed, 142
    taxation of earnings under, 10
    treatment of investments under,
        10-11
    treatment of private and cor-
        porate business under, 10
    on yield and savings, 31
Income tax reform
    appeal of, to business men, ix-x
    need for, 3, 93
Industry, rapid advance of, 72
    in Japan and Russia, 82

Inflation, 228
  retarded by savings, 197
Inheritance tax, 70, 87, 160, 169,
    186-187, 195
Injury, compensation for, 238-239
Insurance, 241-242
  against bombing, 95
  workmen's, 96
Insurance premiums, deduction of,
    201
Interaction, 213
Interest
  accrued, 214
  on loans, 155
  proportionate, change of, 135-137
  in tax return form, 10
  taxing of, 60, 208
Interstate Commerce Commission,
    151n.
Inventions
  commercial laboratories for, 86
  harmful, 227
  importance of fostering, 78-82,
    86, 226, 227
  new, government promotion of,
    90
  new, profits necessary to, 80-82,
    83-84, 85
Inventories, 156-157, 170
Inventors and Money-makers, by
    Taussig, 79n.
Investment, 21, 22, 23, 155
  appreciation of, 116
  combined with spending, 203
  double taxation of, 161
  effect of yield tax on, 47-48
  gain on, not viewed as income in
    England, 178
  by the government, 89-91
  under present law, 10-11, 228
  yield from, 7

Joint returns, 205-207
Jordan, Chester A., 209n.
Journal of Political Economy,
    103n., 207n.
Justice
  concept of, 92

Justice—(Continued)
  in payment, 97-98
  social, 95-97, 196

Keynes, John Maynard, 228-229
King, Eldon P., 177
King, Willford I., xii
Kuznets, Simon, 233

Laso, Luis E., xii
Le Deuc, C. A., xiii, 29, 76-78, 233
  on income concept, 123-124
Legal Aid Societies, 97
Legal complexion, change in, 133,
    135, 137, 138, 166
Liabilities, 7, 174
Life insurance, 239-242
  proceeds of, not regarded as in-
    come, 191
Life insurance premiums, deduc-
    tion of, 201
Living
  cost of, 25, 26
  standard of, 25
    improvement in, 80, 94, 104,
      195
Loan transactions, 153-155, 158,
    202-203
Loans, in tax return form, 10
Loder, Walter M., xii
Lolini, Ettore, 215, 216
Lowerdos, Alexander, xiii
Lutz, Harley L., xii, 104, 206n.
Luxuries, tax on, 5, 35, 94

McCormick, 80
McReynolds, Justice, 138
Magill, Roswell, xiii, 134, 138n.,
    141, 144n., 151n., 158n., 163n.,
    165, 177, 180n., 184, 236, 237,
    245
  on income concept, 121-122, 126,
    129
Malthus, 212
Marconi, 79
Marginal desirability, 101-103
  measurement of, 102, 207
Maroder, Edmond C., xii, 110

Marriage exemption, 205-207
Marshak, Jacob, xii
Marshall, Alfred, 4, 39, 101, 218, 232
Marshall, Chief Justice, 61
Martell, Albert A., Jr., xii
Masci, Guglielmo, 215, 217
Maturity, 241n.
Mayo Clinic, 97
Mill, John Stuart, xi, 4, 39, 101, 218-219
Mills, Ogden L., x, 34, 186
  proposed spendings tax of, 208-209
Minimum exemptions, 5, 205-207
Minus (negative) yield, 18, 20, 21, 22
"Mixed Claims Commission," 242
Money (*see also* Cash)
  as capital, 149, 151
  destination of, 149
    when it counts, 150-151
    when it does not count, 151-152
  embezzled, as taxable income, 236
  as real income, 149, 151-152
Money income, measured by real income, 24
Monograph on Common-Stock Indexes, 230
Montgomery, Robert H., on income concept, 125
Morgan, J. P., 60
Mount Joy, Penna., 88
Murray's English Dictionary on Historical Principles, 109
Musgrave, Richard A., 215, 217

National income, 44-45, 104, 231
National Tax Association, 144
Nature of Capital and Income, The, by Fisher, 39, 43n., 44, 70n., 128n., 209n., 218
Negative property, 7
Net cash yield
  defined, 6
  divisions of, 6-9
  tax on, 5-6

New Methods of Measuring Marginal Utility, by Frisch, 102n., 207n.
New Principles of Political Economy, by Rae, 79n.
New York Medical Journal, 84
New York Times, 149n., 176

Obsolescence, 162
  British tax treatment of, 180-182
Omnibus clause, 237-238
Operating losses, 157-159, 171
Ophelimity, 101
Oversaving, 228-229
Owner-occupancy, 182-183, 189, 190, 244

Panama Canal, 89
Pareto, 101
Parker, L. H., 177
Partnership, 162
  and corporation, compared, 29-30
  taxation of, 10
  Uncle Sam in, 58
Patent laws, 85, 100
Patents, increase in number of, 86-87
Paterson, Justice, 187n.
Payment in kind, 145-146
Peace after the war, 197-198
Periodicity of income, 210, 214, 234, 245-246
Personal holdings companies, 164
Personal Income Taxation, by Simons, 75n., 212n., 232n.
Personal-use goods, *see* Consumption
Persons, Warren, 90
Pettengill, R. B., xii
Pfeiffer, Eduard, xiii, 218
Philanthropy, 123
  exemption of, 89
  a motive for big savings, 88-89
  and new inventions, 84
Pierson, N. G., 215, 216, 217
Pigou, Arthur C., 4, 39, 218, 219
Pitney, Justice, 130-131, 133

Planning for Tax Economy, by
Schachtel, Crow, and Greene,
xiii
Plus (positive) yield, 18, 20, 22
Political Science Quarterly, 232n.
Post Office, 89
Prato, Guiseppe, 218
Preservation of the source, 213
Prices
curb on, 84
fall of, 149
rise of, 149
Primogeniture, 93
Principles of Economics, by Mar-
shall, 232n.
Principles of Economics, by R. T.
Bye, 232n.
Principles of Political Economy,
by John Stuart Mill, 218n.
*Proceedings of the National Tax
Association,* 104n.
Producers' capital, 41
Producing source of income, 18
Production, defined, 43
Profits
book, 156-159
corporate, 6, 162-164
double tax on, 34
high, necessary for rapid expansion, 83, 85, 86
rate of, 80-82, 83
and the consumer, 81-82
undistributed, 32, 51, 73, 80, 118,
163-165, 214, 230, 231
creative influence of, 82, 83
and wherewithal, possible equality of, 157
Progressive taxation, 31, 70-71, 101-
105, 187, 205-207
Property
as capital, 40
damages to, 240-242
exchanged for stock, 165
negative, 7
value of, 46-47
as earnings or as yield, 51, 55
yield from, 6-7, 15
Property taxes, 186, 245

Proportional taxation, *see* Regressive taxation
Protection
legal, for all, 97
mutual, 96
Psychic income, 43n., 99-100
Public opinion, 89
Public welfare, 226
business expansion and, 80
effects of tax system on, 105
Pulido, Proceso, xii

Quintuple taxation, 163-164

Rae, John, 79
Rate of Interest, The, by Fisher,
79n.
Read, Eaton Van Wert, 81n.
Reader's Digest, 90
Real estate
improved, taxation of, 140-141,
161
income from, in England, 182
Real income
exemption of, 188
to the layman, 119-120
measured by money income,
24-27
as personal uses, 25, 41, 43-44
under present law, 244
relationship of spendings to, 15
as tax base, x, 27, 33, 39-40
under yield system, 159
Realism, deviations from, 230-231
Realization, 139-141, 184, 185
Receiving source of income, 18
Reciprocation, foreign, 205
RFC, 95, 230
Recovery after the war, 197-198
Reductions, 236
double, 58-60
Reform, income tax
appeal of, to business men, ix-x
need for, 3, 93
Regressive taxation, 102, 104
Reinvestment, 6, 9, 11, 21, 47-48,
73, 81, 82, 83, 130, 139, 197,
223, 224, 229, 230

274 GENERAL INDEX

Reinvestment—(*Continued*)
deduction for, 181-182
destructiveness magnified by, 61-62
double taxation of, 161
exemption of, 242-243
Rent and owner-occupancy, 182-183
Rents, in tax return form, 10
Reorganization cases, 131-134, 148
Research laboratories, 86
effect of present tax law on, 87
Retail Executive, 81n.
Revenue
increased, with yield tax, 35, 62-69
loss of, under present law, 73
from taxes, *see* Yield tax, revenue from, *and* Income Tax law, present, revenue from
Revenue Act of 1940, amendments to, 174
Ricci, Umberto, 215, 217
Robertson, Thomas E., 86
Roosevelt, Theodore, 96
Royalties, in tax return form, 10

Sales
profit on, 85, 86
tax on, 10
of stock, taxes on, 186
Savings (*see also* Capital-increase)
bank, considered as cash by layman, 112, 118
compulsory, in wartime, 197, 228
discouragement of, 73, 84, 196
double taxation of, 161
encouragement of, xi, 195, 216
injurious, 228
lessening of, 226-227
motives for, 88
not thought of as real income, 120
"perpetual," 69-70
tax on, 3, 31, 56, 57, 58, 195, 216-217, 229
destructiveness of, 61-74
1%, 222
10%, 222

Savings, tax on—(*Continued*)
20%, 68, 72, 230-231
50%, 67-68, 72, 220
80%, 65-67, 72
90%, 222
100%, 63-64, 66-71, 222
Schachtel, Irving I., xiii
Schanz, Georg, 232
Schock, Clarence, 88
Schumpeter, Joseph A., 79, 228n.
Schwab, Charles M., 88, 99
Securities
dates of selling, 146-147
exemption of, 34
Security, taxation of, 99-101
Seligman, E. R. A., xii, 39, 218
Seller-user deals, 203
Service-disservice, interaction between, 41-44, 213
Services, 25, 26, 210, 211
aggregates of, 43-44
future, as value of property, 46-48
measurement of goods by, 211
negative, 41-43, 44
sources of, 40-41
value of, 50
as yield-income, 212
Shoup, Carl, xii
Simons, Henry, xii, 75, 212n., 232
Sixteenth Amendment, 184, 185, 186, 191, 192
adoption of, 127
Smith, Adam, 16n., 229
Snyder, Carl, 79
Soak-the-rich policy, 80, 195
Social consequences of present law, 92-105, 195
Social justice, 95-97, 196
Social mobility of the individual, 93, 196
Social Security, 239
Social vs. individual income, 44-45
Society, original purpose of, 96
Sociological Theory of Capital, The, by Rae, 79n.
Spencer, Herbert, 84

Spendings
checked with yield, 14-15
combined with investment, 203
and consumption, discrepancies between, 203
discouragement of, 227
lessening of, 72n.
marginal desirability of money a function of, 103
measurement of, 4-5, 15, 25-27, 39-40
measurement of money by, 33
as tax base, 4-5
tax on, *see* Yield (spendings) tax
and yield, equality of, 20
Spendthrifts, tax on, 76, 89, 189
Staehle, Hans, on marginal utility, 103, 207n.
Stamp, Sir Josiah, x, 215, 216, 233
Stamp Scrip, by Fisher, 228n.
Statisticians, income according to, 233
Stevens, Chase, xii
Stevenson, 79
Stockholders, 28-32, 132, 133, 214
taxation of, 162, 163, 165
Stoppage at the source, 30, 31
Straddle tax, *see* Capital gains tax
Succession taxes, 70, 195 (*see also* Estate tax *and* Inheritance tax)
Successive double taxation, 161-162
Summary of The British Tax System with Special Reference to its Administration, A, by Magill, Parker, and King, 177, 180n., 181n., 182n., 183n.
Sumner, William Graham, 96, 104
Sun, Nien-min, xii
Supreme Court, 16, 119, 147, 184, 185, 188, 236
and the common man, 190-192
and debt reduction, 155
definition of capital by, 241
on dividends tax, 130-138
on double taxation, 160-161

Supreme Court—(*Continued*)
on Edwards v. Cuba R.R. case, 150-151
efforts of, to define income, 127-129, 130
failure of, to distinguish between capital and income, 189-190
flexibility of, 191, 245
inconsistency of, in tax rulings, 133-135, 140-141
interpretations by, 185, 186, 187, 234, 235, 240, 241, 242
on obsolescence, 162
and periodicity, 245-246
Surrey, Stanley S., 185, 190, 246
Surtaxes, corporate, 164, 173
Survey of income concepts held by the man in the street, 110-120
Sweepstakes winnings as taxable income, 236

Taft, Chief Justice, 234, 239-240
Taussig, Frank W., 79, 90
Tax base, 15, 190
accretion as, 58-59, 75-77, 120, 194, 232
book profits unsuitable as, 156
"broader," fallacy of, 75-78
real income as, x, 27, 33, 39-40
spendings as, 4-5
yield as, 46, 194
Tax evasion, 35, 129, 147, 166-167, 195, 207-208, 235n., 236
Tax Magazine (now *Taxes*), 203n.
Tax rates, 63-72, 220, 222, 230-231
profusion of, 172
punitive, 173
Tax reform, need for, 3, 93
Tax return form for yield (spendings) tax, 8-14, 28
comparisons of, with existing forms, 9-11
interpretation of, 11-14
Tax systems
compared, 104-105
rival, discrepancy between, 156
Tax Systems of the World, 206n.

Taxable Income, by Magill, 121,
134n., 138n., 141n., 144n.,
151n., 158n., 163n., 165n.,
180n., 185n., 236n., 237n.,
245n.
Taxation (*see also* specific forms
of taxation)
double, 3, 56-60, 120, 129, 160-163
avoided by yield tax, 194
constitutionality of, 160-161
controversy over, 215-219
of corporate profits and stockholders' dividends, 29, 34
identical, 162-163
involving more than one state,
161n.
remedy for, 30, 31-32
vs. destructiveness, 222
progressive, 31, 70-71, 103-104,
187, 205-207
quintuple (former), 163-164
regressive, 102, 104
successive, 161-162
triple, 163, 165-166, 195
Taxes (formerly *Tax Magazine*),
xiv, 75n.
Taxes
corporation, *see* Corporation income taxes
deductibility of, 201-202
direct, 126-127, 184, 186
discriminatory, in wartime, 228
indirect, 126, 186, 187, 237
and wherewithal, failure of, to
synchronize, 153-159
Taxpayer, capital and labor of,
234-236
Technological improvements, 86,
226
Thelander, P. W., xii
Theory of Interest, The, by Fisher,
79n.
Triple taxation, 163, 195
avoidance of, 165-166
Trusts, 162, 235

Undistributed profits, 32, 51, 80,
118, 163-165, 214, 230, 231

Undistributed profits—(*Continued*)
creative influence of, 82, 83
investment of, in government
bonds, 197
tax on, abolished, 173
United States Steel Corporation,
30
Uses, 25, 26, 40

Van Devanter, Justice, 138
Vickrey, William, xiii, 202

Walker, Francis, 149n.
Wall Street Journal, 149n.
Wallace, Ralph, 90n.
War profiteers, 84
Wartime
discriminatory taxes in, 228
necessity for creative effort in,
82, 83-84, 196-197, 231
shorter bracket ranges in, 207
Wash sales, 147-148
Waste
discouragement of, 84
encouragement of, 230
Watt, James, 79, 86
Wealth, *see* Capital
Weaver, Donald V., 215
Webb, Beatrice, 96
*What Social Classes Owe Each
Other,* by Sumner, 96
Wherewithal to pay tax
availability of, xi, 15-16, 34, 153
and profits, possible equality of,
157
White, Justice, 186n.
Whitney, Eli, 79, 86, 100
Windfalls, 235, 238
Window tax, 73
Woodbridge, Frederick W., xiii
Work, yield from, 6, 15, 19, 22
World Wars I and II, 231
Wueller, P. H., 232
Wynhausen, Frits, xiii

Yield (*see also* Earned income)
cash, 5-6, 18-23, 211

Yield—(*Continued*)
checked with spendings, 14-15
contrasted with earnings, 50-51
discounted
as capital, 46, 49
vs. discounted accretion, 54-55
future, 49, 51
measured by real income, 178
negative (minus yield), 18, 20, 21, 22
positive (plus yield), 18, 20, 22
preferable for entry in tax return, 15
source of, 212-213
and spendings, equality of, 20
as tax base, 46, 194
Yield-income, 40-45, 50, 52-53, 120
conditions defining, 210-214
marginal factor in, 103
net cash, 18
relation of, to capital, 40-41
Yield (spendings) tax
advantages of, 194
annually computed, 149
British approximation to, 172-181
compounding of, 47-48
constitutionality of, 184-193
deductions under, 239

Yield (spendings) tax—(*Cont.*)
departures from, by Supreme Court, 139
discouragement of waste by, 84
and double-entry accounting, 18-23
effect of, on investment, 47-48
encouragement of philanthropic giving by, 89
explained, 3-17
gradual adoption of, 16-17
gross, 111, 113, 116, 119
as income in Supreme Court's view, 131
increase in revenue effected by, 62-69
and loss carry-over, 158
opponents of, 99-101
philosophy of, 195-196
precision of, 33
questions to the layman on, 110-120
revenue from, 75-78, 87
simplicity of, 34, 209
subsidiary problems of, 201-209
support for, 218-219
a tax on real income, 194
and wherewithal, xi, 15-16, 34, 153, 156